Sexual Science and the Law

# Sexual Science and the Law

## Richard Green

Harvard University Press
Cambridge, Massachusetts
London, England
1992

**Library of Congress Cataloging-in-Publication Data**

Green, Richard, 1936–
Sexual science and the law / Richard Green.
p.   cm.
Includes bibliographical references (p.    ) and index.
ISBN 0-674-80268-3 (acid-free paper)
1. Sex and the law—United States.   I. Title.
KF9325.G74   1992
345.73′0253—dc20
[347.305253]
92-10458
CIP

For Adam Hines-Green, conceived in a joint venture with Melissa Hines, before this book was. Adam was eight months old when I agreed to write it and two years older when I had written it. This legacy is for Adam so that, in his later years, he will know what his daddy did when he went "to work" during his early years.

# Contents

# Acknowledgments

In the early 1970s when he headed Basic Books, Arthur Rosenthal signed the contract for my book *Sexual Identity Conflict in Children and Adults*. Before it was completed, he moved on to Harvard University Press. In the late 1980s, at Harvard, Arthur signed the contract for this book. Then, before it was completed, he moved on to Hill and Wang. I am hopeful that the next time Arthur is ready to move he will let me know, so I can prepare another book proposal.

Richard Whalen deserves special recognition for his critical reading of the first version of the manuscript and his enormously helpful suggestions for revision. Thanks, too, to two anonymous reviewers for Harvard University Press, whose comments spurred me on toward a final draft. And that would not have been completed without the (nearly) endless typing of Laurel Mallet and Sylvia Bliss. For their sakes, I am grateful that word processing has replaced correcting ribbon and "whiteout." I also thank Angela von der Lippe and Linda Howe at Harvard University Press.

Bob Stoller read the beginnings of this book as it trickled down the hall from my office to his. As always, for over thirty years, his enthusiasm fueled me. His comment after reading the first draft chapters ("There's nothing else like it") encouraged me to develop them into a book. His death as it was reaching completion is a profound tragedy impossible to express here.

I thank, too, the following publishers for permission to reprint material that appeared in an earlier version in their publications: *Anglo-American Law Review* for "'Give Me Your Tired, Your

Poor, Your Huddled Masses' (of Heterosexuals): An Analysis of American and Canadian Immigration Policy" and "Fornication: Common Law Legacy and American Sexual Privacy"; *Ohio Northern Law Review* for "Griswold's Legacy: Fornication and Adultery as Crimes"; Record Press Inc./Federal Legal Publications, Inc. for "The Immutability of (Homo)sexual Orientation: Behavioral Science Implications for a Constitutional (Legal) Analysis" in *Journal of Psychiatry and Law*; and Yale University Press for "Exposure to Explicit Sexual Materials and Sexual Assault: A Review of Behavioral and Social Science Research" in *The Psychology of Women*, edited by Mary Walsh.

Sexual Science and the Law

# Introduction

The televised hearings on the nomination of Robert Bork to the Supreme Court in 1987 riveted public attention to the question, "Is there a constitutional right to 'sexual privacy'?" Nonlawyers learned that, beginning with a case in which a Connecticut law forbidding married couples to use contraceptives was declared unconstitutional, the Supreme Court has fashioned a zone of sexual autonomy. Law students had already been studying some privacy cases in courses on constitutional law. However, many areas of "sexual privacy" were not covered and state court decisions were often ignored.

Until recently, there was little interest among law students in sexual behavior and the law. It took the gay liberation movement, launched in the early 1970s, to attract political and legal attention to the behavior of sexual minorities. Today, the work of gay activist lawyers and other civil libertarians has brought this area into the mainstream of legal analysis and has expanded the scope of sexual privacy beyond "gay rights" to much of heterosexual behavior.

A more traditional academic focus has been the bridge between law and psychiatry. Especially in the area of insanity and criminal conduct, psychiatry has received considerable attention. Missing from this integration of behavioral science and law, however, has been the discipline of sexual science, which did not begin to emerge as a new subspecialty until the best-selling "Kinsey Reports" of 1948 and 1953, and the best-selling Masters and Johnson studies of 1966 and 1970. Together with the explosion of sex research in the 1980s, these works provided the legal profession with material from which to fashion a new subject of jurisprudence.

This book is the result of twenty years as a psychiatric researcher in human sexuality and an interest in law that led me to pursue a law degree. Prior to attending law school, I was an expert psychiatric witness in dozens of legal cases in which I reported on sexual science data. Now, with training in legal principles, I hope to bridge these two disciplines. What follows here is a brief overview of some of the topics I will consider.

Discrimination against homosexuals in housing and employment is legal in nearly every American state, and the sexual behavior of homosexuals is criminalized in nearly half the states. Two approaches in law that could grant equal rights to homosexuals can be informed by sexual science data. One approach examines whether the feature for which a group is stigmatized is "immutable" or unchangeable, such as race. Research can address the question of whether homosexuality is inborn or acquired (perhaps by choice) and can clarify the results of psychotherapy and other efforts at changing sexual orientation. The other approach determines whether the expression of homosexual behavior is of such personal significance as to be deemed "fundamental." Here too, research can assess the impact of a homosexual identity to determine whether it is comparable to other legally determined "fundamental rights," such as the right to marry or whether or not to have children.

Divorcing parents committed to pursuing a homosexual life-style are often denied child custody and have major restrictions placed on the time they share with their children. In deciding custody, courts attempt to determine the "best interests" of the child. Should the fact that a parent is lesbian or gay influence custody or visitation? Research can provide information on the social, psychological, and sexual development of children raised by lesbian mothers or gay fathers.

"Age of consent" law sets the age for legal participation in sexual intercourse. Its purpose is to protect the young against victimization through participation in sexual acts whose significance they may not sufficiently appreciate. Age of consent, a legal concept, intersects with meaningful consent, a psychological concept. Psychological science can determine the extent to which minors understand specific sexual behaviors at varying ages.

Reports of sexual abuse have skyrocketed. Increasing numbers of adult psychiatric patients report that their current difficulties derive from early sexual abuse. Penalties for a wide range of sexual involvements with children, which are believed to be uniformly damaging, are severe. Research on the short- and long-term effects on children of sexual interaction with older persons can consider the age of the child, the type of sexual behavior, and the relationship of the child to the older person as they relate to outcome. Researchers can also examine the impact of society's condemnation of the sexual behavior, and the accompanying legal investigation, on the child, as distinct from the sexual act itself, and address ways to reduce further trauma through law enforcement, psychiatric investigation, or court trial.

The high percentage of sex offenders who re-offend after psychotherapy or incarceration or both has led to efforts to control assaultive sexuality by blocking testosterone, the male sex hormone, which facilitates male sexual motivation and behavior. But to what extent is sexual assault sexual? To what extent is it aggressive? Studies can reveal whether surgical or chemical castration reduces the likelihood that offenders will re-offend.

Immigration law has excluded aliens with specific antisocial psychiatric features, including homosexuality, which was categorized in general as a mental illness, and in particular as an expression of a psychopathic personality. Homosexual men and women can be evaluated to determine whether they meet the criteria for these exclusionary diagnoses.

Persons who want to change their sex face several legal obstacles. In preparing for sex reassignment, transsexuals need to experience cross-gender living on a trial basis (the "real-life test"). This includes employment. But employers often will not hire a transsexual, and courts have ruled that transsexuals are not protected under statutes that prohibit discrimination based on gender. Research can clarify to what extent this "real-life test" for preoperative transsexuals is necessary for postsurgical success. Sex-reassignment surgery is expensive. Medical insurance companies contend that the procedure is experimental or cosmetic and thus excluded from reimbursement. The long-term effects of sex-change surgery can be determined.

Transsexuals want to change their legal status as male or female. They may want to marry in their new status. Sexual science can elucidate the several criteria according to which an individual's sex is determined—sex chromosomes, genital organs, hormones, and psychological identity—and address which should receive priority when there is a conflict.

Many persons believe that exposure to pornography leads to sexual aggression and the sexual victimization of women and children. The effects of various types of explicit sexual portrayals on attitudes and behaviors can be studied. Psychologists evaluating normal volunteers in the laboratory, psychiatrists studying sex offenders in prison, and sociologists conducting research in countries where pornography may be more or less available are providing data that could influence how—and if—we regulate pornography.

Moral issues related to the formal exchange of money for sex aside, sexual scientists can study the effects of prostitution on the prostitute and on the customer to determine whether either or both is benefited or harmed, the extent to which prostitution is associated with other criminal behaviors, and its role in transmitting sexual diseases.

In the controversy over abortion, sexual scientists can gather facts about the psychological effects on pregnant women of allowing or denying the termination of pregnancy, as well as the status of children born to women who requested but were denied abortion.

The controversy over sex education in public schools is another area in which sexual science can inform the debate. Two target behaviors with which sex educators and some parents predict opposite effects can be studied: Does education raise or lower rates of unwanted adolescent pregnancy? Does it raise or lower rates of venereal disease?

Criminal law permits excuse or mitigation for criminal acts when a person's ability to control the act is absent or compromised. In this regard, four sex-related mental states have been advanced as legal defenses. In men, the anomaly of an extra male chromosome has spurred interest in whether these "supermales" are compromised in their ability to control aggressive acts. In women, severe alterations in psychiatric status resulting from premenstrual hormone-induced changes have been proposed to mitigate or excuse crime. For women charged with infanticide, an insanity defense has been advanced based on a diagnosis of postpartum psychosis. And some men, charged with killing a homosexual man, have argued that the threat of a homosexual assault precipitated a panic state that should excuse the homicide. Sexual science research can provide data for evaluating all four claims.

I have selected these topics both because they are controversial and because they represent the contemporary coupling of sexual science and the law. Some are rich in sexual science data; others are ripe for further study. With some, courts have respected the findings of science; with others, the findings have been ignored. The court decisions I have chosen to discuss reflect relevant case law and, where possible, the use of scientific data.

Both the legal system and sexual science focus on human behavior. Both disciplines honor the impact of sexuality on the individual and on society. But, to a major degree, the law has not kept pace with the advances of sexual science. In a classic example, although Kinsey reported in 1948 that homosexual acts occur in the lives of a third of males from adolescence to adulthood, every state continued to criminalize such behavior into the 1960s, and nearly half the states continue to do so into the 1990s.

The chapters that follow suggest ways in which sexual science research should influence legislators and the courts. They also indicate the directions in which sexual science research must proceed in order to answer the questions of legislators and courts. They demonstrate the vitality of the interface between sexual science and the law for both interdisciplinary research and jurisprudence.

# · 1 ·

# Fornication

In *Griswold v. Connecticut,*[1] the contraceptive use case that set in motion a train of sexual privacy cases, Supreme Court Justice Arthur Goldberg remarked that the State of Connecticut "does have statutes, the constitutionality of which is beyond dispute, which prohibit . . . fornication." The anti-fornication law did not have to await a constitutional challenge in that state. Connecticut's legislature repealed it in 1967. The situation in New Jersey was different. In a race to the finish line, the state supreme court, two years before the legislature was prepared to decriminalize fornication, ruled the two-century-old statute unconstitutional in *State v. Saunders.*[2] I was an expert psychiatric witness in *Saunders.* I testified to the significance of fornication and the emotional and behavioral consequences of its proscription.

## Fornication and Sexual Privacy

Fornication is generally defined as sexual intercourse between consenting unmarried persons.[3] A fornication statute is at the threshold of those laws that attempt to regulate sexual conduct.

A continuum of sexual behavior may be constructed, reflecting varying levels of conventionality as well as religious and moral concerns. At one end of this continuum is masturbation. This is behavior so private that generally only one individual is involved, so that discovery and law enforcement are nearly impossible. Notwithstanding the history of psychiatric pronouncements linking masturbation to insanity,[4] the Boy Scout manual's concern that this activity undermines the physical health of young men,[5] and the view of some religions that it is a nonprocreative surrender to the flesh,[6] the law ignores autoerotic behavior when it occurs in private.

Fornication is next on this posited continuum. The persons involved are consenting adults. The behavior is extremely common and, except for the persons' marital status, is comparable, when conducted in private, to behavior engaged in by hordes of other persons with whom the law is not concerned.

Next is adultery. This can be seen as undercutting the sanctity of marriage and the family. A potential victim exists in the person of a nonparticipating spouse. Here, private behavior may become public knowledge in subsequent divorce litigation.

Finally, there is homosexual behavior. Here, there is considerable concern among the general public and in religion and psychiatry. It is probably less common than heterosexual adultery because of the disparity between the number of heterosexuals who engage in adultery (50 percent)[7] and the number of homosexuals and bisexuals in the general population (about 10 percent).[8]

If fornication stumbles under the weight of the law and sexual science cannot lift it to protected standing, then surely private, consenting expressions of sexuality further along this posited continuum are in jeopardy.

The proscription of fornication has a venerable history. While prostitution may be the oldest profession, fornication may be one of the oldest crimes. It is forbidden in the Bible.[9]

In England, fornication was at times punishable by death; at other times it was not considered an offense under the common law, although when ignored by the common law, it could still be punished by the ecclesiastical courts. Blackstone reported on the vacillation of official concern:

> In the year 1650, when the ruling power found it for their interest to put on the semblance of a very extraordinary strictness and purity of morals, not only incest and willful adultery were made capital crimes, but also the repeated act of keeping a brothel or committing fornication were (upon a second conviction) made a felony without benefit of clergy. But at the restoration, when men, from an abhorrence of hypocrisy of the late times, fell into a contrary extreme of licentiousness, it was not thought proper to renew a law of such unfashionable

rigor. These offenses have been ever since left to the feeble coercion of the spiritual court according to the rules of the canon law.[10]

The legal meaning of fornication varied according to whether it was defined under ecclesiastical or common law. To the church, it was the act of illicit sexual intercourse by an unmarried person with a person of the opposite sex, whether married or not. Under the common law, it was illicit sexual intercourse between a man, whether married or not, and an unmarried woman. Fornication was not generally recognized as a crime under the common law unless committed "openly and notoriously so as to constitute a public nuisance."[11]

The Puritan colonies of New England developed a unique approach to fornication. Violators could be enjoined to marry, they could be fined, or they could be pilloried and whipped. It was customary to force fornicators to wear a "V" (for Uncleanness) displayed conspicuously on their clothing.[12] The Massachusetts Bay Colony was singularly dedicated to the suppression of fornication. In Middlesex County alone from 1760 to 1774, such suppression was the basis for 210 of 370 criminal prosecutions.[13]

The colony of New Jersey was quick to enact a statute against fornication, and "An Act for Suppressing Immorality" was implemented in 1704. Its preamble claimed that immorality had "abounded too much" and "to the shame of Christianity and the great grief of good and sober men." In 1796, the 1704 act was repealed by the state of New Jersey and replaced by a "general crimes act," which maintained the prohibition against fornication and fixed a fourteen-dollar fine for its violation.[14] As statutes were periodically revised the fornication provision remained, the major variation being in the penalty. "Morality" reentered the title of the statute in 1898 when fornication was classified as a crime "against public morals and the institution of marriage,"[15] but the statute itself remained essentially unchanged until the latter half of the twentieth century. In its 1970s version it read: "Any person who commits fornication is guilty of a misdemeanor, and shall be punished by a fine of not more than $50 or by imprisonment for not more than six months, or both."[16]

The brevity of the statute and the absence of a definition of the offense led to a landmark judicial interpretation in 1790.[17] In *Smith v. Minor* Mary Smith brought an action of slander against Isaac Minor. She alleged that he had said, "Mary Smith is with child by Stephen Jones," that she "had been begot with child by [him]"[18] and that "Ezekiel Smith's daughter [Mary] is like to have a little one."[19] Counsel for defendant Minor contended that "in order to make words actionable in themselves without proof of special damage, they must contain a charge, which, if true, would subject the plaintiff to a criminal prosecution."[20] The issue was whether the criminality of fornication depended on whether a child was born of the act. The court ruled that the New Jersey legislature "says no such thing."[21] It found that English cases regarding bastardy did not apply:

> Their statutes only relate to the security of the parish, not at all to the criminal act, which is considered as altogether a *spiritual* matter and is subjected to the cognizance of another tribunal. Our act of assembly, however, provides for both cases: it prescribes a punishment for the offence, and, in that respect, provides a substitute for the *spiritual court,* and it follows the English statutes in taking care of the township. We have no *spiritual court* with us, and, therefore, unless the interpretation for which we contend be given to the act, the crime of fornication will be committed here with impunity."[22]

The defendant argued that the words uttered did not say that the plaintiff was delivered of child and were therefore not actionable if no penalty followed from the act of fornication, nor did they say that "the child was chargeable or likely to become chargeable to the township."[23] The court ruled that fornication per se was not indictable under the Act of 1704 unless a child was born. This, in the court's view, was the way the law "ought to be," because "where the fornication is productive, the crime may be proved in some measure by this circumstance, and by other facts which would not render the trial indecent." Otherwise, "it would subject behavior perhaps at worst merely imprudent to critical investigation."[24]

State concern for the "issues" of fornication is evident in the fate of the fine levied for violation of the statute: it was "to be paid to the overseers of the poor of the town where the offence was committed, for the use of the poor of the said township."[25] Indeed, prevention of illegitimate (and presumably indigent) births continued to be a "legitimate state purpose" of the statute as late as 1970. The birth of an illegitimate child was ruled not to be an element of the offense, however, and the state did not have to prove the birth of a child who became a burden on the community.[26]

## Constitutional Challenges: Failed Cases

For nearly two centuries after *Smith v. Minor,* the statute remained. Not until the 1970s were serious constitutional challenges mounted. A 1970 challenge was turned back in *State v. Barr,* [27] where it was held that the constitutional "right to privacy" was not violated. Justice Goldberg's remark, mentioned at the beginning of this chapter, was quoted. A year later, in *State v. Lutz,* which involved *conspiracy* to commit fornication, the statute was again held not to penetrate the individual's protected zone of privacy.[28] The court did not enunciate its reasons; it merely referred to the opinion of Justice Goldberg.

The two-hundred-year-old statute remained timely in another 1971 case, that of *State v. Clark:*[29]

[We] cannot accept the suggestions that the statute ought to be regarded as such a relic of ancient times, so out of tune with presently existing notions of morality, so discriminatorily administered and so invasive of a perfected zone of privacy as to require a holding that a person accused under it is denied equal protection and due process contrary to the Federal Constitution.

One year later, and only two years before *Saunders* was tried, a New Jersey court continued to maintain that "public policy still, even in this 'enlightened' era, opposes any illicit relationship, including cohabitation without benefit of marriage."[30]

## Sexual Science Testimony and the Successful Case

The New Jersey statute's ultimate test came about in an unlikely manner. In the course of a prosecution in which two women with prostitution records charged two men with rape after a series of sexual acrobatics involving all four in the back of a parked car, the jury was instructed that if they found that the women, both of whom were unmarried, had *consented* to sexual intercourse, the men could be convicted of fornication. The jury convicted. The

New Jersey Civil Liberties Union then entered the case and attacked the constitutionality of the statute.

*Saunders* provided the opportunity for an application of sexual science data to the constitutionality of a statute prohibiting fornication.

Two components of the sexual science testimony were the psychosexual significance of nonmarital intercourse and the frequency and acceptance of such behavior. My testimony addressed the first component, and the testimony of Morton Hunt, author of *Sexual Behavior in the 1970s*,[31] addressed the second. The following summaries of the testimony are taken from the defense counsel's brief before the appellate court.

> Dr. Green . . . testified that the sex drive is instinctive, and is a biologic force that is a central factor, not only in personality development, but also at the practical office level of treating problems. When this drive is involuntarily proscribed, guilt and anxiety problems can arise and frequently create residual problems many years later. The involuntary proscription of the sexual drive can interfere with sexual function and can most dramatically manifest in the male by the inability to achieve erection, so-called impotency in the male, sometimes by what is called premature ejaculation; that is, the male cannot maintain erection long enough without achieving climax . . . And in the female the most common manifestation which is the product of years of guilt and taboo about sexuality is what used to be called 'frigidity,' . . . sometimes with accompanying pain, painful intercourse, or if not painful, just not pleasurable to the point of sexual climax.
>
> Dr. Green further added that prohibition from premarital sex can interfere with a very important part of the marital state, once the parties enter that state. He said . . . Masters and Johnson have repeatedly asserted that strong moral prohibition against sexuality in the earlier years of training is probably the primary agent responsible for sexual dysfunction within the marriage . . .
>
> Dr. Green added [that] the criminal statutes could be a strong prohibition which gives a negative connotation to the sexual behavior.[32]

Sociological data were stressed by Morton Hunt, who

> detailed for the court the differences in American sexual mores and attitudes between 1938 and 1949 (when the Kinsey survey took place), and the contemporary data . . . [These] data [were] obtained as a result of a 1972 survey . . . The survey found that half of the

college males had premarital coitus by age 17. That is double the percentage in Kinsey's time . . . The current survey found that one-third of the single women queried had premarital intercourse by the time they were aged 17 . . . This was more than double Kinsey's findings . . . Mr. Hunt also indicated that the frequency of episodes of premarital intercourse had almost doubled from Kinsey's time. Among the younger unmarried women, the episodes were anywhere from 3–10 times as frequent.[33]

Mr. Hunt's survey revealed even more radical changes concerning America's attitudes toward premarital intercourse . . . 59 percent of the people in 1959 and 56 percent of the people in 1937 disapproved of premarital sex for both men and women . . . However, by 1972, . . . three-quarters of the men felt it was acceptable to have premarital intercourse. Two-thirds of the men also felt it was acceptable for women. Fifty-five percent of women felt it was acceptable for a man, and 41 percent of them felt it was acceptable for a woman to engage in premarital intercourse.[34]

The testimony showed that fornication is a normal, common, and accepted behavior. Furthermore, not only is it part of a typical person's psychosexual development, but when proscriptions are applied against it, the effect may be psychologically injurious.

The trial court upheld the constitutionality of the fornication statute.[35] On appeal, however, the New Jersey Supreme Court held that the statute was unconstitutional:[36]

Any discussion of the right of privacy must focus on the ultimate interest which protection the Constitution seeks to ensure—the freedom of personal development . . . We conclude that the conduct statutorily defined as fornication involves, by its very nature, a fundamental personal choice.[37] Private personal acts between two consenting adults are not to be lightly meddled with by the State.[38]

Did the behavioral and social science testimony have an impact on the courts? To ascertain this, I interviewed the trial judge and a Supreme Court justice.

TRIAL JUDGE

"I didn't feel that [the science data] had any influence at all." To the trial judge the social science data pointing to the common practice of fornication and the general lack of societal condemnation represented but a temporary artifact of the times. "As far as I was

concerned, it was a lot of the stuff of the 1970s and the wild pen-
dulum of the 1960s that's going to go back. [Those data] didn't take
into account change and the historical fact that things go back and
forth." Pointing to the short-sightedness of the 1970s Supreme
Court, the judge observed, "The court would not have declared the
statute unconstitutional in 1878. Popular appeal has no place in the
judicial scrutiny of a statute. For anyone to decide a constitutional
issue based on a Gallup poll is impossible and wrong."

Changes in the laws regulating such behavior should rest with the
legislature. "I felt my role as a judge was not to interfere in a legislative function. I said, 'Let the legislature do it.' I personally dis-
agree with the activism in the Supreme Court. They have no right
to do what they are doing."

The trial judge was not concerned that ruling the fornication statute unconstitutional would have a ripple effect, washing away the
adultery and homosexuality statutes. "I was not too happy with the
trend of permissiveness, but at the same time I didn't think it would
make that much difference in the overall thing. I can't say I felt I
had my finger in the dike!"

His comments underscored the significance of the personal view
of a judge in deciding such matters. "My personal philosophy was
important, which I think you're going to find with most judges. It
might be interesting to see how [the others on this case] split along
personal, religious background, rather than on legal philosophy or
privacy."

In response to the question about whether there is any place for
behavioral or social science data in cases of this type, he indicated
that there was, "but you'd better have fertile ground with the judge
himself, with the prejudices of the judge, the orientation of his background. If you're talking contrary to his own background, you'd
better have pretty strong stuff that has no rebuttable argument."

SUPREME COURT JUSTICE

In contrast to the trial judge, for the justice who authored the concurring opinion overturning the statute contemporary morals were
important. "Today's morals are different, and the state doesn't have
the right to regulate that. No one was being offended by that."

The right of privacy was pivotal. "Fornication falls within the
zone of privacy and therefore it might well be beyond the scope of

legislative action, unless there is some rational relation between the legislative action and some wrong."

The historical foundation for the statute was without adequate contemporary weight. "The statute was apparently initially adopted for religious reasons and the query was whether or not the reason for the statute would support today's viability. I think behind the court's action was that the court was satisfied that the conduct was not antisocial."

To this Supreme Court justice, the extent to which a behavior is common is not of sufficient weight to include it within the zone of privacy. "They're not necessarily related. If conduct is such that it doesn't affect anybody else, no third person is affected, or the state isn't affected, then we're getting into the zone of privacy. Whether it's being done frequently or infrequently wouldn't really make very much difference."

The question of whether the frequency of a proscribed behavior shifts the responsibility for reform to the legislature rests with the "personality of the court." There are some courts "that act very conservatively and wait for the legislature. Some courts will adhere to the traditional legal functions of handling only dispute resolution. Other courts are more active and will attempt to step in and attempt to solve the problem immediately."

As for the concern that repeal of the fornication statute might have a ripple effect on other sexual behavior statutes, the justice considered it unlikely. "The opinion was written quite narrowly. I think there might have been some different thinking if you're talking about adultery. There were some comments made about adultery. There, again, it affects a third person."

## Sexual Science Data and Its Implications for the Law

The nature of sexual conduct generally, or of any pattern specifically, may be informed by sociological data. How common is a particular pattern of sexuality? Is its prevalence changing? If so, why? To what extent does the frequency of a behavior reflect on its "normalcy?"

What is considered "normal" in statistical science is distinct from what is considered "normal" in medical science or in moral debate. One discipline speaks to frequency, the others to an absence of pathology or sin.[39] Commonality per se is not convincing evidence of normalcy in the nonstatistical sense, or of societal acceptability. Tax evasion or driving under the influence of alcohol occurs within a substantial segment of the population, but society still wants to penalize these behaviors.

In the sexual area, research could show an increasing frequency of father-daughter incest. Would such findings influence a legislature or a court? Would incest be seen as "normal" and thus be decriminalized? Certainly, if society valued the proscription of certain sexual acts as much as it does the proscription of drunken driving, the power of the argument that the high prevalence of a particular sexual behavior militates against law enforcement would be weakened.

The effects of decriminalization on the prevalence of a behavior can also be studied. Does the behavior increase, by objective measures? Does it appear to increase by becoming more visible? Has fornication, for example, become more common in states in which these behaviors are no longer criminal? Have the rates of illegitimate births or venereal disease risen? Or, is this approach invalid due to previously low rates of enforcement? If so, what purpose of the state was served by the proscribing laws?

A state's purpose could be communicating to the young of the community that certain types of behavior are disapproved of by a majority of society. Again, sexual science could be informative here. Consider another proscribed sexual behavior: homosexuality. Have rates of homosexuality increased among young adults growing up in states in which this behavior is not a crime? Homosexuality has not been criminal in Illinois for two decades. Are there proportionately more young adult or adolescent homosexuals in that state?

Would the prevalence of fornication decrease if laws prohibiting such behavior were more strictly enforced? Isolating cause and effect would be problematic here. For example, if fornication is increasing at a time when fornication statutes are little enforced, is it the result of a later age of marriage? Is it the result of a greater dissociation of intercourse from pregnancy? If the last factor is relevant, what of the historic basis of the fornication statute—prevention of illegitimacy? Here the undesirable consequence of a behavior *diminishes* concomitantly with an *increase* in the behavior.

Both the trial court judge and the Supreme Court justice acknowledged the significance of religious views and personal subjectivity in interpreting law. When the trial judge, in discussing his opinion in *Saunders,* acknowledged the role of expert opinion in sexuality cases, he warned that it would have to find fertile ground in the views of the judge.

Selecting data to justify a particular view of sexuality is exemplified by the United States Supreme Court in a pornography case, *Paris Adult Theatre I v. Slaton.*[40] In a posture deferential to legislative wisdom, Chief Justice Burger wrote, "Although there is no conclusive proof of a connection between antisocial behavior and obscene materials, the legislature of Georgia could quite reasonably determine that such a connection might exist." The chief justice supported the possibility of such a finding by citing the *minority* report of the Commission on Obscenity and Pornography.[41] This minority labelled the Commission's majority conclusion that pornography did not lead to sex crimes as "fraudulent." The minority report was authored by *two* members of the commission. The majority report was authored by *seventeen* members of the commission.[42]

Consider, too, "expert" opinions on homosexuality. Homosexuality per se was considered a mental disorder by American psychiatry until 1973. What changed? Was it the data available to science? Was it the interpretation of the data? Was it the definition of mental illness? Was it the political power of the gay rights movement? The answer is in part all of these.[43] It may not matter so much why homosexuality per se is no longer considered a mental illness, however. The important point is that the "scientific" view changed. And if it changed then, it could change again.

The reluctance of the trial judge in *Saunders* to decide judicially in response to the latest opinions in a Gallup poll is telling in view of how the question of whether homosexuality constitutes a mental illness was ultimately decided by American psychiatry: by *referendum.* All American psychiatrists were invited to vote on the question.

\*     \*     \*

Public appreciation of the salience of sexuality has evolved during the past eighty years. Freud described what he considered to be the essence of the human condition in the sexual terminology of libido theory.[44] Kinsey collected an exhaustive body of interview data documenting the panorama of human sexual diversity.[45] Masters and Johnson observed and documented the physiology of sexual response and developed ways to enable individuals to fulfill their interpersonal sexual potential.[46] The behavioral and social science data proffered in *Saunders* are the legacy of these advances in sexual science. In some of the chapters that follow, sexual science data are given more weight than they received from the New Jersey courts in considering whether a developmentally normal pattern of sexual behavior is a privacy right to be constitutionally protected.

# · 2 ·

# Child Custody and
# Homosexual Parents

As more bisexual parents divorce to follow homosexual life-styles, courts have become child custody battlegrounds. When courts decide what is in the best interests of the child with a homosexual parent and a heterosexual parent, they focus on the psychosexual development of the child.

What do we know about the roles of parents generally in the psychosexual development of children? What do we know specifically about the influence of a parent's sexual orientation on the child? Of what relevance is it that the homosexual parent is father or mother? That the child is son or daughter? That the child is in preschool, grade school, or high school? That the parent is openly or secretly (to the child) homosexual? That the parent lives with a same-sex romantic and sexual partner? That the social climate in which the family lives is generally tolerant or rejecting of homosexuality?

The processes by which the child develops an early sexual identity and a later sexual orientation are at the core of the legal determination of the "best interests of children" in cases where one parent is homosexual. Perhaps if current theories of psychosexual development emphasized a genetic or prenatal hormonal organization, the homosexual or bisexual orientation of one parent would concern courts (and the heterosexual parent) less, since the sexual orientation die would have been cast by the time of the litigation. Perhaps if ultimate sexual orientation was clearly discernible early in life, before parents divorce, there would also be less judicial and parental concern. But because popular theory holds, and sexual science suggests, that influences on the ultimate parameters of sexual orientation continue to operate throughout childhood, heterosexual parents emphasize the detrimental influence of a homosexual parent on the emergent sexuality of the child.

In the following sections I will examine research on children of homosexual parents and analyze cases involving child custody and visitation with homosexual mothers and fathers, focusing on the ways in which research findings can be introduced and received in court. I participated as a psychiatric expert witness in several of the cases. Excerpts from the testimony in three of them illustrate the application of sexual science to family law.

## Research Studies

Research on the development of children of lesbian mothers must discount two collateral variables that could adversely affect the children and thus bias results: the effects of divorce and the effects of living in a one-parent household. The short- and longer-term trauma of divorce is well documented and includes an array of problems both social and academic.[1] The psychosexual problems of children who experience early separation from their fathers, notably boys, have also been documented.[2] Thus, if children from lesbian mother households are compared to children from intact households, the first group may show more evidence of psychosocial and psychosexual disorder, and an erroneous conclusion may be drawn indicting the mother's sexual orientation. A "control group" must be used for comparison, incorporating the variables, other than the mother's lesbianism, that may affect the children. Divorced heterosexual mothers living in households without an adult male constitute the control group.

A few studies have addressed the emergent sexual identity of these children and by implication the likelihood that they will become heterosexual or homosexual. Although the American Psychiatric Association has not listed homosexuality as a mental disorder since 1973, the courts (and much of the public) continue to regard a homosexual orientation as a less favorable outcome. Thus, charged with determining the best interests of the child, courts may be receptive to these research findings.

Three studies that compare boys and girls from lesbian mother households with children being raised by divorced, single heterosexual women are frequently cited, two from the United States and one from the United Kingdom.

In the late 1970s our research group began a ten-state study of children aged three to eleven living in two types of single parent households.[3] One group consisted of fifty lesbian-identified mothers and their fifty-six children; the other consisted of a demographically matched sample of forty heterosexual divorced mothers and their forty-eight children. There were thirty daughters and twenty-six sons of homosexual mothers and twenty-eight daughters and twenty sons of heterosexual mothers. The average age of the children was eight. Mothers had lived as single parents for an average of four years. The majority of lesbian mothers lived with another female adult in addition to their children. In just over half of the lesbian mother families, the two women were sexual partners.

As part of the study we administered the Draw-a-Person test (DAP) to the children. In this test, the child is told to draw a person but no indication is given as to which sex it should be. The sex of the first figure the child draws is presumed to reflect the drawer's own sexual identity. Most children in both groups drew their own gender first. The figures were also analyzed for signs of emotional problems such as the omission of body parts.[4] Again, no group differences were found.

We also tested the children using the It-Scale for Children. Here, a child is presented with a neuter stick figure, "It," and then asked to select an activity for "It" from a series of sex-typed activities portrayed on cards.[5] The test discriminates between typical boys and girls and has been shown to distinguish between cross-gender identified and typically masculine boys.[6] No differences were found between the children in the two groups of families. Both groups of boys scored as typical boys and both groups of girls scored as typical girls.

We also looked for other indicators of the children's discontent with their gender role. When they were asked whether they wished to be a person of the other sex, no group differences were found. There was also no difference in the extent of the boys' interest in cross-dressing. Although daughters of lesbian mothers were more likely to wear boy-type clothing, they showed no aversion to traditional girls' clothes. As for toy preferences, both groups of boys preferred typically masculine toys, while girls in both groups showed more mixed preferences. Daughters of lesbians showed more interest in boy-type recreational activities compared to daughters of heterosexuals, but doll play did not differ for the two groups of girls, nor did participation in sports.

Peer group composition and status were assessed by asking children to identify their best friend and to rate their popularity among the peer group. Most children in both groups reported a same-sex best friend, which is typical for children of this age group not experiencing sexual identity conflict.[7] There were no differences on ratings of popularity between the two groups of boys or girls.

These findings address both the short- and longer-term effects of living in a lesbian mother household that concern the courts. Neither the boys nor the girls, who were being raised in these households without an adult male for an average of four years, showed peer group rejection. Nor did they show evidence of significant cross-gender identification. To the extent that homosexuality in adulthood has childhood behavioral forecasters, such as extensive cross-gender identification and behavior,[8] the boys and girls in the households with lesbian mothers appear to have no higher probability of emerging as homosexual than the children from the families with heterosexual mothers.

The second U.S. study evaluated ten boys and ten girls, aged five to twelve, living with their lesbian mothers, and twenty children of the same ages living with their heterosexual single mothers.[9] Half of the lesbian mothers were living with a female sexual partner. Two children of lesbian mothers had never had a father living in their home.

Children were evaluated in a playroom interview by a psychiatrist who did not know whether a child's mother was lesbian or heterosexual. As in the previous study, the children's human figure drawings were evaluated for signs of cross-sex identity and psychopathology. Children were also given a test in which they interpreted ink blots, another measure of psychopathology, and were rated on a scale as severely, moderately, minimally, or not emotionally disturbed. On none of the measures were there any differences between the boys or girls from lesbian or heterosexual mother families.

Gender identity development was evaluated through toy preferences, roles taken in fantasy play, and reports of cross-dressing or other cross-sex activities. One girl and two boys showed "some concern over gender issues" in their histories or playroom responses and in their drawing of the opposite sex first on the DAP. The girl was from the lesbian mother group and the boys were from the heterosexual mother group. This study's conclusion was that the prevalence of psychological disturbance found in these children was not related to the mother's sexual orientation.

The U.K. study[10] assessed seventy-five children, aged five to seventeen, of twenty-seven lesbian mothers and twenty-seven heterosexual mothers. Nine of the lesbian mothers lived without a sexual partner in the home, twelve lived as a lesbian couple, two lived in a lesbian shared household (not as sexual partners), two as a lesbian couple sharing the home with a husband, and two in a mixed-gender shared household (not as sexual partners). Three children of lesbian mothers had never lived in a heterosexual home. One third of the children of lesbian mothers had spent at least five years in a heterosexual home prior to the parents' divorce, and another third had lived with both parents for at least two years. Standardized interviews were utilized with parents and children, and sex role scales were constructed for the children listing sex-typed activities such as toy, reading, activity, and media preferences.

There was no evidence of cross-sex identity in any of the children. On the sex-role scales the boys in the two groups were similar, as were the two groups of girls. The boys scored as conventionally masculine and the girls as conventionally feminine. The peer groups of both groups of prepubertal children were primarily same-sex, and in both groups, the quality of the child's peer relationship was good. Among the pubertal and postpubertal children, romantic crushes or friendships revealed that of the nine children with lesbian mothers, six had heterosexual interests, two reported no sexual interests, and one girl had a crush on a female teacher. In the families with heterosexual mothers, four older children reported heterosexual interests, and seven reported no sexual interests. Although no group differences were found on measures of emotional problems, there was a trend for more children with heterosexual mothers to have a psychiatric disorder. The study concluded that "rearing in a lesbian household per se did not lead to atypical

psychosexual development or constitute a psychiatric risk factor."[11]

Studies of children of homosexual fathers are more limited. Custodial gay fathers are less common (as are custodial heterosexual
fathers). One study evaluated nineteen children of homosexual
fathers (six males and thirteen females, aged fourteen to thirty-
five).[12] Two sons reported being homosexual, and one daughter
considered herself bisexual. A second study assessed the sexual
orientation of twenty-seven daughters and twenty-one sons of
homosexual fathers. By fathers' reports, one son and three daughters were homosexual.[13]

## Cases: Mothers

In 1947, an Ohio trial court permitted a presumably lesbian mother
to retain custody only if her woman companion left the home.[14] The
court ruled that "the plaintiff, Olesa Holland, [shall] discontinue all
association whether business or social, with the said Dorothy Roesler, until further order of this court."[15] In a later hearing, the court
noted, "From the evidence produced at the hearing and from the
report of the Bureau of Domestic Relations, it is found that the
plaintiff has continued to live with Dorothy Roesler, and that
she is found to be an unfit person to have custody of the children
born of the marriage of the plaintiff and defendant . . . therefore . . .
the former order of this court . . . is hereby modified in respect to
the custody of the children . . . the children formerly awarded
to the plaintiff, Olesa Holland . . . [are] hereby awarded to the
defendant, Donald Holland."[16] On appeal, after much procedural
squabbling, including a suggestion by the court that one attorney
take his case to the World Court, it appeared that the change of
custody had been based on a report that was not consented to by
both parties. Then the court, pointing to an absence of evidence on
which to base the change of custody, reversed the order.[17]

In an early California case the trial court ruled that evidence of
the mother's homosexual activity was inadmissible and awarded
her custody. On appeal, however, custody was changed because
"moral character, acts, conduct and disposition . . . are relevant
matters."[18]

Eight years later the California Court of Appeals held that homosexuality was not a preclusive factor to the granting of child custody.[19] The trial court had ruled that "as a matter of law" a lesbian mother was to lose custody to the children's heterosexual father, although the court had the authority to exercise its discretion by hearing all the evidence directed toward the child's welfare. The Court of Appeals held that "not until the trial court has considered *all the evidence* [may it] exercise its discretion . . . the trial court failed in its duty to exercise the very discretion with which it is vested by holding as a matter of law that petitioner was an unfit mother on the basis that she is a homosexual."[20] When the case returned to the lower court, custody was again awarded to the father. The mother's visitation rights were restricted so that she could see the child only in the presence of a chaperon, but she was assured that if she took "therapeutics," the chaperon might no longer need to be present.[21]

Court decisions for lesbian mothers had not improved in California by 1975. In one ironic custody award, the children went to the mother's mother, who had not only raised a lesbian daughter but a gay son as well.[22]

A landmark Ohio case was *Hall v. Hall*.[23] In one of her exceptional reviews of lesbian mother child custody cases, law professor Rhonda Rivera characterized that case as "the beginning of the use of experts on homosexuality."[24] I was the expert witness in *Hall*. Excerpts from the testimony follow:

*Mother's Attorney:*

EMOTIONAL STABILITY OF MOTHER

Attorney: Did you find [the mother] to be a stable person?

Green: Yes. With respect to her sexual relationships that she has had, I would say [she is] traditionally stable, being committed to the people with whom she has been involved romantically and sexually . . . She was married at a young age. In fact, she was married twice to the same individual in an effort to continue that relationship. She has currently been involved in a romantic and sexual relationship for some three years which indicates stability in maintaining a significant interpersonal relationship . . . This is a sign of maturation and sexual health.

## SEXUAL INTERACTION OF MOTHER VISIBLE TO THE CHILDREN

Attorney: In your examination how did [the mother] say she expresses herself regarding her sexual attraction to another female in front of the children?

Green: . . . She indicated that both she and [her partner] were particularly careful in terms of not exposing [the girl] to explicit sex acts between the two of them; that what might be available to [the child's] view from time to time could be common kinds of affection frequently shown by adult females in our culture, perhaps an occasional hug or kiss, but certainly nothing of a graphic sexual nature . . . With respect to sexual activities conducted by them in their own bedroom, this is absolutely off limits.

## MOTHER'S ATTITUDE TOWARD MALES

Attorney: From your interview with [the mother] is she hostile towards men?

Green: Not at all . . . Her feeling is that she gets along better with men in terms of a working relationship, in terms of colleagueship and close companionship . . . It is with respect to the sexual part of her life that women are preferred, but her feelings toward men are not at all hostile, but in fact, quite warm and positive. This I feel is particularly important in this situation.

Attorney: Why?

Green: One concern that one would have with respect to a young female growing up in a home in which there were two women who have a sexual and romantic commitment to each other, to the exclusion of males, is the kind of imagery that might be painted of males, generally. This image may have a bearing on how a young child sees males in our culture, and may . . . have a bearing on subsequent relationships, both interpersonal and sexual . . . A danger could exist in which one has two female homosexual parents who dislike men intensely and overtly convey this image to the child. This can have a destructive influence on the child's development.

## PSYCHOSEXUAL REARING OF THE DAUGHTER

Attorney: Do they encourage [her] to act in an anti-male way?

Green: No, based on the kind of toys they [the two women] provide for her and the kind of clothing they provide, if anything, they adhere to rather traditional stereotypic ways of what is considered to be "appropriately" feminine and "appropriately" masculine.

The toys available for [her] are primarily Barbie dolls and classically female-type toys which some feminists, in fact, would object
to, and say it was sexist and we shouldn't be programming little
girls into playing with Barbie dolls. With respect to clothing,
dresses primarily are provided, and the child delights in that. In
fact, she has a wedding gown which was bought for her by her
mother; a wedding gown that she utilizes in her fantasy play. She
role-plays as a bride. It is a very pro-female identity and pro-femi-
nine kind of child raising that [she] is having.

## MOTHER'S PARTNER

Attorney: Tell us what the results of your examination and interview
were with [the mother's partner].

Green: . . . She has been employed at her current occupation now for
some twelve years . . . I was particularly impressed with the degree
of stability in [her] past sexual relationships. She first engaged in a
homosexual relationship at approximately eighteen, a relationship
which lasted some five years. A second relationship, again a female
homosexual relationship, lasted some ten years, and then the current relationship with [her partner] has been ongoing for three
years. With respect to the number of sexual partners and the duration of the relationships she has been engaged in, this demonstrates
a remarkable capacity for commitment to another person, and a
mature capacity to maintain a longstanding relationship with a significant other person.

Attorney: What is her feeling about [the little girl]?

Green: Her feeling is positive and strong.

## EVALUATION OF THE CHILD

Attorney: Would you tell us the results of your interview with [the
little girl]?

Green: She is a rather delightful little child. I asked her to draw a
picture of someone, which is sort of an icebreaker for children
before one begins a formal interview, asking a child to draw a person. It is a simple thing that is within the competence of children.
It tells you something about sexual identity in children. In the age
group around five or six, little boys with a male identity typically
draw a boy or male first, and little girls with a typically female identity draw a female first. I was impressed in this instance that not
only did [she] draw a female, but she also drew her mother. I asked
her whether she plays house and typical mother-father type games

with anyone, . . . and she said, "Yes." She said the role she plays is the mommy and [the other child] plays the daddy. Her favorite toys are Barbie dolls, and the wedding gown which she wears. I asked her about her friends at school. She quite proudly told me she has not only one but two boyfriends. One of them in particular she says she would like to marry. I forget the little boy's name, but there is one she has a crush on. She considers him to be her boyfriend.

The significance of all these issues is with the respect to the first two components of sexual identity. The first is the basic awareness—"I am male—I am female." There is no question but that [she] has a sexual identity of being female. With respect to the second component, masculine or feminine behavior, there is no question but that she is a feminine little girl. With respect to the third, sexual preference, I think that [she] is exploring child fantasies playing the female role, and it is a fairly traditional male-female role—husband-wife, heterosexual role relationship. That is where the earlier seeds of her sexual identity are.

Attorney: And you believe that to be?

Green: I would predict that she will be a female feminine heterosexual lady.

DEVELOPMENT OF SEXUAL ORIENTATION

Attorney: Will you explain what causes a person to become homosexual according to the scientific evidence available today?

Green: I will be brief. There are a number of theories. They can be divided into genetic or inborn ones, biochemical ones, and social learning theories.

The genetic theory was best expounded by Dr. Kallman of Columbia many years ago. He studied identical twins. He found that in about forty pairs of identical twins, when one twin was homosexual, the other was also homosexual. From these studies Dr. Kallman concluded that homosexuality was an inborn genetic condition. Since that time other investigators have found identical twins who are discordant, where one is heterosexual and one is homosexual. I think the issue remains unsettled, but most investigators feel that there is probably some degree of genetic loading, if you will, of characteristics which predispose certain people to homosexual life-styles.

A second theory which has gained interest in the last four or five years is the levels of sex hormones, male and female sex hormones. There has been a series of papers indicating that homosexuals have higher or lower male or female hormones, that is, higher or lower than their heterosexual counterparts. The conclusion drawn from these studies is that in some way sex hormone levels attained before birth or in early childhood influence sexual identity and sexual orientation. Again, these studies, in scientific terms, remain inconclusive.

The third category is social learning theory. What researchers are looking at is the quality of the relationship during the first three to five years of life between the mother and child and father and child. With respect to male homosexuality, people frequently look at a too close relationship between the young boy and mother or an alienated relationship between the young boy and father. They feel it predisposes to male homosexuality. Contrariwise, with respect to female homosexuality, people look for a distant or alienated relationship between the mother and daughter and encouragement of tomboyism or masculine-type behavior from father to daughter. The thinking here is that children, as they establish sexual identity, need to identify with the appropriate parental figure, and the appropriate parental figure for the young male is the father and the appropriate parental figure for the young female is the mother. It is this identification which takes place during the first two to three years, and clearly by the onset of the grade school years, that is the critical period which later shows itself as heterosexual or homosexual.

Whether one ascribes to the genetic viewpoint, to the hormonal theory, or to the social learning viewpoint, if there is a consensus, it is that the critical issues are the ones decided early in life. They are decided at an age in which the actual sexual expression doesn't show itself, but the seeds are sown. Probably the most sober view today is that there is an interactional effect between a genetic predisposition, and some hormonal contributions, perhaps, and primarily the relationship between the significant parent and child.

## HOMOSEXUAL PARENTS AS DETERMINING A CHILD'S HOMOSEXUALITY

Attorney: You didn't mention one possible cause of homosexuality, and that is having homosexual parents, and living with them. What is your opinion as to that as a possible cause of homosexuality?

Green: It is an erroneous view to say that because the parents are homosexual the children will be. If that were the case homosexuality would have died out long ago. Almost all, if not all, homosexuals have had heterosexual mothers and fathers. So if it is merely parent role modeling, how do we explain that ten percent or more of the population is homosexual? It has to be something beyond that. Frankly, I don't know of any theory which has been advanced which has suggested that having homosexual parents in and of itself is going to be a significant contributor to a homosexual orientation.

EFFECTS ON CHILDREN OF LIVING IN A
HOMOSEXUAL HOUSEHOLD

Attorney: If a child were to see homosexual parents and had a loving relationship with them, what would the reaction of the child be?

Green: The most significant effect in the long haul would be that the child would tend to view homosexuality in others in a more tolerant and less prejudiced manner than the child who grows up with the typical kind of myths they may get from street corner gossip that most of us grew up with. An analogy can be made to a child that grows up in a racially integrated neighborhood or with a very restricted background. It doesn't mean the child who comes from a Protestant family growing up next to the Catholic is going to convert to Catholicism, but it can mean they could have a greater understanding of the two religions and be more tolerant of the two and the two different viewpoints. I think the same thing is true with respect to homosexuality. Children cannot grow up today in a social vacuum. They recognize their own family, and they also recognize cultural standards. They see male-female role modeling portrayed in movies and television. They read children's stories and what they do is put their own family into perspective with the rest of the culture. And what comes out of that is that they adopt the standard and traditional cultural perspective with greater tolerance of people whose life-style is atypical. The only significant change would be a tolerance of homosexuality in others.

Attorney: What is the likelihood that this mother . . . will sexually molest [the child]?

Green: It is pretty unlikely. Sexual molestation in our culture is pretty much by males . . . It is essentially a male act, and it is in most cases by heterosexual males on children, and since neither [women] are male heterosexuals, I would say the probability of child molestation is trivial.

HOMOSEXUALITY AS A MENTAL DISORDER

Attorney: Have there been recent changes by the medical profession in their views of homosexuals, especially as to whether it signifies emotional disorder?

Green: Yes. Traditionally, homosexuality was considered by medicine and psychiatric science as being a mental disorder. One of the reasons this was so is that classically the case reports which got into the psychiatric and psychological literature were based upon patients who were troubled with their sexuality, who came to physicians requesting help . . . This clearly does not represent the average person. The average heterosexual and average homosexual never seek out psychiatric help. If one were to look at the psychiatric files of most of us one would find most of the people there are heterosexual. Of course, this doesn't mean we have mental disorders because we are heterosexual. Just recently the American Psychiatric Association officially decreed homosexuality per se is not a sign of mental illness or emotional disorder, and that the individual needs to be evaluated as an individual. One's sexual orientation, be it heterosexual or homosexual, does not signify mental disorder.

STIGMA

Attorney: Is the child embarrassed by the mother's lesbianism at this point, to your knowledge?

Green: Not to my knowledge . . .

Attorney: Could she possibly be so in the future?

Green: I would say it is a possibility. I think it is going to depend upon the degree to which our culture continues to change with respect to its view of alternative life-styles. We are going through a period of dramatic social change, and it depends upon how young children view the way people behave and act. Homosexuality, which was so much of a taboo twenty years ago, is much more open to discussion today. We know people live a variety of life-styles. They do things today they didn't do ten years ago, and in the next five or ten years we will continue to see evolution in this direction. So the degree of their embarrassment, if any, will depend upon the way it is looked upon and the biases of people. Perhaps [they will have] a certain degree of embarrassment, but that is relatively insignificant and will be so, so long as there is a solid relationship in the home.

Some of us grow on a degree of adversity. I don't believe the child is going to be stigmatized more than all children who, for a variety of reasons, are teased, for example, because they are short or tall, fat or skinny, athletes or sissies. Some children get taunted throughout their childhood, and we all have labels that we have been taunted with, but it doesn't destroy us. Weighing the possible embarrassment she may experience against continuing in a solid home relationship, I would come out on the side of continuing the home relationship.

## Questions from the Court

Court: *Dr. Green, how is the sex act between lesbians accomplished?*

Green: That would vary just like with non-lesbians. It would vary depending upon the individual couple. There is a range of practice between them.

Court: How would you expect it to be accomplished?

Green: The most common form of sexual expression between two females is by mutual manipulation of the genitalia.

Court: Do you consider that normal?

Green: Well, the act itself is the act which is also practiced by heterosexuals. Oral-genital sex is practiced by some eighty percent of heterosexuals, so the act itself is that which is practiced by most people. The incidence of same sex acts between male persons after puberty, based on the Kinsey data, is one in three, so while it is minor, it is very substantially minor. We are talking about a lot of people.

Court: Would you consider it to be normal copulation?

Green: Normal in terms of statistics or psychologically healthy?

Court: Let's take them one at a time.

Green: In a statistical sense it is atypical . . . With respect to its being psychologically a healthy or unhealthy experience, I would say the current thinking of behavioral scientists, including psychiatrists, is that the sex of one's partner is not really the essential ingredient of psychological health. We know heterosexuals who have terrible relationships and terrible adjustments sexually, and we also know there are homosexuals who are very healthy psychologically, and who have very good relationships. I don't think without knowing the individual couple one could say the act between two females or two males is psychologically abnormal. One has to examine the individual.

The mother was awarded child custody. The transcript became an early reference for attorneys in other cases.

Neither parent was found to be suitable for custody of the children in another Ohio case in which I testified a year after *Hall*.[25] In awarding custody to the father's mother, the trial court stressed societal disapproval of homosexuality: "Society as a whole disap-

proves of sexual aberration of any kind, particularly homosexual-
ism, and that is a very ancient disapproval. You read in the old
testament of Sodom and Gomorrah . . . there can be no question in
the Court's mind that the conduct revealed here is against the mores
of our present day society."[26]

The court also indicated that if the mother had abstained from
lesbianism she might have received custody. "Had the defendant
indicated that until her children were reared she would abandon the
practice of lesbianism, I am not asking her to abandon being a lesbian, I think she probably couldn't, the Court might be tempted to
experiment with the mother." The court emphasized concern about
teasing by other children: "Children are cruel in their relationship
to other children. They will be teased, they will be confronted with
the remark 'Your mother is queer' . . . that cannot be helpful in the
rearing of these children." Disregarding my testimony regarding
sexual orientation of children raised by homosexual parents, the
court continued, "the Court is not expert enough to know whether
they will be more likely themselves to be homosexual because of
living in that environment." And here again, the mother's insistence
on continuing her relationship was scored by the court. "I would
think that a lesbian, for the sake of the children, would have abandoned the practice, if not the aberration . . . But I am struck by the
primacy that lesbians, at least the two lesbians who testified here,
give to multiple *organisms* [sic]."[27]

After the lower court had awarded custody to the father's
mother, the Court of Appeals of Ohio had its say. It reviewed the
lower court testimony that during a nine-day vacation the mother
and her partner and the children had slept in one motel room, that
the couple had exchanged vows of love in a chapel and had granted
newspaper and television interviews, that the children were aware
of the lesbian relationship and that the oldest child had been teased.
The court recounted that the women "made love as many as five or
six times in one day."[28]

The appellate court ruled on several questions, including whether
the trial judge erred in excluding my testimony on the good mental
health of the mother's partner and whether there was trial court
error in "compelling [the mother] to answer questions about the
intimate details of her sex life."[29]

The mental health of the mother's partner was deemed irrelevant, as it "had not been placed in issue." Descriptions of the mother's sexual actions were held to be necessary because "the trial court did not know precisely what occurred in this lesbian relationship" and it was appropriate for the trial court and father's counsel to receive "a primer education in the sexual techniques of lesbians,"[30] although it was not made clear why this was necessary. The appellate court reviewed the trial court transcript, including the excerpts cited above, and ruled that "the trial court's decision was not tainted by bias."[31]

A much sensationalized 1974 case in which I was a witness involved the consolidated custody battles of two families.[32] The two lesbian mothers and their children, living as a combined family, had appeared on television and in public demonstrations, and had made a movie, *Sandy and Madelein's Family,* that featured the anthropologist Margaret Mead.

In the earlier divorce of both couples in 1972, the mothers, already romantic partners, were ordered by a Washington State court to live "separate and apart," with their sets of children. Not exactly complying with the letter of the ruling, and certainly not with its spirit, they took adjacent apartments and essentially lived as a combined family. As the publicity extolling the success of their alternative family life-style increased, the fathers returned to court to effect a change of custody. The mothers counterpetitioned to modify the divorce decrees so that the women and children could live together.

At the outset the trial judge noted the publicity and the need to evaluate its effects on the children.

(The mothers) . . . have violated in spirit and in fact the terms of the decree requiring them to live separate . . . they have publicized their homosexual relationship and their lesbian parentage in newspaper stories, radio and television shows and a motion picture and numerous speeches, appearances, presentations and publications relating to their cause of homosexuality. [Under the 1973 Marriage Dissolution Act] . . . I must decide . . . whether the children's present environment is detrimental to their physical, mental or emotional health and [whether] the harm likely to be caused by a change in the environment is outweighed by the advantage of a change to the child."[33]

The testimony of experts was considered and respected.

In this case almost all of the testimony of all the people who actually saw, examined, talked to the children was that the children are healthy, happy, normal, loving children. And I must so find. Their living situation during the past twenty months with custody in the mothers and visitation with the fathers has proved to be in the best interests of the children as shown by the way they have turned out . . . Testimony introduced by [the fathers] . . . suggests that children raised by homosexual mothers may be more likely to become homosexuals than if raised by heterosexual parents. [Mothers'] witnesses discredited this theory.[34]

The trial judge was concerned about the extent of any publicity. "I would caution [the mothers] that if in the future they put the children on exhibition for the cause of homosexuality or if they spend too much time on that cause as to the neglect of the children, these circumstances could jeopardize future custody."[35]

Finally, in an understatement, the trial judge concluded, "I don't think this case should be regarded as any landmark decision or as any stamp of approval by the Court on homosexuality. I think that it is a case just like cases that we decide every day."[36]

On appeal, the Washington Supreme Court ruled that the children could remain with their mothers but that the mothers must live apart.[37]

Several years after this case, the Washington State Supreme Court addressed the issue of homosexual parenting more directly. It ruled that "homosexuality in and of itself is not a bar to custody or to reasonable rights of visitation."[38]

Psychiatric testimony attesting that a mother's lesbianism did not have adverse effects on her children was also heeded by a Vermont court.

Counsel for the children urges the Court to find and the Court does find that there is no evidence from which the Court could reasonably conclude that the defendant's relationship with another woman has had any negative effect on the children nor is there any evidence from which the Court might reasonably infer that this relationship will if continued in the future adversely affect the children. In particular, the expert testimony which the Court has received indicates that all of the research on this subject, although sparse, concludes that the children living with a parent having a homosexual relationship are at no greater risk to suffer adjustment or psychological disorders as children living in a heterosexual parental relationship.[39]

Termination of the mother's lesbian relationship was the price the father demanded for her continued visitation in a Michigan case. The "friend of the court" expert testified that he believed that if the sexual nature of the relationship was openly expressed in the presence of the children, it would have a harmful effect. The trial court found that the lesbian relationship was detrimental to the health and upbringing of the children, especially to the son who was eight, and that it would only be a matter of time until the younger five-year-old girl became aware of the relationship. The court had no objection to the plaintiff's lesbian relationship, provided that it was not "exercised in the children's presence." The trial court's order continued visitation as it existed but provided that while the children were visiting the mother no "intimate sexual conduct was to take place and that the children could not remain overnight if the mother's sexual partner were present overnight." On appeal, these limitations were upheld.[40]

A different result was obtained in Oregon. There visitation restrictions were imposed on the mother as the price for retaining or seeing her children. The Oregon Court of Appeals, however, struck down the restriction. "So long as the mother's sexual practice remains discreet—a requirement whatever the sexual preferences of the parties might be . . . and the presence of lesbianism in the home from time to time does not of itself create difficulties for the children of a greater magnitude than that suggested by the record, restriction is inappropriate."[41]

A father's sexuality was also disfavored in Louisiana, where the courts were not impressed with the "high moral standards" of either parent. The father had admitted to an adulterous relationship with his girlfriend, while the mother was found to be engaged in "discreet lesbian activities." The courts took a dim view of both relationships. The appellate court noted, "In his custody award, the trial judge did not see fit to favor one form of adultery [sic] over another; we do not find his decision erroneous."[42]

The appellate court's analysis focused on the nexus between "immoral" parental behavior and the child's welfare. In a statement reflecting society's double standard on cohabitation, the court observed that "although the mother and Ms. Greenwood are still roommates, the presumptions society makes when an unmarried man and woman share living quarters do not apply in situations where members of the same sex are roommates. While the child may suffer from the opprobrium of society when living in the same house with her mother and the mother's homosexual lover, such is not the case unless the relationship is notorious. Such does not appear to be the case, at least presently, in the situation at hand."[43] The mother retained physical custody.

A Detroit case elicited considerable newspaper coverage. The *Detroit Free Press* characterized the parental relationship in soap-opera fashion: "Mrs. Stamper brought first one and then another woman into their house to live . . . [Mr.] Stamper moved to a new home with the woman who was his wife's former lover. [Mrs.] Stamper's current lover has, meanwhile, continued to live in the home with her and the two children for the past two years."[44]

The newspaper also reported the diverse testimony of the behavioral science experts. "All but one [of the experts] said homosexuality was not a mental illness." One psychiatrist called it a "character disorder." A psychologist "recommended that the children remain with the mother, provided her lover moves out of the house." Another psychologist "counseled against putting the mother's lover out of the house if the children were to remain there." I was cited as having "made no recommendation other than saying I saw no reason why a homosexual parent could not raise children." (Excerpts from my actual testimony follow.) The other psychiatrist recommended custody with the father "lest [the children] be harmed by [what he called] their mother's 'homosexual evangelism.' "[45]

*Father's Attorney:*

MOTHER'S DESIRE REGARDING SEXUAL ORIENTATION OF HER CHILD

    Attorney: Could those parents in some degree influence the child's [sexual behavior]?

    Green: They might.

    Attorney: They're committed to having a daughter or son that is heterosexual?

Green: . . . If you ask people . . . do you want your son to be hetero-sexual or homosexual, you get one or two categories of answer. Either parents will say that they want their son to be happy or they would like the child to be heterosexual. You don't get people who want their child to be homosexual. The real question is, can parents influence the child and to what degree can parents influence the adolescent?

Attorney: I'm dealing in terms of heterosexual.

Green: Let's consider the mother or father who is very concerned about premarital intercourse in the adolescent female because of pregnancies out of wedlock, abortion, venereal disease. Parents, whether they like it or not, are notoriously unsuccessful in effecting influence on their children in the area of sexuality. I don't know that the parents want their children to have babies out of wedlock, and yet the rate of illegitimate births is soaring. I don't know that parents want their children to get venereal disease, but we are hav-ing a gonorrhea epidemic and a revival of a syphilis epidemic. Par-ents' expectations and desires in many areas of adolescent behav-ior, including sexual or educational, are frequently unfulfilled.

Attorney: Now, a homosexual parent, would that parent be commit-ted to a homosexual way of life? Would that parent feel that a homosexual life would be better than a heterosexual life?

Green: My experience with homosexual adults is that their feeling is that it is a better way of life for themselves, and it has been dem-onstrated to themselves that it is. Homosexuals are not out to con-vert the heterosexual world into a homosexual world. Even the most rabid, most militant faction aren't out to try to convert the other 90 percent to homosexuality. They're concerned with civil rights.

Attorney: . . . Are you saying that the homosexual parent would not encourage his or her life-style on someone that they loved?

Green: I would say that they would essentially leave the choice of life-style to the decision of the person they love.

PUBLIC EXPOSURE AND STIGMA

Attorney: What do you believe or perceive the effect on the children of this age forward of the criticism that they will face from their peers and society as a result of their mother's sexual preference?

Green: . . . It depends first on the degree to which this family unit becomes public. The degree to which the mother involves herself and the children in a public display of homosexuality and lesbian motherhood and public demonstrations and makes a celebrity case out of it. I don't think that's wise, it exposes the children to mass public exposure. Based upon my experience in other families, there may be some degree of teasing from the peer group. That will not be as much teasing as you would think because society is continuing to liberalize its views towards all racial, religious, and sexual preferences and styles. Also when children have siblings to rely on as well as a comforting home, a lot of support emanates which reduces the effect of peer group testing. And all kids get teased about something.

In its decision the court hardly embraced the life-style of either parent: "[The lesbian mother] has had two long term love affairs within the confines of her home, while the children were there. The first affair, with a teenage girl, was more intermittent but, the evidence shows, no less intense than the second affair. It went on for years with the husband present in the house . . . The second relationship, the one that continues to the present, was started at the time the wife's first lover was away at school . . . The present lover of the wife had just had a long standing affair of her own . . . The second relationship was commenced in the home while [the father] and the children were still in residence. Almost immediately upon the cessation of his relationship with his wife and upon the termination of the relationship of his wife with her first lover, [the father] upon moving out of the house, commenced a relationship with his wife's first lover which appears to continue to the present time. This brief narrative to extensive testimony indicates that as to the question of 'moral fitness' there is very little to choose between the parents . . .

"[However,] both girls expressed a preference for living with their mother. They were very protective of their mother but very careful not to be too critical of their father."[46]

Custody went to the mother.

A Massachusetts trial judge took "judicial notice" of what he considered the adverse effects of lesbian motherhood, even though *both* mother and father introduced evidence "to the effect that a mother's sexual preference per se is irrelevant to a consideration of her parenting skills."[47] As the appellate court observed, "a clinical psychologist and professor of psychology . . . testified that '[T]here is no evidence at all that sexual preference of adults in the home has any detrimental impact on children . . . [M]any other issues influence child rearing. Sexual preference per se is typically not one of them.'" The father's counsel questioned further: "[T]here is nothing to prove that a homosexual relationship would make or in any way influence a child to be a homosexual rather than a heterosexual?" The witness responded, "There is no evidence that children who are raised with a loving couple of the same sex are any more disturbed, unhealthy, maladjusted than children raised with a loving couple of mixed sex."[48] A psychologist witness for the father concurred with the opinion of the mother's expert that homosexuality per se is irrelevant to parenting ability.

In a ringing affirmation of the necessity of a trial court's objectivity, the appellate court held that

> [a] finding that a parent is unfit to further the welfare of the child must be predicated upon parental behavior which adversely affects the child. The State may not deprive parents of custody of their children "simply because their households fail to meet the ideals approved by the community . . . [or] simply because the parents embrace ideologies or pursue life-styles at odds with the average." In the total absence of evidence suggesting a correlation between the mother's homosexuality and her fitness as a parent, we believe the judge's finding that a lesbian household would adversely affect the children to be without basis in the record. This is not a matter about which the judge could take judicial notice. 'Matters are judicially noticed only when they are indisputably true . . . Judicial notice is not to be extended to personal observations of the judge . . .'"[49]

But in a subsequent Massachusetts case in which I was a witness, the court held that the mother's time with her daughter was not to be shared with any female romantic partners.[50] The court was concerned that the mother's lesbianism could have "an indirect effect in many ways. For example, time spent away from home with lovers could mean less time spent with children . . . Also a general attitude of permissiveness in matters of sex could be considered detrimental to a child's welfare, in spite of current trends in TV and movies."[51]

On the other hand, two years later the Massachusetts Appeals Court upheld a trial court's decision for joint custody between a lesbian mother and the child's heterosexual father while giving physical custody to the mother.[52] The husband had sought custody in consequence of his wife's having a "deviant life-style." The appellate court assessed whether the child's living conditions "adversely affect[ed] his physical, mental, moral or emotional health."[53]

Four psychiatrists testified that the mother's sexual orientation per se would not adversely affect the child. The appellate court noted: "One of these three witnesses testified to a study he had conducted comparing single parent heterosexuals with minor children to single homosexual parents with minor children. He found 'no difference in the minor children and no evidence of sexual dysfunction to a minor child reared by a single homosexual parent.' "[54] The court discounted the opposing psychiatrist's testimony because "he had no supporting studies and his exposure to single parent lesbians was limited."[55] The court also noted the absence of any stigma on the child: "There is no evidence to show that the wife's life-style will adversely affect [the son] . . . we think this an important fact, that [the son] 'has not been tormented by his friends in regard to his mother's life-style.' "[56]

Stigma has been cited by courts when awarding custody to the heterosexual father: "[T]he court must determine whether and to what extent the emotional and mental health of the child has been affected by the mother's deviant behavior . . . the court finds on the basis of the clinic report, its interview of the child and the testimony of the witnesses that the social stigma of having a lesbian mother has had a traumatic emotional impact on [the boy] and that he should not be forced to return to his mother and the environment of her home."[57]

In addressing the issue of stigma, the Alaska Supreme Court referred to the United States Supreme Court case of *Palmore v. Sidoti*.[58] There, a white father of a white child from an earlier marriage sought custody after his ex-wife married a black. The Supreme Court ruled that even though stigma might attach to the child, the Court would not enforce bigotry. "The Constitution cannot control such prejudices but neither can it tolerate them. Private biases may be outside the reach of the law, but the law cannot, directly or indirectly, give them effect."[59] The Alaska court held it impermissible to rely on any real or imagined social stigma attaching to the mother's status as a lesbian.[60]

Two New Jersey cases in which I testified are linked.[61] They are unique in that their tandem custody disputes involved two sets of cohabiting families, as distinct from the previously described consolidated litigation in Washington State, and in their disparate outcomes.

In *Belmont v. Belmont,* the father demanded a change of custody, contending that the mother's cohabitation with a lesbian, who also had children, was harmful to his children. "The court heard from a psychiatrist specializing in human sexuality," however, "who testified that the children suffered no sexual identity problems, and in fact were extremely well adjusted." The court ruled that "the mother is not to be denied continued custody merely because of her sexual orientation. Her sexual preference and her living arrangement with her lover are only two of the many factors to be examined in determining the best interests of the children."[62]

Ms. Wales was the romantic partner of Ms. Belmont who won custody of her children at trial. By contrast, she settled her case, before trial, a settlement she states was "forced on her by the court."[63] Physical custody went to the father.

Another New Jersey case in which I testified is memorable for its vindication of the rights of a homosexual parent. After seven years, during which a lesbian mother had had custody of two daughters, the father won a lower court decision and regained custody. But the appellate court, in reviewing the trial court record, observed that all experts, including the one appointed by the court, were favorable to the mother. "These witnesses were qualified, their opinions were unrefuted and were not inherently implausible . . . Nowhere do we find documented in the record any specific instances of sexual misconduct by defendant or evidence that she tried in any way to inculcate the girls with her sexual attitudes . . . The only conclusion to be drawn is . . . that the custody order was modified for the sole reason that she is a homosexual."[64]

On appeal, the father argued that the change in circumstances that warranted a change in custody was the mother's sexual orientation, which caused "embarrassment to the girls in the eyes of peers."[65] Observing that the girls would have a lesbian mother whichever parent had custody, the court wrote: "Neither the prejudices of the small community in which they live nor the curiosity of their peers about defendant's sexual nature will be abated by a change in custody. Hard facts must be faced. These are matters which courts cannot control, and there is little to gain by creating an artificial world where the children may dream that life is different than it is."[66]

In a stirring decision more eloquent than that of the Supreme Court in *Palmore v. Sidoti,* the New Jersey court wrote that one result of societal intolerance could be that the children

> will emerge better equipped to search out their own standards of right and wrong, better able to perceive that the majority is not always correct in its moral judgments . . . Taking the children from defendant can be done only at the cost of sacrificing those very qualities they will find most sustaining in meeting the challenges inevitably ahead. Instead of forbearance and feelings of protectiveness, it will foster in them a sense of shame for their mother. Instead of courage and the precept that people of integrity do not shrink from bigots, it counsels the easy option of shirking difficult problems and following the course of expedience. Lastly, it diminishes their regard for the rule of human behavior, everywhere accepted, that we do not forsake those to whom we are indebted for love and nurture merely because they are held in low esteem by others."[67]

The New Jersey court's view stands in stark contrast to that of the supreme court of North Dakota:

> Sandra's homosexuality may, indeed, be something which is beyond her control. However, living with another person of the same sex in a sexual relationship is not something beyond her control. It may be argued that to force her to dissolve her living relationship in order to retain custody of her children is too much to ask. However, we need no legal citation to note that concerned parents in many, many instances have made sacrifices of varying degrees for their children.[68]

In a Colorado case in which I testified, four children had been born of the parties' fourteen-year marriage.[69] Excerpts from the testimony follow.

*Mother's Attorney:*

TRANSSEXUAL PARENTS' EFFECT ON
CHILDREN'S SEXUALITY

Attorney: Doctor, are there any studies of which you are aware in progress with regard to sexuality development as it relates to the children of the homosexual parent . . .

Green: I have evaluated sixteen children who were living in the home with a parent who, in addition to being, strictly speaking, homosexual, had an even more dramatically atypical sexual identity. These are parents that had undergone so-called "sex change surgery." That is for about half the parents, a person who now appears as the father had formerly been a woman and in some cases had actually been the mother of the child and was now in the role of the father. With about half of the other children the person now apparently in the role of the mother to the child either had previously been a male or had previously been the father of the children. We are also evaluating a series of fifty lesbian mother families and their children.

Attorney: Doctor, have there been any conclusions reached?

Green: The conclusions so far do not show any significant difference between the children being raised in homosexual or even transsexual settings compared to the children being raised in the traditional heterosexual settings. With respect to sexual identity of these children, so far, all the evidence that we have does not show that there is any significant influence.

*Father's Attorney:*

DIFFERENCES OF CHILDREN IN LESBIAN
MOTHER HOUSEHOLDS

Attorney: Is there any difference whatsoever with children in lesbian mother households?

Green: The only difference we see so far is that these children seem more tolerant of adult people who have different kinds of sexual preference from the majority.

Attorney: How do you know that they show more tolerance?

Green: By what they tell me.

Attorney: What do they tell you?

Green: "People should have the right to live the way they want to. If they want to live with a person of the same sex instead of another sex, that's fine with me. It is not something I would like to do." Which is what one of the children [in this case] told me.

Attorney: Which one?

Green: It's a quote from the twelve-year-old. I asked him how he felt about his mother living with another woman instead of another man. "I don't feel nothing bad about it. There is nothing wrong, but I wouldn't want to live with another man myself."

Although this Colorado-based case was decided in favor of the lesbian mother, in a later Colorado case, the trial judge ignored the recommendations of experts: "I think the homosexuality of the mother is severe now, with the oldest child being ten and can't help become more severe as the children go into puberty . . . The court is not bound by the testimony of experts."[70]

Not all expert testimony is supportive of custody by a lesbian mother, nor does it always reflect the most prevalent research findings. In Kentucky, a court-appointed psychologist testified that "[the daughter] will have additional burdens to bear in terms of teasing, possible embarrassment and internal conflicts . . . there is excellent scientific research on the effects of parental modeling on children. Speculating from such data, it is reasonable to suggest that [the daughter] may have difficulties in achieving a fulfilling heterosexual identity."[71]

## Cases: Fathers

In an early case involving a homosexual father, the father lost custody in the trial court but was granted visitation rights. He appealed and then lost visitation. The appellate court disapproved of his lifestyle, which revealed an "erotic engrossment." There was concern that the children "may be exposed to improper conditions and undesirable influences."[72]

A much-cited case in which I testified involving a gay father focused on the father's political activism (he was the director of the National Gay Task Force).[73] The central issues as defined by the New Jersey court were whether parental rights of visitation should be restricted because a father is homosexual, whether granting visitation would serve the children's best interests, and whether visitation of this father should be restricted.

At the outset the court affirmed the rights of homosexual parents: "The parental rights of a homosexual, like those of a heterosexual, are constitutionally protected. Fundamental rights of parents may not be denied, limited or restricted on the basis of sexual orientation per se."[74] But it was downhill for this father from that point on.

The court recounted that all experts who testified agreed that homosexuality per se was not a mental disorder and that "a balanced exposure would not be harmful to the children."[75] The experts all endorsed visitation with the father and agreed that the father had been a good parent. The mother, however, requested limitation of visitation because the father's "total involvement with and dedication to furthering homosexuality has created an environment, exposure to which in anything more than a minimal amount would be harmful." Responding to this allegation, the court noted that the father lived with a male sexual partner and had "involved the children in his attempts to further homosexuality. They have accompanied him on protest marches, at rallies and were filmed with him for a television show . . . [They] have been present with him at . . . a meeting hall for homosexuals . . . [furthermore] homosexuality and gay rights are a common if not the most common topic of conversation when the children are with defendant."[76]

Although the three experts agreed that "there was very little chance that exposure to a homosexual environment would alter the children's sexual orientation and that at the present time they were well adjusted,"[77] the mother's expert opined that "the total environment to which the father expose[s] the children could impede healthy sexual development . . . the father's milieu could engender homosexual fantasies causing confusion and anxiety . . . it is possible that these children upon reaching puberty would be subject to either overt or covert homosexual seduction."[78]

The court acknowledged that my testimony and that of the father's other witness "[did] not concur with [the mother's expert's] conclusion regarding the possible ill effects on the children."[79] Nevertheless, the court ordered that, during visitation, the father was not to be in the presence of his lover, and that he was not to involve the children in any homosexual-related activities or publicity. The decision was upheld on appeal.[80]

In a later New York case the children's visitation to their homosexual father in the presence of his male partner was also denied by the trial court. The court's visitation was conditioned on "the total exclusion of [father's] lover or any other homosexuals during such visitation periods . . . [and] . . . during [the father's] periods of visitation the child will not be taken any place where known homosexuals are present."[81] Five appellate judges reversed this decision.

A homosexual father in Maine was also challenged because of his live-in or regularly present sexual partner. In the lower court, the overnight visitation of his daughters was restricted to times when no male or female visitors were present.[82] The appellate court disagreed with the lower court analysis: "The issue is not the possible effects of homosexuality, generally, but of [the father's] specific homosexual behavior in so far as it affects the character of the environment to which the girls were, or would be exposed."[83] The lower court's order barring overnight visitation when the father's partner was present revealed "concern[s] about the possible effects of [father's] sexual activities,"[84] but no evidence had been presented of possible "deleterious impact" on the children, only "that there *may* be an effect and the effect is not good."[85] Bias by the trial judge was seen as the basis of the ruling: "Because there is no showing or finding of effect of that behavior on the children, I can only conclude that the Court, rather than focusing on the best interests of the children or the evidence presented, based its decision on its personal dislike of the father's sexual behavior."[86]

Two homosexual men, one of whom was the child's biological father who had co-parented a girl for five years, engaged a Virginia court.[87] The divorced mother had filed a petition for a temporary restraining order in which she alleged that it had come to her attention that the father was living with a man as sexual partners, that the two men occupied the same bed in the house in which the father lived with the child, and that the child had reported seeing the two men "hugging and kissing and sleeping in the same bed together."[88]

To the appellate court, the father's continuous exposure of the child to his "immoral and illicit relationship rendered him an unfit and improper custodian as a matter of law."[89] The court noted the mother's contention that the "influences to which the child is exposed here are far more deleterious than those [involving an adulterous mother]." She had also pointed out that, "as an illustration of the relative degree of abhorrence by which our society regards such conduct, adultery is a class four misdemeanor in Virginia, which is seldom prosecuted, while the conduct inherent in the father's relationship is punishable as a class six felony which is prosecuted with considerable frequency and vigor." The appellate court observed, "[h]owever that may be, we have no hesitancy in saying that the conditions under which this child must live daily are not only unlawful but also impose an intolerable burden upon her by reason of the social condemnation attached to them."[90] The "selfish" nature of the father's sexuality was then addressed. "The father's unfitness is manifested by his willingness to impose this burden upon her in exchange for his own gratification."[91]

In another case, however, a California appellate court overruled a trial court's decision to bar a homosexual father's visitation with his son in the presence of any other person "known to be homosexual" because "no current harm to the child can be attributed to [the father's] sexual orientation. [Further] there is no evidence of future detriment."[92]

Similarly, the Iowa Supreme Court ruled that a trial court erred by restricting a homosexual father's visitation to times when no "unrelated adult" was present.[93] A joint friend of the court brief had been filed by Lamda Legal Defense and the National Center for Lesbian Rights "centering on scientific research on gay parenting and child rearing."[94]

Sexual science experts are not always heeded, however. They were thoroughly discounted in a case in Missouri.[95] There, the court stated that the "experts" (court's quote) testified that there was "no consensus as to the cause of homosexuality . . . They were espousing only their opinion upon theories of causation, which they both admitted were not subject to any demonstrable scientific proof."[96] Expert testimony on the minimal risk of child molestation by a homosexual father or a friend of the father was discredited. "The experts' testimony with respect to molestation of minors is likewise suspect. Every trial judge, for that matter, every appellate judge, knows that the molestation of minors by adult males is not as uncommon as the psychological experts' testimony indicated."[97]

This diversity of custody rulings when a parent is homosexual reveals the injection of court subjectivity into the application of the standard, "best interests of the child." Although research findings indicate that children of homosexual parents do not appear more likely to grow up homosexual (a political concession by the homosexual parent that this is a less than optimal outcome), this fear has been only one concern of the courts. The misconception remains that the homosexual parent or partner will sexually assault the child, even though the vast majority of sexual abuse is perpetrated by heterosexual males, or that the parent will attempt to proselytize the child into a homosexual life-style, even though homosexual parents nearly always prefer that their children become heterosexual. The misconception that equates homosexuality and mental illness also remains, although it is more than eighteen years since the mental health professions have declared that equation false.

While nearly all sexual science expert witnesses attempt to counter these misconceptions, when a witness is found who will testify to the potential adverse effects of homosexual parenting, courts are often predisposed to accept that minority viewpoint. Occasionally, the anti-homosexual prejudice of the trial court is so clear that the difficult legal standard for reversal, an abuse of discretion, is reached, and the homosexual parent is vindicated on appeal.

One concern for the child's interests that is less easily answered by the experts is the question of the stigma attaching to the child as a result of the parent's homosexuality. Some courts follow the lead of the United States Supreme Court in the interracial custody dispute of *Palmore v. Sidoti* and hold that courts cannot acquiesce to societal prejudice. Others attempt to resolve conflicting testimony as to whether the child will be teased and, if so, whether its consequences are distinguishable from those of the teasing that assaults all children for myriad reasons. Still others consider it their responsibility to insulate the child from any potential stigma arising from the parent's sexuality and so attempt to remove the child from its posited path.

The romantic partners of homosexual parents are particularly worrisome to courts. Although a few judges have permitted the homosexual parent to cohabit with the partner and retain custody, others have predicated visitation on the absence of the partner from the environment when the child is visiting. Still others demand sexual abstinence from same-sex partners as a requirement of custody. Courts appear to believe that the presence of the homosexual partner will increase the likelihood that the child will become homosexual, perhaps by rendering more obvious the sexual orientation of the parent, or perhaps by "doubling the dose" of the offending influence. Perhaps the court's rationale is that a homosexual parent deserves to pay a sacrifice, his or her significant socio-sexual relationship, or make a commitment to celibacy, to be entitled to the privilege (not the right) of parenting.

More research may resolve some of these issues. The sexual orientation of children raised in lesbian mother households who were examined in the three studies described earlier remains to be reported. As adults, these children may recount the extent to which they were subjected to teasing because of their parent's sexual orientation and any negative or positive effects of that teasing. We may also be able to answer the question, "Have the children evolved more accepting attitudes toward persons with a homosexual lifestyle, or are they 'homophobic'?"

Some trends in contemporary lesbian parenting may test theories of psychosexual development. Donor insemination by a male who assumes no other parenting responsibility after conception and is absent from the child's environment from birth is becoming more common. What is the effect on the sexual identity of girls and boys when there is no male who relates to them as a parent, and whose mothers do not have romantic or sexual relationships with men? A genetic influence on sexual orientation may be tested as well. What is the effect on sexual identity when not only the mother is homosexual but the semen donor is as well?

Missing from these child custody cases are the contests that never take place in the courts. In these, homosexual or bisexual parents have abdicated custody or conceded to limitations on visitation, including dissociation from romantic partnerships, without a court ruling. The heterosexual parents' winning edge was the homosexual or bisexual parents' reluctance to have their sexuality revealed in a public forum or their fear that they would not prevail if their sexuality, rather than their parenting, went on trial.

# · 3 ·

# Homosexuality as a
# Fundamental Right

As defined by the ancient civil or canonical codes,
sodomy was a category of forbidden acts: their perpetrator was nothing more than the juridical subject of
them. The nineteenth century homosexual became a
personage, a past, a case history, and a childhood, in
addition to being a type of life, a life form, and a mor-
phology . . . The sodomites had been a temporary
aberration; the homosexual was now a species.

Michel Foucault, *The History of Sexuality*

Fundamental rights receive special protection in constitutional law.
For a law legitimately to curtail a fundamental right, it must serve
a compelling state interest. Supreme Court cases have held that fundamental rights in the area of sexuality include the right to pro-
create, to use contraception, to have an abortion, and to marry.

What determines whether a right is fundamental? In striking
down a state law that mandated sterilization for men after a third
conviction for a felony involving "moral turpitude," the Supreme
Court wrote in 1942: "We are dealing here with legislation which
involves one of the basic civil rights of man. Marriage and procreation are fundamental to the very existence and survival of the race
. . . [Without them a person] is forever deprived of a basic liberty."[1]

In 1965 the right to use contraceptives was held to be fundamental. It was seen as a private decision "concern[ing] a relationship
lying within the zone of privacy created by several fundamental
constitutional guarantees . . . a law . . . forbidding the use of contraceptives . . . seeks to achieve its goal by means having a maximum destructive impact upon that relationship."[2]

The right to abortion was declared fundamental in 1973, in part because otherwise "[t]he detriment that the state would impose upon the pregnant woman by denying this choice altogether is apparent (and profound)."[3]

Marriage was held to be a protected right in 1978. "The right to marry is of fundamental importance. *Griswold* [the contraceptive use case and others] established that the right to marry is part of the fundamental 'right of privacy' implicit in [the] Due Process clause."[4]

## Sexual Identity

If there is a fundamental right to some aspects of human sexuality, is sexual orientation included? How personally "fundamental" is sexual identity?

Sexual identity encompasses three components. The first is the core awareness of belonging to one of two categories of persons— male or female. The second is more diffuse—an array of behaviors that are more or less commonly expressed by males or by females; the shorthand terms being masculinity and femininity. The third concerns the sex of those persons sought as romantic and sexual partners. This is sexual orientation.[5]

The first component is a bedrock human feature, permeating nearly all behavior. It is as basic a personality element as can be identified, classifying persons into one of only two primary groups. The age at which this feature becomes psychologically incorporated is not known with precision, but it is very early. Some evidence points to recognition of two classes of humans based on gender at thirteen months.[6] Firmer evidence derived from studies of anatomically intersexed children (pseudohermaphrodites) documents the emergence of this concept in the third year of life.[7]

Medical anomalies in which children are born with either sexually ambiguous genitalia or deceptively sex-typed genitalia are "experiments of nature." They document the early emergence and immutability of the sense of being male or female. In the androgen-insensitivity syndrome, the fetus has the male sex chromosome pattern of XY and develops male gonads, the testes, that secrete male hormone. But, because of a metabolic defect, the body's cells are unable to utilize this hormone. In the absence of the effects of male hormone, the body develops along female lines (no female hormone from the female gonads, the ovaries, is necessary for the fetal genitals to develop as female). The newborn infant appears to be a female and is designated "a girl."[8] The early, irreversible nature of the first component of sexual identity is demonstrated when physicians discover that an "error" was made in the initial sex assignment of a "male" infant and attempt to reassign sex. Efforts at reassignment from female to male after about two-and-a-half years are generally not successful.[9] Core sexual identity as a female has been set.

Similar evidence can be derived from the medical syndrome of congenital adrenal hyperplasia.[10] The adrenal gland of a fetus with the female sex chromosome pattern of XX and female gonads, the ovaries, overproduces male-type hormone. Consequently, what would have been female genitalia become masculinized. At birth such an infant may be considered male. If subsequent medical examination reveals the "error" and an attempt is made to reassign the child as female, again, the reassignment will probably not take if it is not effected during the first two or three years.[11] Core sexual identity as a male has been set.

Research on anatomically normal children also demonstrates the early emergence of this fundamental sense of self-definition. Gender constancy is a phase in cognitive development in which children not only know their own sex, they also know that this feature is not changeable. Through testing with dolls and pictures showing variable sex characteristics, children indicate whether they are boys or girls and whether they think they will grow up to be men or women. This happens by about age six.[12]

Nearly everyone takes this feature of sexuality, being a male or a female, "for granted." But a small percentage are grossly discontent with having been born male or female. Their distress is overwhelming. It forces them from early childhood onto a path of "sex-change" surgery. They are the transsexuals of Chapter 6.

Masculine and feminine behavior, the second component of sexual identity, generally evolves in accord with the basic self-concept as male or female. It is also manifested early. Thus, the social and solitary play of boys and girls differs somewhat in preschool years and becomes substantially more separate in early grade school.[13]

Because a person's identity is influenced by the manner in which others interact with that person, based on these sex-typed behaviors, this second component also has a profound impact. Children whose behaviors are markedly atypical experience distress, especially boys ("sissy" boys), who are more stigmatized by age-mates than are "tomboy" girls. Furthermore, children of both sexes who show extensively atypical sex-typed behavior have a substantially higher probability of maturing into homosexual or bisexual adults.[14]

The third component of sexual identity, selection of male or female sexual partners, or sexual orientation, is so profound that it is commonly used to define the person. Thus, when the word for sexual orientation is used as a noun, the person is "a homosexual," and little else need be said. When used as an adjective, as in "a homosexual lawyer," it is meant to convey a great deal about the person's totality interpreted through the lens of sexual orientation: "We have allowed the homosexual's sexual object choice to dominate and control our imagery of him. We have let this single aspect of his total life experience appear to determine all his products, concerns, and activities."[15]

The age at which sexual orientation emerges is still being debated, but most of the debate is about how *early*. Research I have conducted since the early 1960s demonstrates that men who are homosexual or bisexual can often be identified by behaviors beginning in early childhood. A study of forty-four boys, aged four to twelve, who demonstrated extensive cross-gender behavior (feminine on the second component of sexual identity) revealed that three-fourths were homosexual or bisexual men at follow-up fifteen years later. By contrast, only one out of thirty-five boys whose early behaviors were conventionally masculine was bisexual at follow-up.[16] This finding could mean that sexual orientation (the term for adults) is frequently expressed in early years as gender-typed behavior. If so, then sexual orientation may be evident in childhood. Alternatively, we may be witnessing a developmental sequence in which gender behavior in childhood, because of its effects on socialization with peers and parents, promotes emotional needs in the child that are expressed later as sexual orientation.

The extent to which sexual orientation is inborn or evolves from life experience remains controversial after decades of research. The extent to which sexual orientation is modifiable (from homosexual or bisexual to heterosexual) is also a subject of dispute. (A review of current data on both issues can be found in Chapter 4.) The enormous amount of time and money patients have spent in psychotherapy exploring their sexual orientation is evidence of its significance to personal identity. The extensive library of books and professional papers on the issue are a testament to those who have vigorously confronted conflicts over their sexual orientation.[17]

Together, then, these three components—a person's identity as male or female, the public expression of that identity, and the sex of those who are the objects of romantic and sexual desire—constitute a fundamental personal domain.

## Impact of Sexual Orientation

The degree to which homosexual orientation is self-defining to the individual is demonstrated by the "coming out process." Here "closeted" homosexuals declare their true orientation. "Coming out," a political term, is more properly a process of "acceptance and appreciation."[18]

"Coming out" can have a dramatic impact on men previously living as heterosexually married fathers: "Openly gay fathers . . . [w]ith the move out of the nuptial closet . . . report a stabilization of self-concept and a greater sense of psychological well-being . . . Several report that, following the dissolution of their marriages, they began to use their seat belts when driving, claiming they now had more reasons to live."[19] Comparable significance is found among female homosexuals: "[T]he coming out process provide[s] a common sense rhetoric or explanation for the variations in identity that exist in the gay world. Identity rules in the lesbian world also provide a method for locating the 'true self,' because here, as in the heterosexual world, gayness is considered definitive of the self in an essential way."[20]

This process of defining one's homosexual orientation to self and others is described as "an integrating factor in personality functions." It provides "a psychological sense of self-identity."[21] The centrality of a homosexual identity is additionally demonstrated by those who define themselves as homosexual, although celibate or engaging in only heterosexual behavior (with homosexual fanta-sies).[22]

Mental health studies illustrate the potentially positive impact of a homosexual identity. The extent to which homosexuals socialize with other homosexuals reflects their increased acceptance of their sexual orientation.[23] In a study of over two thousand homosexual men in the United States, the Netherlands, and Denmark, who responded to a questionnaire, those with a greater degree of this gay "acculturation" into the homosexual community reported less depression, loneliness, guilt, shame, and anxiety, and a higher degree of self-acceptance.[24] "Normalization" occurs when the homosexual person does not view homosexuality as an illness. Those with greater normalization report greater psychological well-being on several measures, including a higher self-concept, fewer psychosomatic symptoms, lower depression, and less loneliness, guilt, shame, or anxiety.[25]

Laws proscribing homosexual conduct have an impact on mental health and identity as a result of governmental policy and public stigma. Nearly half of the states in the United States continue to criminalize homosexual behavior.[26] It remains a criminal act in heavily populated nations (for example, in the former Soviet Union and in the People's Republic of China). The cross-national study cited above concluded: "for the majority of homosexuals in the societies studied (the U.S., Netherlands, and Denmark), the most universal . . . effect of legal repression is to symbolize society's rejection of the homosexual. This rejection seems to be a major source of the homosexual's problems."[27]

The stigma of homosexuality attaches early in life. Many homo-sexual men were called "sissy" in childhood and otherwise teased by their peers. During adolescence their awareness that they were different from most peers on the major life parameter of sexual ori-entation set them further apart. In adulthood they continue to expe-rience a negative self-concept because of the general societal rejec-tion of homosexuality evidenced in part by laws that criminalize their sexual conduct. Thus, recognizing the personally fundamental nature of a homosexual orientation may help "the process of heal-ing the narcissistic injury of disparaged sexuality of otherwise healthy gay[s] or lesbian[s]."[28]

Although sexual science underscores the personally fundamental nature of sexual identity, its protection must be grounded in constitutional doctrine.

## Legal Theories

The contours of an organizing principle that can engage laws regulating patterns of sexual conduct—the "freedom of intimate association"—have been delineated by Kenneth Karst. In his attempt to couple sexual privacy to freedoms already recognized by constitutional case history, Karst sees a relationship between homosexuality and speech.

> [W]hatever may have been the original purposes of laws forbidding homosexual sex, it seems clear that today one of the chief concerns underlying the maintenance of those laws is a concern to regulate the content of messages about sexual preference. It is said that the state, by repealing its prohibition on homosexual conduct, will itself be seen as making a statement approving that conduct . . . The laws are rarely enforced against behavior carried on entirely in private; it is those persons who advertise their sexual preference by frequenting gay bars and the like, or who openly display their homosexual affections, who are likely to be punished. The immediate practical effect of such a law enforcement is thus to penalize public expression.[29]

Deciding to " 'come out of the closet' and avow one's homosexual association is certainly a statement of great personal importance and may also be a political act."[30] However, "[f]or the homosexual individual, it is typically the very act of self-identification that results in the loss of a material benefit."[31] In addition, denying a "formal association status," such as marriage, to the homosexual couple has "immense symbolic value."[32]

Karst emphasizes the significance to the homosexual of state sodomy laws, even if they are not regularly enforced.

> Not only is the forbidden conduct expressive; for a homosexual, a violation of the law is the principal form that a sexual expression of her love can take. The total denial of this expression thus invades the associational values of intimacy, caring, and commitment to a degree that exceeds the invasions condemned in (the contraceptive cases) *Griswold* and *Eisenstadt*.[33]

The "unwritten constitution" is the basis for protection of sexual orientation according to the analysis of David A. J. Richards.[34] This is the spirit in which the Constitution was formulated. Certain structural features of the Constitution, such as judicial review, should protect sexual orientation. This counter-majoritarian measure has as its basis basic human rights that government cannot transgress. For the framers of the Constitution it was "[t]he idea that an enforceable charter of human rights requires a special set of government institutions that, in principle, protect these rights from incursions of the governing majority . . . the Bill of Rights was part of and gave expression to a developing moral theory."[35] This "radical vision of human rights" that the Constitution was intended to express is the "unwritten constitution."[36]

A concept of morality guides this privacy doctrine, putting constraints on what may be regarded as ethical. "Children, because they lack rational capacities, do not have full rights to privacy."[37] Furthermore, "[o]btrusive or forced sexuality is not protected since to permit otherwise would deny equal opportunity."[38] Homosexuality, however, is protected. The only way homosexual behavior could be denied protection would be if it led "directly to disease, social disorder and disintegration."[39]

Freud's contributions to our understanding of sexuality are honored by Richards in his elevation of sexuality to a position of fundamental legal protection. Freud wrote, "Hitherto we have left it to poets and imaginative writers to depict for us the 'conditions of love' under which men and women make their choice of [a love] object, and the way in which they reconcile the demands expressed in their phantasy."[40] And further, "may all those who from their exalted standpoint look scornfully upon psychoanalysis remember how closely the extended sexuality of psychoanalysis corresponds with the Eros of the divine Plato."[41] Building on Freud's base and extending it to possible governmental constraints, Richards adds, "[T]o understand the powerful role of sexuality . . . is to acknowledge the central role of sexual autonomy in the idea of a free person . . . Sexuality, in this view, is not a spiritually empty experience that the state may compulsorily legitimize only in the form of rigid, marital procreational sex, but one of the fundamental experiences through which, as an end in itself, people define the meaning of their lives."[42]

Freud's romantic exposition of the power of biological libido, amplified by evolution's most sophisticated system of symbols, provides the substrate for this elemental human essence. "[H]uman sexuality, rooted in the high degree of cortical control of sexuality, serves complex imaginative and symbolic purposes . . . Freud . . . introduced into scientific psychology what artists have always known and expressed: that for humans to experience sex is never, even in solitary masturbation, a purely physical act, but is imbued with complex evaluational interpretations of its real or fantasied object, often rooted in the whole history of the person from early childhood on."[43]

## Cases

In the face of sexual science research on the fundamental nature of sexual identity, including sexual orientation, the United States Supreme Court ruled in 1986 that there is no fundamental right to engage in homosexual conduct.[44] In *Bowers v. Hardwick*, the five to four majority wrote: "We . . . register our disagreement . . . that the Court's prior cases [of sexual privacy] have construed the Constitution to confer a right of privacy that extends to homosexual sodomy." Earlier cases finding fundamentally protected areas of sexuality were held to be inconsistent with genital behavior conducted by persons of the same sex. "No connection between family, marriage, or procreation on the one hand and homosexual activity on the other, has been demonstrated . . . Proscriptions against [sodomy] have ancient roots . . . The law . . . is constantly based on notions of morality."[45]

An earlier Supreme Court case concerning nonsexual behavior, however, hinted at a principle that could protect sexual orientation. Protected relations, according to the Court's analysis in *Roberts v. United States Jaycees* (forbidding the Jaycees to exclude women), are characterized by their "relative smallness, a high degree of selectivity in decisions to begin and maintain the affiliation and seclusion from others in critical aspects of the relationship." The Constitution "afford[s] . . . certain kinds of highly personal relationships a substantial measure of sanctuary from unjustified interference by the state . . . [Because] individuals draw much of their emotional enrichment from close ties with others . . . [p]rotecting these relationships from unwarranted state interference . . . safeguards the ability . . . to define one's identity that is central to any concept of liberty."[46]

But some members of the Supreme Court had earlier ruled out sexual privacy as a fundamental, and thus specially protected, right: "Neither our precedents nor sound principles of constitutional analysis require state legislation to meet the exacting 'compelling state interest' standard whenever it implicates sexual freedom."[47]

Long before the current debate on sexual orientation and the right to privacy, Justice Louis Brandeis issued a general rallying cry for privacy. His dissent in *Olmstead v. United States*[48] regarding the public disclosure of personal information concluded that "the makers of our Constitution undertook to secure conditions favorable to the pursuit of happiness . . . They sought to protect Americans in their beliefs, their thoughts, their emotions, and their sensations. They contend, as against the government, the right to be let alone— the most valued by civilized men."[49]

The Brandeis dissent, with its clear civil libertarian ring, preceded Justice Harry Blackmun's resonant dissent in *Hardwick*,[50] the homosexual sodomy case, by nearly seventy years. There Blackmun wrote,

Our cases long have recognized that the Constitution embodies a promise that a certain private sphere of individual liberty will be kept largely beyond the reach of government[51] . . . We protect those rights not because they contribute, in some direct and material way, to the general public welfare, but because they form so central a part of an individual's life[52] . . . Only the most willful blindness could obscure the fact that sexual intimacy is "a sensitive, key relationship of human existence, central to family life, community welfare, and the development of human personality"[53] . . . The fact that individuals define themselves in a significant way through their intimate sexual relationships with others suggests, in a Nation as diverse as ours, that there may be many "right" ways of conducting those relationships, and that much of the richness of a relationship will come from the freedom an individual has to *choose* the form and nature of these intensely personal bonds . . .[54] what the Court [in this case] . . . has refused to recognize is the fundamental interest all individuals have in controlling the nature of their intimate associations with others[55] . . . the issue raised by this case touches the heart of what makes individuals what they are."[56]

Although the United States Supreme Court has not recognized a fundamental right to engage in private consenting homosexual behavior, some state courts have. The basis of these rulings has been not only the state's constitution but also an interpretation of the federal Constitution.

New York found that "[t]he right to privacy is a right of independence in making certain kinds of important decisions, with a concomitant right to conduct oneself in accordance with those decisions, undeterred by governmental restraint."[57] The New York law criminalizing sodomy was found to infringe on the "right of privacy which is a fundamental right." Although the New York holding was based on the series of federal privacy cases decided before *Hardwick* and subsequently repudiated as extending to sodomy, the law has not been reinstated.

The right to privacy found in the fornication case *State v. Saunders*[58] detailed in Chapter 1 was the foundation on which New Jersey summarily held its sodomy law unconstitutional.[59] *Saunders* was also cited by New York in its holding.[60]

In 1980 a Pennsylvania statute prohibiting "deviate sexual intercourse," which it defined as "sexual intercourse per os or per anus between human beings who are not husband and wife,"[61] was challenged in court. Although the suit was brought by heterosexual unmarried parties, the statute clearly applied to homosexuals as well. The court held that the state's proper role in regulating sexuality is limited to "protecting the public from inadvertent offensive displays of sexual behavior, in preventing people from being forced against their will to submit to sexual contact, in protecting minors from being sexually used by adults, and in eliminating cruelty to animals."[62] The statute regulating "deviate" sexual intercourse between unmarried but not between married persons failed to meet the threshold of state power and was an irrational distinction based on marital status. Thus, it violated the equal protection clause of both federal and state constitutions.

\*     \*     \*

The authority of science and the logic of common sense attest to the fundamental nature of an individual's sexual orientation. Justice Blackmun recognized this when he called for the early reversal of *Hardwick:* "It took but three years for the Court to see the error in its analysis [in the case involving the requirement of student to salute the flag] . . . I can only hope that here, too, the Court soon will reconsider its analysis and conclude that depriving individuals of the right to choose for themselves how to conduct their intimate relationships poses a far greater threat to the values most deeply rooted in our Nation's history than tolerance of nonconformity could ever do."[63]

According to most sexual science estimates, a homosexual orientation is the predominant sexual pattern of 3 to 4 percent of the population of the United States.[64] Overruling *Hardwick* would legitimize the sexual identity of six million Americans.

# · 4 ·

# Homosexuals as
# a Suspect Class

In constitutional law it is established doctrine that classifications which discriminate between groups are subject to varying levels of court scrutiny. Most classifications merely require some rational basis. When the class being discriminated against possesses certain features, however, that classification becomes "suspect." To justify discrimination against a "suspect class," the law authorizing the classification must serve a compelling governmental interest.

The characteristics of a class or group deemed suspect by courts and thus receiving enhanced protection are that the group has been subjected to a long history of persecution because of irrational stereotypes, that it has been unable to obtain relief from the nonjudicial (that is, legislative) branch of government, and, often, that it has been discriminated against for a trait that is "immutable" or unchangeable.[1] Race represents one suspect class, as does national origin and alienage (under state law), and to a lesser degree, illegitimacy and gender.[2]

Whereas a 1986 Supreme Court case unsuccessfully sought to insulate persons engaging in private, consenting homosexual acts from state laws, the Court's ruling was not based on the suspect class rationale.[3] It was based on the "substantive due process" component of the Fifth and Fourteenth Amendments to the Constitution, which forbids government to abrogate any "fundamental" right, absent a compelling state need. Consequently, those who continue to seek a constitutionally based protection for homosexual persons must, for now, travel the avenue of the "equal protection component" of the Fifth and Fourteenth Amendments. This avenue will require heightened court scrutiny for laws that discriminate against gay men and lesbian women.

Homosexuals easily meet two characteristics of a "suspect class." First, there is little doubt that they have been subjected to a long history of societal discrimination. Homosexuality has been condemned by religion as a sin and labeled by psychiatry as a mental illness.[4] Second, the political process has not provided homosexuals with an effective remedy for discrimination. Nearly half the states have laws prohibiting private, consenting homosexual acts, and only six states and a few municipalities prohibit employment and housing discrimination based on sexual orientation.[5] The third characteristic, immutability, is more controversial. The following review of research on the development of sexual orientation, in particular male homosexuality, and its amenability to change addresses this issue.

## Biological Research

Sigmund Freud maintained a conviction that many answers to questions about the origins of homosexuality would be found in the biological laboratory.

> It is not for psychoanalysis to solve the problem of homosexuality. It must rest content with . . . tracing the paths leading from [psychical mechanisms] to the instinctual basis of the disposition. There its work ends, and it leaves the rest to biological research.[6]

### Twin Studies

The study of twins holds a venerable place in psychiatric research attempting to dissect the relative influences of nature and nurture. Monozygotic (identical) twins have a genetic composition as close as can be found among human beings, so that the extent to which the twins differ in behavior may be ascribed to environmental influences. Dizygotic (fraternal) twins, however, are genetically no more similar than any pair of siblings born of different pregnancies from the same parents.

Earlier categorical theorizing about a range of psychiatric conditions simplistically ascribed causation to either nature or nurture. But the optimistic hope of finding a single gene or set of genes that would fully explain the development of any syndrome has met with failure except in the case of some chromosomal disorders (such as Down syndrome, formerly known as "mongolism"). With other behaviors, such as schizophrenia, for which there was once great hope that a genetic etiology would be demonstrated, research has found that, although there is some contribution from genetics, this is far from the entire story. Many of the contributory factors appear to be either the result of environmental influences or of some complex interaction between nurture and nature.[7]

Nevertheless, interesting studies relating genetics to homosexual orientation have been reported. The first, in 1934, described six pairs of monozygotic twins, both of whom were homosexual, and only two pairs in which only one twin was homosexual.[8] The most provocative data resulted from a 1952 study of thirty-seven male monozygotic twins, each of whom was bisexual or homosexual (rated 3 to 6 on the Kinsey sexual orientation scale, where 0 is exclusive heterosexuality and 6 is exclusive homosexuality).[9] When their thirty-seven co-twins were interviewed, all were also found to be bisexual or homosexual. For the twenty Kinsey 6 (homosexual) twins, sixteen co-twins were also rated 6 and three were rated 5. For the nine Kinsey twins rated 5, three co-twins were rated 6 and three were rated 5. The investigator noted that

> the majority of one egg pairs not only are fully concordant as to the overt practice and quantitative rating of their aberrant sex pattern, but they even tend to be very similar in both the parts taken in their individual sex activities and the visible extent of feminized appearance and behavior displayed by some of them. It also seems significant that most of these index pairs assert to have developed their sexual tendencies independently and often far apart from each other."[10]

By contrast, of the dizygotic or fraternal twin pairs, over half of the co-twins of the bisexual or homosexual males reported no history of homosexuality. For those twins with a Kinsey rating of 5 to 6, only 11.5 percent of the co-twins were comparably rated, a percentage similar to the frequency of homosexual orientation reported within the general male population.[11]

Since this astounding study, there have been a few small series or individual case reports of monozygotic or identical twins of whom only one was homosexual.[12] Indeed, a year after the 1952 report of 100 percent agreement between thirty-seven twin pairs, the same investigator described a pair of monozygotic twins of which one was schizophrenic and homosexual and the other was neither schizophrenic nor homosexual.[13] But not all of the more recent reports refute the strong influence of genetics. A 1968 study from England reported one family with three sets of monozygotic twins, two of which were concordant for homosexuality and one for heterosexuality.[14] The authors of this report also pointed out that "the striking similar pattern of homosexual behavior developed in these twins entirely independently."[15] A large 1991 study compared the sexual orientation of monozygotic and dizygotic male twin pairs, raised together, as well as their adoptive (nonblood-related) brothers. About half of the fifty-six monozygotic homosexual twins had a homosexual co-twin compared to only about 20 percent of fifty-four dizygotic twins. Only 11 percent of fifty-seven adoptive brothers were homosexual.[16] A puzzling finding in this twin study is the substantial percentage of monozygotic homosexual twins with an exclusively heterosexual (and not bisexual) co-twin—nearly 40 percent. Finally, in 1992, a major study examined female twin pairs for sexual orientation. With seventy-one pairs of monozygotic twins, where one was homosexual, about half of the co-twins were homosexual or bisexual. By contrast, only 16 percent of homosexual dizygotic twins had a bisexual or homosexual co-twin and only 6 percent of adoptive sisters of homosexual twins were homosexual. Again, the puzzling finding emerged of a substantial percentage of monozygotic homosexual twins with an exclusively heterosexual co-twin (34 percent).[17]

A major methodological hurdle in dissecting the nature/nurture mix in monozygotic twin pairs is the confounding variable of the twins having been raised together, so that their environment may also be nearly identical. Thus, when monozygotic twins are separated shortly after birth and raised in different families, comparing their later behaviors is of great interest. A recent report described a set of male monozygotic twins separated in infancy who had accidentally found each other in their mid-twenties. Both were exclusively homosexual. In a second similar pair, one was homosexual and the other was married, although the married twin had had an ongoing homosexual relationship between ages fifteen and eighteen. Of four pairs of female twins raised apart, in none were both women homosexual.[18]

## Non-Twin Sibling Studies

An alternative strategy for uncovering evidence of a genetic contribution to homosexual orientation is the study of non-twin siblings of homosexuals. In one report fifty-one predominantly homosexual and fifty predominantly heterosexual men served as reference subjects. The sexual orientation of siblings, 115 sisters and 123 brothers, was judged through interviews with the reference subjects, and through interview or mailed questionnaire with their siblings. The homosexual men had about four times as many homosexual brothers as did the heterosexual men. Twenty percent of the brothers of homosexual or bisexual men were bisexual or homosexual. By contrast, only 4 percent of the heterosexual men had homosexual or bisexual brothers. No higher incidence of female bisexuality or homosexuality was found among the sisters.[19] This finding was essentially replicated in another sample: again, about 20 percent of the brothers of male homosexuals were bisexual or homosexual compared to 4 percent of the controls, although siblings were not interviewed.[20] Similarly, higher than expected rates of homosexual or bisexual orientation in sisters of homosexual women have been reported (14 percent), but not in their brothers (5 percent).[21] These findings could, however, suggest a common environmental, rather than genetic, influence on the development of sexual orientation.

Other hints of a family "predisposition" to homosexual orientation derive from the classic Henry data of 1941. In that study, family tree information was collected on forty male and forty female "sex variants." In some cases, more than a hundred persons, over four generations, were included. Of particular interest is the finding on parents, aunts, and uncles of the homosexual persons: of twelve homosexual and bisexual aunts and uncles, eleven derived from the maternal side.[22] More recently, a family study of homosexuality found similarly that ten of the twelve male relatives of male homosexuals who were also considered to be homosexual were related through the mother's or sister's side.[23]

Although these findings do not prove a genetic etiology of homosexual orientation, they cannot be casually dismissed as irrelevant. That not every monozygotic twin pair is similar for sexual orientation is not unprecedented, for few, if any, traits are fully concordant between twins. But the early data on the thirty-seven male twin pairs combined with the recent report of the separately raised male twin pairs and the newer large studies of monozygotic and dizygotic male and female twins argue for a genetic contribution to sexual orientation.

## Hormonal Influences on Sexual Orientation

At the turn of the century, German sex researchers, of whom Richard von Krafft-Ebing was the most prominent, postulated that the locus of sexual orientation was the central nervous system. Simply stated, male homosexuals had a predominantly female sex center in the brain.[24] This thesis fell into disrepute during the advent and heyday of the psychological schools, first the psychoanalytic, and then the behaviorist. A brief revival of belief in the biological (now hormonal) basis of sexual orientation occurred in the two decades following the Second World War. Postwar scientists developed primitive tools, such as nonspecific urine assays, for measuring sex hormones or their end products. But tests gave nonspecific results, and soon this avenue of research drifted into a period of quiescence. In more recent decades, however, new techniques have permitted sensitive, specific assays from blood. A wide range of chemicals, including the relevant "sex hormones" and their related compounds, can now be measured. Thus, there was a resurgence of interest in the role of hormones in sexual orientation. Studies tested male and female homosexuals for their levels of "male" and "female" hormones, particularly testosterone and "his" relatives, and estradiol and "her" relatives.

### BLOOD LEVELS IN ADULTHOOD

Blood androgen (male hormone) levels for male homosexuals have been reported in over two dozen studies. In the majority, homosexual males apparently had testosterone levels within the range of male heterosexuals. Only three studies reported significantly lower levels in homosexuals,[25] and of these, two lacked adequate control groups and the third may have been confounded by the high number of drug users in the homosexual group. By contrast, twenty studies reported no differences between homosexuals and controls or among homosexuals with varying degrees of homosexual commitment, and two studies showed elevated levels of testosterone in homosexuals.[26] Because it is the "free" (not bound to a blood protein) component of testosterone in blood that is believed to be the active constituent and not the total level, this vital fraction has been measured in more recent studies. Two that compared heterosexual and homosexual males found that, whereas total testosterone levels did not differ, free testosterone was lower in the homosexuals (but within the typical male range).[27] A third however, found an elevated level in homosexuals.[28]

As for estrogen (female hormone) levels in homosexual men, one study reported elevated plasma estradiol and estrone (both estrogens),[29] whereas another showed elevated estradiol but normal estrone.[30] Still others found no differences.[31]

Studies of female homosexuals, too, have failed to show consistent differences in these hormone levels compared with heterosexual women. There may be a subgroup of homosexual women with elevated testosterone levels, but these levels are far below those found in males.[32]

It is not surprising that studies of sex hormone levels in blood have been inconsistent and generally uninformative. Many obstacles stand in the way of understanding the correlates or causes of sexual orientation using this research strategy. The "normal" range of these hormones, that is, the levels found in most "normal" people, is wide. Thus, a statistically significant difference may be found between two groups, but the average of both groups may be within the "normal" range. Furthermore, an individual's measured hormone level may be irrelevant, since the tissue need for the hormone may vary from person to person: a level within the "normal" range for one person may represent a deficiency for another. The significance of the findings is further compromised by the fact that hormone levels fluctuate throughout the day and from season to season, while blood samples stop the action at only one point in time.

And, if these stumbling blocks are insufficient to dissuade the most intrepid researcher, there is also an array of environmental factors that affect hormone levels. "Stress" is only one of them.

PRENATAL INFLUENCES

The quest for a hormonal answer did not stop with these less than clear-cut results. The increasing understanding of chemical mediators in the body, beginning with secretions from the hypothalamus in the brain, which influences secretions from the pituitary gland, and their subsequent influence on the gonads (testes and ovaries), led to more sophisticated assessments. Concurrently, nonhuman research contributed a greater understanding of the effect of hormonal manipulations before birth. These have been found to lead to modification not only of the genitalia, but also of sex-typed behaviors.

An important fundamental finding of this research is that the basic mammalian state is female. Thus, remove the evolving gonads, which would become either testes or ovaries, from the developing fetus and the fetus progresses along female-appearing lines.[33] Similarly, in the absence of male sex hormones acting in the developing fetus, the body evolves as female.

The next step was to extend these findings to the behavioral system. Researchers looked at rodents and found that depriving the developing male of male sex hormones at critical early periods of development, or exposing the developing female to male hormones, would reverse aspects of sex-typed mating behavior. They then looked at the nonhuman primate. The rhesus was a good research model because rhesus monkey childhood behaviors differ for males and females in a manner comparable to that found in humans, that is, the young male is more often involved in rough-and-tumble and aggressive play than is the young female. When the fetal female was exposed to elevated levels of male hormone through injections of testosterone to her pregnant mother, she behaved more like a male (the "tomboy" monkey).[34] This suggested that, at the primate level, a behavioral phenomenon parallel to the anatomic phenomenon may exist. In the absence of sex hormone, femaleness, and "femininity," evolves, whereas with male hormone, maleness, and "masculinity," evolves. A follow-up on these "tomboy" females as adults, however, revealed that they responded in a generally typical female manner when sexually paired with males, although there were some minor differences from normal females.[35]

## Inherited Defects

### CONGENITAL ADRENAL HYPERPLASIA

The next research strategy was to look for a human model comparable to the rhesus monkey study. One was found in the medical condition known as congenital adrenal hyperplasia (CAH). In this inherited disorder, beginning before birth the adrenal gland secretes an excess of masculinizing hormone. Thus, when the fetus is female, exposure to these high levels of male hormone results in masculinized genitalia at birth.[36]

The social play of these CAH girls was compared with the social play of their sisters who did not have this medical syndrome and thus had normal prenatal hormones. The masculine hormone–exposed girls were more involved in rough-and-tumble play and less involved in play with newborn babies or its surrogate activity, doll-play. They were "tomboys."[37]

These females have also been studied in adulthood. One report examined the most extreme patients, those whose medical treatment to suppress male hormone did not start until adolescence or adulthood and who had thus experienced excessive male hormone exposure both before and after birth. Homosexuality was more common among these women than in the typical female population, although it did not predominate.[38]

Even more provocative findings emerged in a study of females treated shortly after birth to suppress excessive male hormone production. Hormonal therapy was instituted within the first year with over two-thirds of the girls. Later, 17 percent described themselves as either exclusively or predominantly homosexual, 20 percent as bisexual, and 40 percent as heterosexual, while 23 percent could not be rated.[39]

This medical syndrome is also found in males. They too are exposed prenatally to excessive male hormone. Theory would predict, and findings confirm, that nearly all have grown up to be heterosexual.[40]

ANDROGEN-INSENSITIVITY SYNDROME

In what was formerly called the "testicular feminizing syndrome," an individual has the typical XY male chromosomal pattern, testes (within the abdomen but not descended into the scrotum as in a normal male), and normal levels of the male hormone testosterone, but the person's body is unable to utilize testosterone. The infant therefore appears to be female at birth and is raised as a girl. These persons usually develop a sexual attraction for males (and are thus "homosexual" in the chromosomal or gonadal, but not the psychological, sense). In cases like these, however, it is difficult to distinguish the socializing influence of having been raised as a female from the lack of androgenic influence on the brain.[41]

FIVE-ALPHA-REDUCTASE DEFICIENCY

In another genetically inherited defect, the body does not convert testosterone into a substance that is masculinizing. Individuals with this disorder appear female at birth, although closer examination reveals some genital ambiguity. At adolescence, persons with this disorder undergo substantial masculinization: what had been an essentially normal-appearing clitoris enlarges to phallic proportions, the voice deepens, and malelike muscular development occurs, while female breast development does not. During adolescence, these persons assume societal roles as males and manifest sexual interest in females. It has been posited that the availability of testosterone before birth, while insufficient for programming the genitalia to appear malelike, was sufficient to program the brain to mediate later sexual interest in females.[42]

A MEDICALLY INDUCED ANOMALY

Recent research on diethylstilbestrol (DES) exposure before birth has also resulted in provocative findings regarding sexual orientation in the female. DES is a synthetic female hormone that was formerly administered to pregnant women with a history of difficulty in maintaining pregnancies. Although DES is a "female" agent it should be a masculinizing drug, since one mechanism in brain cells believed to masculinize behavior is the conversion of testosterone, the "male" hormone, into an estrogen, estradiol, the "female" hormone. This masculinizes when in the brain. Naturally produced female hormone does not reach the developing fetal brain because it is inactivated in the fetal blood. By contrast, the synthetic hormone DES does get into the developing brain.[43]

Thirty DES-exposed women were compared to twelve of their nonexposed sisters and to thirty unrelated nonexposed women. The percentages of DES women rated bisexual to homosexual on the Kinsey scale (rated 2 to 6) was 21 percent for the period of twelve months prior to the study, and 24 percent for their full life, compared to only 3 percent among the unrelated control groups for the preceding twelve months and zero percent for the longer period. Five DES women had a Kinsey score of at least 3 (bisexual) during the preceding twelve months compared to none in the unrelated control group. Two were living with a homosexual partner.

The DES women also had higher homosexual scores than their non-DES-exposed sisters. Five DES women had ratings of Kinsey 2 or higher for both the preceding twelve months and lifelong, compared to one of their twelve nonexposed sisters (a comparison percentage of 42 versus 8). Three DES-exposed women (25 percent) had scores of 3 or higher for the previous twelve months and two (17 percent) had scores of 3 or higher lifelong, compared to none of their nonexposed sisters.[44]

Data from these naturally occurring and medically induced abnormal hormonal states suggest that sex hormone levels before birth contribute to sexual orientation. That not all those so exposed show an atypical orientation may reflect not only the existence of other contributors, but also that these hormonal dosages may have been too low, or that exposure occurred at less than optimal developmental periods.

## Indirect Biological Measures

Although the evidence increasingly points to the importance of prenatal hormonal influences on postnatal sexual behavior, assessing these influences directly is highly problematic. To address the problem researchers began to look for hormonal influences that operate differently in males and females before birth and can be measured after birth. In the middle 1960s, a research strategy to assess the enduring influences of prenatal levels of male hormone on later sexual behavior was developed. The system studied was the difference between men and women in a hormone response (LH response) to levels of female hormone in the blood. In the typical female, rising levels of estrogen lead to a drop in LH followed by a marked rebound above the starting level (this is the hormonal basis of monthly ovulation). In the typical male, however, rising levels of estrogen, though also followed by a reduction in LH, do not result in the later marked rebound. The basis of this sex difference may be prenatal levels of male hormone that organize or program the developing brain.

Speculating that homosexual males have an insufficiently masculinized brain and hormonal system, the researchers studied the LH feedback response in heterosexual and homosexual males. When subjects were injected with a single injection of estrogen, the LH response in homosexual men differed from that in heterosexual men. More homosexual men showed the positive rebound effect typical of females. Although the response was weaker than that seen in women, and delayed for twenty-four hours, it was nevertheless present.[45]

For many years, these provocative findings lay dormant. In 1984, in a collaborative effort with two colleagues, I sought to replicate the study. We included a heterosexual female control group as well as male heterosexual and homosexual groups. We found that, on average, men declaring a lifelong homosexual orientation had a pattern of LH secretion in response to an intravenous pulse of estrogen that was intermediate between those of men and women declaring a lifelong heterosexual orientation. Nine of fourteen homosexuals demonstrated the positive estrogen feedback phenomenon compared to none of seventeen heterosexual men and eleven of twelve heterosexual women. Furthermore, testosterone concentrations in the men, which decreased after the administration of estrogen, were slower in returning to baseline in the homosexuals.[46] Another study, however, utilizing a somewhat modified design failed to replicate fully the earlier studies. A difference was found in a direction consistent with the earlier results, but the marked rebound phenomenon was not observed.[47] Yet another study, utilizing methods similar to those in the positive reports, also failed to replicate the findings, although a subgroup of four homosexual men appeared to show a response at a low (but not a higher) dosage of estrogen consistent with the earlier reports.[48] Thus this strategy, indirectly measuring the extent of prenatal brain masculinization as a correlate of sexual orientation, has yielded ambiguous and inconsistent results.

## Prenatal Stress

The prenatal stress theory of a homosexual orientation is derived from evidence that stress to the mother may depress prenatal testosterone production. This effect may be triggered by elevated levels of stress hormones from the mother's adrenal gland, which, carried in the blood, cross the placenta and antagonize fetal testosterone. Investigators working with rodents have successfully induced lower fetal levels of testosterone and later femalelike behavior in male offspring whose pregnant mothers were severely stressed (for example, by being confined for hours in an intensely lighted enclosure).[49]

Studies of reported stress in human pregnancy and the resulting sexual orientation of offspring have also yielded intriguing but inconsistent findings. Of the males born in Germany between 1934 and 1953, an unusually high number of homosexuals were reportedly born during and immediately after the Second World War.[50] One possible conclusion is that the extraordinary stress on pregnant women during these years resulted in a greater proportion of homosexual sons. On the other hand, these were the same years in which fathers of young boys were commonly absent, which would support a popular environmental theory of homosexuality.

A second German study questioned male homosexuals, bisexuals, and heterosexuals about stressful episodes described to them by their mothers during pregnancy. Nearly two-thirds of the mothers of the male homosexuals compared to one-third of the mothers of the bisexuals, and less than one-tenth of the mothers of the heterosexuals reportedly recalled such episodes. Only six of the one hundred heterosexual men had mothers who reported moderate prenatal stress, such as an undesired pregnancy or anxiety during the pregnancy because the father was at war. Such prenatal stress was reported, however, by the mothers of ten of forty bisexual men. Among the mothers of the sixty homosexual men, moderate prenatal stress was reported by twenty and severe prenatal stress by another twenty-one.[51]

A U.S. study asked mothers of male students to rate the stress they experienced during their pregnancy with children whose sexual orientation was determined by questionnaire. More stress was recalled by the mothers of more homosexually oriented students during the second trimester of pregnancy.[52] By contrast, other German studies have found no relationship between recalled prenatal stress and the current sexual orientation of male children,[53] nor did a more recent U.S. study, although there was a trend for mothers of female homosexuals to recall more stress.[54] No prospective studies beginning during pregnancy and relating levels of prenatal maternal stress and children's sexual behavior have been reported.

## Anatomic Brain Differences

The basis of homosexuality posited at the turn of the century, the contra-sexed sex center in the brain, has taken on renewed significance. Researchers have discovered differences between males and females in subareas of the hypothalamic portion of the brain as well as differences between male heterosexuals and male homosexuals. In early 1991, the suprachiasmatic area of the hypothalamus of thirteen homosexual men examined after death was found to be twice the size of that in a sample of heterosexual men. This area does not show a consistent male-female size difference.[55] In late 1991 a potentially significant finding emerged from a study that compared an area of the hypothalamus in cadaver brains from homosexual men, presumably heterosexual men, and presumably heterosexual women (a total of forty-one subjects). The area was about twice as large in the heterosexual males as in the heterosexual females, and the size in the homosexual males was similar to that in the females. There is some evidence that this region is related to sexual behavior in the nonhuman primate. Pinpointing the relationship between this area of the brain and the direction of human sexual orientation, however, will require not only replication, but a finding that this area in the brain of female homosexuals is comparable to that of male heterosexuals.[56]

## Cognitive Differences

Nonsexual behaviors in men and women may also be related to structural sites in the brain. A subject of particular interest is cognitive differences—styles and skills in perception. Studies of cognitive patterns have typically found differences between males and females. The hypothesis is that if the same prenatal events that program the brain to mediate cognitive differences also program sexual orientation, then cross-sex cognitive findings should emerge in conjunction with homosexuality.

In these studies, two types of tests employing visuo-spatial abilities are used. Both generally discriminate between males and females. One requires subjects to indicate the level that water will take in a tilted bottle. Here, not only were performances by heterosexual females and homosexual males similar, but both groups were substantially less accurate than heterosexual males. In a second procedure, subjects were required to select the mechanism composed of levels, cogs, or pulleys that would produce a movement demonstrated in test diagrams. They were also required to complete a modified version of the water-level task. On the mechanical diagram test, the homosexual males had an intermediate level of performance between heterosexual males and heterosexual females. The scores of the heterosexual females and homosexual males were different from those of the heterosexual males but not from those of each other. Likewise on the water-level task, the performances of the heterosexual females and the homosexual males were different from those of heterosexual males but not from those of each other. As the authors note, "If we accept that men and women, of whatever sexual orientation, are likely to have equal experiences of liquids in containers, the marked differences recorded on the water level task are intuitively the most surprising."[57]

Heterosexual males have also been found to have a marked left visual field superiority in a dot detection task when the dots were exposed to both left and right visual fields. By contrast, homosexual males and heterosexual females showed no left-right advantage.[58] "Taken together," the investigators note, "these findings establish a link among three phenomena, the etiology of sexual orientation, sex differences in cognitive ability, and sex differences in cerebral asymmetry. In each of these areas there is a growing support for some form of biological determination."[59]

### Immunologic Maternal "Rejection" of the Male Fetus

One method for modifying sexual orientation in laboratory animals involves the induction of an immune response to one or more of the biochemicals necessary for the sexual differentiation of the brain. Immune antibodies exist for nearly all the androgens and estrogens.[60] The more foreign the fetal tissue cells, the more likely it is that there will be a maternal antibody reaction to them. Thus, males are more vulnerable; most spontaneously aborted fetuses are male.[61] The mother may also produce antibodies that compromise the mechanisms responsible for the hormonal organization of the brain in a male direction. These maternal immune responses to a fetus may not be developed fully until a second or third pregnancy, as for example with the Rh blood incompatibility phenomenon, in which the firstborn is spared, but subsequent births are affected.[62] This theory, that the mother's antibody response can compromise the male-hormone potential of the male fetus, though not supported by much empirical work, is compatible with reports that male homosexuals are more often found to be later-born siblings.[63]

## Treatment of a Homosexual Orientation

### "Insight" Therapy

The following sobering words of Sigmund Freud did little to dissuade his psychoanalytic followers from attempting to reorient homosexual patients: "In actual numbers the successes achieved by psychoanalytic treatment of the various forms of homosexuality . . . are not very striking. As a rule, the homosexual is not able to give up the object of his pleasure . . . If he comes to be treated at all, it is mostly through the pressure of external motives, such as the social disadvantages and dangers."[64]

The most detailed research report on the psychoanalytic "insight" treatment of male homosexuality appeared in 1962.[65] Of seventy-two men who were exclusively homosexual prior to therapy, fourteen (19 percent) were reported to be exclusively heterosexual after therapy. Of thirty men who had been bisexual prior to therapy, fifteen were later reported to be exclusively heterosexual. Outcome was related to duration of treatment. Of twenty-nine males reported to be exclusively heterosexual after therapy, only two had less than 150 hours of therapy, nine had between 150 and 349 hours, and eighteen had at least 350 hours. Additional prognostic factors beyond length of treatment were that most who reoriented had made some attempt at heterosexual intercourse prior to treatment and had had heterosexual content in their dreams prior to treatment. Surveying the treatment results, the authors concluded: "The shift from homosexual to exclusive heterosexuality for 27 percent of the patients is of outstanding importance since *these are the most optimistic and promising results thus far reported.*"[66]

Another follow-up report of psychoanalytically treated homosexual patients described fourteen men treated in the early 1950s. Eleven were exclusively or predominantly homosexual prior to treatment, and three were bisexual. An average interval of four-and-a-half years had elapsed since the end of therapy. Of the eleven who were exclusively or predominantly homosexual prior to treatment, four were predominantly heterosexual after therapy. The three who were bisexual prior to therapy were also now predominantly heterosexual. The level of heterosexuality considered to be a successful adjustment was the ability to derive pleasure and satisfaction in sexual intercourse most of the time, or the ability to enjoy "mature, consistently satisfactory heterosexual adjustment without significant conflicts."[67] But as a critic of this study points out, "the criteria for 'success' in this report are highly questionable . . . [and] the self reports of the patients were interpreted by the authors without external validation. This method is insufficient in terms of objective data collection."[68]

A sobering report published in England found that only seven of eighty-one cases referred by courts and other agencies achieved "satisfactory results" of "no homosexual impulses, [or] increased heterosexual interest" through nonanalytic psychotherapy. Furthermore, none of these "successful" patients had initially been exclusively homosexual.[69]

Another English study evaluated a hundred males. Twenty-three had been treated by psychotherapy, eleven with in-patient care and sixty-six with supportive counseling and medication. Less than 20 percent reported less intense homosexual feelings at follow-up. Of those twenty-four who had been exclusively homosexual, there was no change in twenty-three. In addition, there was no difference in sexual reorientation in the men who had received psychotherapy compared to those who had not.[70]

*Behavior Therapy*

Psychoanalytic efforts at changing homosexuality were disappointing for at least two reasons. First, classic treatment is extremely lengthy. It involves fifty minutes a day, five days a week, with the weeks extending into years. Aside from the extraordinary expense, the results, as noted above, were less than overwhelming. The majority of previously exclusively homosexual males remained primarily homosexual, and the rates of those previously bisexual males reorienting to exclusive heterosexuality were no better than 50 percent. Considering that the homosexual males who entered therapy were those most highly motivated to change and that therapists are more likely to report successes than failures, these "gains" are even more modest.

As practitioners gradually became disillusioned with psychoanalytic and other insight therapies in the early 1960s, "behavior therapy" enjoyed a surge in popularity. In contrast to the psychoanalytic approach—uncovering unconscious conflicts and gradually "working through" early life psychological trauma—the behaviorist approach treated the unwanted behavior not as a symptom of some long-repressed conflict but rather as a learned behavior that could be quickly unlearned. Sexual arousal by a male to another male was a learned phenomenon, reinforced by the pleasure of the sexual response, that could be changed by substituting pain for pleasure.

For about fifteen years, individual case studies and group reports flooded the treatment literature. Today it is difficult to find new reports. While this dearth is partially due to the general fall from grace of treatment for a homosexual orientation, a review of the results of treatment suggests that the less than spectacular outcomes also provide a reason.

Painful electric shock was paired with projected slides of nude males in a 1960 study. As treatment progressed, increasing numbers of slides of nude females were also shown that were not paired with shock. The latter slides were used to elicit "anxiety relief" and were thus to be associated with a positive experience. Treatment outcome was measured by reports of heterosexual intercourse. Of nine males who had not experienced heterosexual intercourse prior to therapy, six later "demonstrated decreased homosexual arousal and engaged in heterosexual coitus" at three years' follow-up.[71]

A few years later, a series of forty-three homosexual males were treated using a similar procedure. The subject viewed a projected slide of a male nude that he could remove from the screen. If he viewed the slide for too long (more than eight seconds), however, he would be shocked. A slide of a female nude was shown either after the homosexual slide was removed or after the shock was administered. Of forty-one males, twenty-four had been homosexually active for more than a decade and twenty-five had displayed no heterosexual practice or fantasy. Nine bisexuals were heterosexually active at the initiation of treatment but were utilizing homosexual fantasy in their heterosexual activity.

After treatment, twenty-five of the forty-one men "improved to a sufficient degree for their treatment to be described as successful." At one-year follow-up, thirteen were engaging in heterosexual intercourse unaccompanied by homosexual fantasy and were not engaging in homosexual acts. Only fourteen patients, as compared with twenty-five before treatment, had no heterosexual fantasy or practice. Those who began treatment as exclusively homosexual during the preceding few years were less likely to become heterosexual. This study remains the most positive of any large series behavior therapy report.[72]

Later studies employed physiological measures of sexual arousal, that is, changes in penile circumference. One employed electric shock, which was delivered after penile arousal was evident in response to homosexual fantasies and slides. In this study, five of ten patients showed a reduction in homosexual interest, and four demonstrated a reduction in homosexual behavior. This was followed by increases in heterosexual behavior and interest in about half of the men.[73] Another paired slides of female nudes with previously arousing slides of male nudes. The subject first viewed a series of female nude slides, then a slide of a nude male. During this sequence, the subject masturbated. Over the course of weeks, the number of slides of males was reduced and finally eliminated. At the outset, there were four male homosexual and five bisexual men. The pattern of penile erection in response to heterosexual and homosexual stimuli was reversed during treatment, so that by the end, all the men showed more responsivity to slides of females.

Nine men reported no homosexual behavior one year after treatment, but at eighteen months' follow-up, two were living in homosexual unions, while seven "continued their heterosexual adjustment."[74]

By contrast, a more negative study of the effectiveness of an aversive shock treatment procedure in sixteen men found that only five demonstrated any change and only two demonstrated decreased homosexual arousal accompanied by an increase in heterosexual behavior. Therapy gains were maintained after two years in only two of sixteen patients.[75]

A 1977 review of the status of behavior therapy noted that thirty-seven studies had offered "reorientation services" to a total of 350 homosexuals (346 males) whose history of homosexual preference ranged from six months to thirty-eight years. The authors concluded that "there is no evidence that aversion relief is a direct and potentially effective procedure for increasing heterosexual arousal itself." Furthermore, "the reduction of homosexual arousal and behavior is now being viewed as only one component of an effective treatment program. If treatment gains are to be maintained, other sexual and social behaviors must be instituted to replace the previously reinforcing homosexual patterns."[76]

Candid reports by two clinicians experienced in the behavioral treatment of homosexual orientation also provide sobering views of purported treatment "successes." Their comments reveal that the "heterosexuality" reported for many "successfully treated" patients is not genuine heterosexual orientation. One clinician's report described forty-seven male patients treated with chemical aversion therapy (nausea paired with homosexual stimuli). About a dozen were considered at follow-up to have, in general, a heterosexual adaptation. After the initial brief follow-up period, however, one of the twelve reverted to his previous homosexual orientation, and another could not be traced. Another requested further treatment four years later because of renewed homosexual drives. Another married for six years, then fell in love with a male and became impotent with his wife. Another, who entered the military four years later, claimed, in contradiction to previous statements alleging heterosexuality, always to have been oriented in a purely homosexual way. Another divorced his wife and remarried, but during the last year of evaluation fell in love with a male. Another, who claimed to have been happily married for six years, was having homosexual intercourse about once every ten days. Another, married for nine years, had homosexual intercourse as frequently as heterosexual intercourse, and another, married for three years, had homosexual intercourse once every ten days and intercourse with his wife about once a week. More heterosexually oriented reports were given by others. One man, married and the father of two, claimed to be happily married but would not let the researchers interview his wife. Another, married for seven years, had homosexual intercourse on three occasions over the follow-up period. Another, married for five years, had homosexual intercourse only once during that time. All, however, "claim[ed] that their motivation is still almost exclusively homosexual."[77]

The other clinician's report also challenges the validity of sexual "reorientation" and comes to this pessimistic conclusion: "The significant change in reduction in homosexual feelings and behaviour after aversive therapy, as compared with positive conditioning, is not accompanied by change in the sexual orientation of the patients . . . [as measured by penile responsivity to erotic stimuli]. In all studies, over half the patients continued to obtain a score indicating a homosexual orientation after treatment."[78] The researcher then asks, "Can treatment alter homosexual orientation?" and answers, "The aversive therapies . . . reported would appear not to have altered the patient's sexual orientation . . . it must be assumed that present treatments may reduce or eliminate homosexual behavior and awareness of homosexual feelings *without altering the sexual orientation.*"[79]

*Religious Therapy*

One report of heterosexual reorientation claims a religiously mediated influence.[80] Changes occurred in the context of a crisis service provided by a pentecostal church to its homosexual members. Thirty men who claimed to have changed from homosexuality to heterosexuality were located, and the investigators obtained the cooperation of eleven to collect interview data. The number of years the men reported to be functioning as heterosexual ranged from one to seven.

When the homosexual men came into contact with the church's crisis center, they were invited to commit their life to Christ and the church. All had an explicitly Christian conversion or rededication. Their psychological condition of homosexuality had been "interpreted by these church members as a sign of Christian immaturity."

When interviewed at follow-up, one man acknowledged homosexual dreams, three acknowledged homosexual fantasies, and five acknowledged homosexual impulses. While the Kinsey ratings on all had been at least 4 (predominantly homosexual) prior to this conversion, it was reported as zero for five men, 1 for three men, and 2 for three more (exclusively or predominantly heterosexual). The homosexual impulses of three men were "a source of neurotic conflict." Those who married reported that initially their homosexual dreams, fantasies, and impulses had not vanished, but "as they progressed in a satisfactory marital relationship, their homosexual dreams, fantasies, and impulses gradually diminished over time." None of the unmarried men was engaging in heterosexual intercourse "because of religious prohibitions."

A critique of this report points out that in addition to the fact that nineteen of the thirty men were not interviewed, the thirty "are but 10 percent of the 300 total 'dissatisfied' homosexuals who had initially requested treatment."[81]

All of these reports of treatment outcome involve males. The reasons for this sex disparity may include the greater stigma accompanying male homosexuality, the greater ease with which female homosexuals achieve, on their own, the goals of marriage and parenting, and the greater economic status of men, which facilitates expensive treatment.

## *"Homosexual" or "Prehomosexual" Children*

A fifteen-year study I conducted also points to the very early and essentially irreversible establishment of sexual orientation in the male.[82] That research identified a series of sixty-six boys, aged four to twelve, who displayed extensive cross-gender behaviors. These included statements of wishing to be a girl, preferential cross-dressing in women's or girls' clothes, preferential role-playing as a female in fantasy games, a female peer group, and an avoidance of rough-and-tumble play and sports. Among the two-thirds of the previously cross-gendered boys who were followed up fifteen years later, 75 percent were homosexually or bisexually oriented.

The irreversibility of the prehomosexual behavioral pattern, even when "treated" early, was demonstrated. Approximately one-third of the cross-gendered boys were involved in psychotherapy, with several clinicians, yet the rate of homosexual or bisexual behavior in the treated group is not different from that in the untreated group. Thus, just as treatment during adulthood aimed at reorienting homosexual orientation is generally unrewarding, so is treatment during boyhood aimed at preventing the development of a homosexual orientation.

These data provide some evidence that sexual orientation is innate. They provide even more evidence that it is essentially unchangeable. Coupled with the other requirements for "suspect class" designation—societal prejudice and political powerless-ness—homosexuals would appear to qualify.

## A Court Case

Homosexuals came close to achieving "suspect class" status in the marathon legal battle of Perry Watkins against the U.S. Army. For nearly a decade he fought the Army's refusal to permit him to reenlist because of his stated homosexual orientation (homosexual behavior was not at issue).

A three-judge panel of the Ninth Circuit Court of Appeals held two to one that homosexuals were a "suspect class" and that the Army's discriminatory policy toward Watkins did not meet the required exacting standard.[83] When the case was reheard by a larger panel of judges, Watkins's reenlistment was permitted, but their ruling was based on the fact that the Army had known about his sexual orientation when it had previously allowed him to be a soldier, thus eliminating the need for the court to determine whether homosexuals are a "suspect class."

In dissent, Judge Norris, the author of the earlier majority opinion, restated the case for the previous holding.[84] First, Norris pointed to the history of discrimination: "It is indisputable that 'homosexuals have historically been the object of pernicious and sustained hostility' [and further] 'lesbians and gays have been the object of some of the deepest prejudicial hatred in American society.' "[85] Second, he underscored their political powerlessness: "Homosexuals have historically been underrepresented in and victimized by political bodies . . . by 'coming out of the closet' to protest against discriminatory legislation and practices, homosexuals expose themselves to the very discrimination they seek to eliminate."[86] Finally, he stressed the immutability of sexual orientation: "Although the causes of homosexuality are not fully understood, scientific research indicates that we have little control over our sexual orientation and that, once acquired, our sexual orientation is largely impervious to change."[87]

## Immutability and Sexual Orientation

The negative results of treatment directed at homosexual orientation and the evidence for its genetic or hormonal basis are not reverse sides of the same coin. Learned phenomena may be extremely resistant to change, particularly those learned early in life. The priority of first language is an example. Conversely, a behavior may be inborn and related to brain functioning but still amenable to change. Lefthandedness is an example.

Biological research does not prove that sexual orientation, or at least homosexual orientation, is entirely genetically determined or entirely hormonally induced. The sexual science data, however, do point to some contribution from both of these sources. An objective comparison of the evidence behind genetic and/or hormonal influences reveals it to be at least as strong as the posited Freudian concepts of unresolved Oedipal conflicts and residual castration fear, or the behaviorist idea of "mislearning" homosexual arousal. The outcome of psychotherapy based on these theoretical constructs has been disappointing for proponents of these therapies.

This chapter has focused on "immutability" in the jurisprudential context of what constitutes a "suspect class." The standard dictionary definition of *immutable* is "unchangeable" or "unalterable." Here, however, this definition is too absolute. That an individual can undergo reconstructive genital or "sex-change" surgery (see Chapter 6) does not mean that gender is mutable. Some of the basic criteria for determining the sex of an individual, such as the sex chromosomes, remain the same after surgery. Other traits found to be "immutable" in court decisions are likewise "changeable": aliens can become naturalized citizens, illegitimates can be legitimized, and national origin can be concealed.

Nor does the finding that one can with great effort graft apparently heterosexual behavior onto an earlier homosexual orientation mean that sexual orientation is mutable. The arduous process of "reorientation" is psychologically wrenching and sometimes physically painful. Therapy for homosexuals may not be much more effective than what could be expected from attempts to reorient heterosexuals if penile-vaginal intercourse were to become (frequently) a crime, (usually) a sin, and (for several decades, at least) a mental illness.

# · 5 ·

# Immigration and
# Homosexuality

Excluding undesirable immigrants from entering a potential host nation and denying an alien's continuing residence are generally recognized national prerogatives. The traditional criteria for exclusion address persons who may endanger or burden the host nation—those with criminal histories, those with contagious diseases, those with handicaps that will require host support. But among the classes of excludables there has been another group that does not fit neatly into these traditionally unwelcome categories: homosexuals.

## History

United States immigration policy regarding homosexuals has involved a marriage of one government bureaucracy with another: the Immigration and Naturalization Service (INS) and the Public Health Service (PHS). Not until 1979 when that marriage ended in divorce was any hurdle placed in the way of the INS's exclusion of homosexuals for reasons of "health."

Homosexuals were first excluded by statute from entry into the United States by the Immigration Act of 1917. The Act prohibited the entry of "persons of constitutional psychopathic inferiority."[1] The excluding term was the medical classification for persons "who show a lifelong and constitutional tendency not to conform to the customs of the group." These were persons who "habitually misbehave . . . have no sense of responsibility to their fellow men or to society as a whole . . . succumb readily to . . . a life of crime . . . [and] fail to learn by experience."[2]

The 1918 PHS Manual on the Mental Examination of Aliens defined constitutional psychopathic inferiority as a "borderland between sanity and insanity" populated by persons exhibiting "failures of mental adaptation" who have a "tendency to become actively disordered." Grouped with "constitutional psychopathic inferiors" were "moral imbeciles, pathological liars and swindlers," and persons with "abnormal sexual instincts." Since "the dividing line between these various types is not well defined . . . for purposes of simplicity in classifying the mentally abnormal immigrant they may all be included in one general class and certified as cases of constitutional psychopathic inferiority."[3]

The 1930 PHS revision made little progress toward a more enlightened position: "There shall be certified as cases of constitutional psychopathic inferiority all psychopathic characters such as 'sexual perverts,' 'pathological liars,' 'dipsomaniacs,' [and] 'moral imbeciles.' "[4] Psychopathic inferiors were excluded in order to prevent the entry of persons with "tainted blood" (that is, those "who have medical traits which would harm the people of the United States if those traits were introduced").[5]

In 1947, Congress consulted the PHS in its effort to update medically excludable classes.[6] In 1950, the Senate Committee on the Judiciary reported that the "classes of mental defectives should be enlarged to include homosexuals and other sex perverts."[7] Then a series of proposed bills was drafted providing for the exclusion of "aliens afflicted with psychopathic personality" and "aliens who are homosexuals or sex perverts."[8] Express reference to "aliens who are homosexuals or sex perverts" was eliminated in the proposed new law, however, because "[t]he Public Health Service has advised that the provision for the exclusion of aliens afflicted with psychopathic personality or a mental defect which appears in the instant Bill is sufficiently broad to provide for the exclusion of homosexuals and sex perverts. *This change of nomenclature is not to be construed in any way as modifying the intent to exclude all aliens who are sexual deviates.*"[9]

Although this bill was not enacted, the report accompanying a subsequent bill that became the Immigration Act of 1952 contained a similar reference to the PHS observations. The PHS had noted that "psychopathic personality," which replaced the term "constitutional psychopathic inferior," would satisfy the congressional objective of excluding "homosexuals and perverts" because "ordinarily sexual deviation was a manifestation of a psychopathic personality."[10] Thus "psychopathic personality" became a "legal term of art" and for immigration purposes included the homosexual.

As used by psychiatry in the 1950s, "psychopathic personality" referred to persons whose behavior was "predominantly amoral or antisocial and characterized by impulsive, irresponsible actions satisfying only immediate and narcissistic interests without concern for obvious and implicit social consequences accompanied by minimal outward evidence of anxiety or guilt."[11] The descriptive "medical" characteristics of this disorder were becoming less moralistic. Psychopathic personalities were now characterized by "developmental defects or pathological trends in the personality structure manifested by lifelong patterns of action or behavior, rather than by mental or emotional symptoms. [They may be] persons ill primarily in terms of society and the prevailing culture."[12]

Difficulties in the diagnosis of homosexuality, absent acknowledgment by the alien were also addressed by the PHS:

> Sexual Perverts. The language of the bill lists sexual perverts or homosexual persons as among those aliens to be excluded from admission to the United States. In some instances considerable difficulty may be encountered in substantiating a diagnosis of homosexuality or sexual perversion . . . Ordinarily, a history of homosexuality must be obtained from the individual, which he may successfully cover up. *Some psychological tests may be helpful in uncovering homosexuality of which the individual himself may be unaware* . . . The detection of persons with more obvious sexual perversions is relatively simple. Considerably more difficulty may be encountered in uncovering the homosexual person.[13]

A lawsuit challenging the meaning of "psychopathic personality" as applied to homosexuals provided the Ninth Circuit Court of Appeals with the opportunity to define the term. In *Fleuti v. Rosenberg*,[14] described more fully below, it ruled that the term did not include homosexuals. To eliminate such doubt, Congress then amended the Immigration Act to include "sexual deviates" as an excludable class.[15]

Action by the Board of Trustees of the American Psychiatric Association (APA) set the stage for the next historic phase. In 1973, the APA Trustees voted to remove homosexuality per se from the categories of mental disorder. In the next year, a referendum upholding the decision was passed by the full APA membership.[16]

The contradiction between the position of the APA, which declared that homosexuality was not a mental disorder, and that of the PHS, which continued certifying homosexual aliens as medically ill, continued for another five years. Then, on August 2, 1979, the surgeon general of the PHS announced a dramatic new policy: PHS personnel would not issue medical certificates certifying an alien as afflicted with a medically excludable condition solely because the alien was homosexual. The old policy was revised because homosexuality per se was no longer a mental disorder and the determination of homosexuality was not made through a medical diagnostic procedure.[17]

In response, the INS initially allowed suspected homosexuals to enter the country conditionally under "parole status," deferring their medical examinations until the resolution of the dispute.[18] Then the assistant attorney general in the Office of Legal Counsel of the Department of Justice opined that the surgeon general had overstepped his authority. As to "policies regarding the description and diagnosis of disease," the PHS was limited by Congress's "specified intent to bar homosexuals."[19] The Office of Legal Counsel informed the INS that it was still required to enforce the homosexual exclusion.[20]

The new INS policy was described in the Department of Justice press release of September 9, 1980. If an alien made an "unsolicited, unambiguous admission of homosexuality" to an INS inspector or was identified as a homosexual by a "third party who arrived at the same time," the alleged homosexual would be subjected to a "secondary inspection." At that inspection, the person would be asked whether he or she was homosexual. If the person answered, "no," entry would be permitted. If the person answered, "yes," a formal exclusionary hearing would follow.[21]

Until 1990 the Immigration Act continued to exclude aliens afflicted with "psychopathic personality, sexual deviation, or mental defect,"[22] and the U.S. visa questionnaire continued to ask whether the alien applicant for entry was a "sexual deviate." Applicants who knew that the APA did not consider homosexuality a mental disorder could truthfully answer "no." Those unaware of the APA change, and who thought they were included, might answer "yes." This answer would amount to "an unambiguous oral or written admission of homosexuality," and thus would constitute grounds for exclusion.

Another way the INS could bar homosexuals was through testing aliens for the Acquired Immunodeficiency Syndrome (AIDS). Aliens with AIDS, a disease that was added to the list of "dangerous contagious diseases," could be barred. An alien seeking admission to the United States can be required to undergo a medical examination at the discretion of a consular officer overseas or an immigration officer at a port of entry if there is reason to suspect such a disease.[23]

In 1990, the INS announced rule changes for visa applications by HIV positive visitors. Formerly, if they were permitted entry their passports were marked to identify their HIV status. The new regulation permitted foreign visitors to reveal this entry waiver information on a separate form. It also allowed visitors to request waivers from American personnel at foreign consulates and embassies rather than from local nationals employed as clerks.[24] In 1991 HIV positive persons could enter the United States only for brief periods. Whether to abolish HIV exclusion remained a topic of debate in the Bush administration.

## Cases

Over the years courts have grappled with the meaning of the term "psychopathic personality." In a 1962 case, *Fleuti v. Rosenberg*,[25] a resident alien was ordered deported because at the time of entry he was a "psychopathic personality." But he contended that the order was invalid because it was not based on reasonable substantial and probative evidence and was overly vague, thus violating the

Due Process Clause of the Fifth Amendment, which mandates that a person be given sufficient information about what is required or prohibited by law.

The Court of Appeals found that "psychopathic personality" is not defined in the statute and asked whether the language of the statute conveyed adequate warning of the proscribed conduct. Noting that medical experts are in disagreement about the meaning of the term, the court ruled that it did not sufficiently convey the warning that homosexuality and sex perversion are included within its meaning. When the case got to the Supreme Court, however, the Court avoided judging whether the term was unconstitutionally vague and addressed only the question of whether when Fleuti returned to the United States after a two-hour trip to Mexico his return constituted "entry" into the United States, thus triggering application of the statute. The Court held that it did not.[26]

To remedy the ambiguity of the term "psychopathic personality," Congress revised the Immigration and Naturalization Act to include "sexual deviate." Then, in 1967, the courts had another opportunity to grapple with the meaning of the term. First, the Second Circuit had its turn.

In *Boutilier v. Immigration and Naturalization Service,* Judge Kaufman began his decision in an astounding manner: "Although a relatively young segment of contemporary society prides itself on its readiness to cast off conventional and tested disciplines and to experiment with nonconformance and the unorthodox merely to act out its contempt for traditional values, certain areas of conduct continue to be as controversial in modern and *beau monde* circles as they were in bygone and more staid eras."[27] Kaufman went on to say that the above notwithstanding, the court would embark on a course guided by "personal detachment."

This was the case: Boutilier had been admitted into the United States at age twenty-one for permanent residence. Four years later in his application for citizenship he acknowledged an arrest and admitted that the circumstances leading to it involved acts of anal sodomy and fellatio with a seventeen-year-old-male. Boutilier subsequently acknowledged that his first homosexual experience had occurred when he was fourteen and that such experiences continued up to the time of his entry into the country.

The Public Health Service stated that Boutilier "was afflicted with a Class A condition, namely, psychopathic personality, sexual deviate, at the time of his admission." Boutilier argued that he was not, by psychiatric definition, a "psychopathic personality." But the term was deemed by the court to be a "legal term of art," interpreted as referring to "any alien shown to be a homosexual,"[28] and not a "medical formulation." Although psychiatrists testified that homosexuals were not psychopaths, their testimony was irrelevant to the court: "We believe the term 'psychopathic personality' reflects a Congressional purpose to prevent alien homosexuals from obtaining admission into this country. It was employed as a term of art to be interpreted by what Congress intended as a guide, and not to be left to the vagaries and honest but conflicting theories of psychiatry for determination."[29]

Then came the Supreme Court's turn.[30] The Court ruled that the legislative history of the Act "indicates beyond a shadow of a doubt that the Congress intended the phrase 'psychopathic personality' to include homosexuals."[31] The Court noted that the PHS had advised that the provision for excluding aliens afflicted with psychopathic personality was sufficiently broad to exclude homosexuals and sex perverts.[32] Justice Douglas dissented along with Justice Fortas, stating that the term "'psychopathic personality' is a treacherous one like 'communist' or in an earlier day 'Bolshevik.' A label of this kind when freely used may mean only an unpopular person."[33]

Female homosexuals have received equal treatment. In a 1961 case, *Quiroz v. Neelly,* a Mexican lesbian was ordered deported because she was considered a psychopathic personality. This was so in spite of the fact that two doctors, one a psychiatrist, testified that homosexuals are not necessarily psychopathic personalities within the meaning of the term. The doctors' views were disregarded by the court: "Whatever the phrase 'psychopathic personality' may mean to the psychiatrist, to the Congress it was intended to include homosexuals and sex perverts. It is that which controls here."[34]

The next major sequence of court battles followed the Public Health Service's refusal to certify homosexuals as medically excludable. In one case, the INS sought to bar the entry of a British alien who voluntarily stated upon attempting entry that he was homosexual. No PHS examination was conducted.[35] The district court analyzed the history of homosexual exclusion to determine the *necessity* of the PHS medical exclusion certificate:

> A reading of the applicable portions of the Immigration and Nationality Act, and corresponding legislative history, indicates the intent of Congress that homosexuality be a medical exclusion, and that therefore a medical certificate is required . . . The excludable aliens statute places persons afflicted with a psychopathic personality, sexual deviation, or a mental defect among six other classes of aliens excludable for medical reasons. The statutes governing the detention, observation and examination of arriving aliens also reaffirm the medical basis for the exclusion of homosexuals, and point out the requirement of obtaining a medical certificate to exclude.[36]

The court cited several statutory examples in support of its contention that the exclusion of homosexuals was medical business only. One section provides for the detention of aliens suspected of being afflicted with a physical or mental defect and calls for a determination by medical officers. Another provides that the physical and mental examination of arriving aliens be made by medical officers. The power of the immigration officer in medical matters is specifically limited by another section, which states that "the inspection, other than the physical and mental examination, of aliens seeking admissions . . . shall be conducted by immigration officers." The court noted that the Act "nowhere provides that an immigration officer may make the determination that an alien is afflicted with a medical condition that constitutes a medical exclusion to admission."[37]

The INS appealed. The Ninth Circuit Court of Appeals reviewed the language and structure of the Act, its legislative history, its administrative interpretation, and its interpretation by the judiciary. Regarding legislative history, "[t]here is no indication . . . that Congress or the PHS believed that homosexuality should be determined by admissions [by the alien] any more than schizophrenia could be self-diagnosed."[38]

The court then reviewed prior INS decisions purportedly supporting INS reliance on medical certification. They were found wanting. In *In re Hayes*,[39] certification was issued without strict compliance with the surgeon general's regulations and was declared an insufficient basis for exclusion of the alien, despite an admission of homosexual behavior. In *In re Caydam*,[40] the Board of Immigration Appeals (BIA) reversed a deportation order because of a defective medical certificate and ruled that the BIA lacked the authority and expertise to make medical determinations. In *In re Berger*,[41] certification without actual examination of the alien, and based "only" on an admission of homosexual acts and two convictions for homosexual acts, was held insufficient to establish that the alien was "afflicted" with a proscribed medical condition. In *In re Flight*,[42] the acknowledgment of five homosexual acts was deemed insufficient to bar the alien without medical certification. On the other hand, for deportation, as opposed to exclusion from entry, a medical certificate was not deemed necessary.[43] The court held that "the INS' attempt to exclude [the alien] from entry into the United States as a person afflicted with a sexual deviation without [their obtaining] a medical certificate . . . constitute[d] an abuse of discretion."[44]

But there is disorder in the courts. The Fifth Circuit reached the opposite conclusion in *Matter of Longstaff*.[45] There, an applicant's admission that he fell within the excludable class of homosexuals was ruled competent evidence on which to exclude, notwithstanding absence of a medical certificate. The court raised the question of whether Congress ordered the exclusion of everyone it considered a sexual deviate or "only persons so classified at any given time by the PHS medical officer or some other physician."[46] The court would not "conclude that a medical certificate was indispensable to bar a professed homosexual from entry to the United States."[47] To the court, "[t]here is no reason why an informed applicant's admission that he falls within an excludable class is not competent evidence on which to base an exclusion decision."[48]

On the other hand, a federal district court held that naturalization should not be denied simply because the applicant engaged in private, consensual homosexual acts. In *In re Labady*,[49] the INS asserted that the alien had not sustained his burden of establishing that he was a person of good moral character. These were the facts. Labady entered the United States at age fourteen and told the INS that he was homosexual but was not certified as a "sexual deviate" or "psychopathic personality." Since he had entered the country "without deceit" he was not deportable on that basis.[50] He could, however, be deportable if he failed the test for "good moral character." The court found that "although he has engaged on occasion in purely private homosexual relations with consenting adults, he has not corrupted the morals of others . . . [Therefore], [u]nder all the circumstances, setting aside our personal moral views, we cannot say that his conduct has violated public morality or indicated that he will be anything other than a law-abiding and useful citizen."[51]

Court views of whether engaging in homosexual behavior eliminates the required provision of "good moral character" necessary for naturalization have not been consistent. In a New York State Court Case,[52] *In re Petition of Schmidt*,[53] the court ruled with regard to an alien lesbian: "Although her activities were confined to her home and with persons with whom she lived, her admitted practices of these sexual deviations continually during the five years preceding the filing of her petition, are not, in the court's opinion, consistent with good moral character as the 'ordinary man or woman sees it.'"

By contrast, in *In re Brodie*[54] Judge Burns succinctly summarized his findings: "Paul Brodie, a citizen of New Zealand, and a veteran of the United States Army, wants to become a citizen of this country. He is a homosexual. Is he by that single trait shut out from citizenship? I have concluded that he is not." The court dispassionately observed: "Although his partners have been men, his social and sexual behavior has not otherwise differed from that of many other persons 20 years old. Like most people, he is not sexually involved with minors. He does not use threat or fraud. He does not take or give money. Nor does he engage in sexual activity in parks, theaters, or any public places . . . In short, he is neither a public nuisance nor a private danger."

State sodomy laws and the question of "good moral character" arose in *Nemetz v. Immigration and Naturalization Service*.[55] There, an alien admitted engaging in sodomy in private in violation of a Virginia ordinance. Conviction for a crime involving "moral turpitude" is a bar to citizenship. But sodomy is not a crime in all states. The court asked, "Since [this alien's] 'crime' is a Virginia one, should he be held to a federal standard of moral turpitude based on that state law? Had he lived in Illinois, the INS could not oppose his petition."

The court concluded:

> Congress did not intend to bar a finding of good moral character merely because of an alien's private consensual sexual activities. Rather than making the categories of exclusion and a finding of bad moral character coextensive, Congress instead absolutely barred a finding of good moral character for only 6 of the excludable classes . . . Not referred to is the excludable class of [a]liens afflicted with . . . sexual deviation . . . Had Congress intended homosexual acts to evince bad moral character, it could easily have incorporated (that) by reference . . . its failure to do so leads us to the conclusion that it did not intend purely private sexual activities to act as an absolute bar to a finding of good moral character.[56]

Thus, a state's prerogative to criminalize consenting, private, homosexual acts, later upheld by the Supreme Court,[57] was an insufficient basis for foreclosing (good) citizenship.

The American attitude toward homosexual aliens has been unique: "The United States, alone among the nations of the world, statutorily excludes homosexual persons from admission into the country for any purpose whatsoever, from casual visitor to would-be permanent resident."[58] The United States immigration system initially adopted the medical profession's designation of homosexuality as a disease in order to exclude it "legitimately" along with other medically unwelcome conditions. That the INS had more in mind than merely abiding by the medical profession's concern for illness was later made strikingly clear: When psychiatrists declared that homosexuals were not "psychopathic personalities" (the medical diagnosis previously ascribed to homosexuals), the INS argued that the term was being used as a "legal term of art," rather than as a medical diagnosis. Later, any semblance of reliance on the medical profession was dropped when the INS persisted in attempting to exclude homosexuals even after the Public Health Service abandoned the enterprise, stating that homosexuals were not afflicted with an illness under any terminology.

Prejudice against homosexuals among some members of the U.S. Congress is revealed in the *Congressional Record*. In 1965, after a court ruled that "psychopathic personality" did not include homosexuality, Representative Richard Poff of Virginia declared: "[T]he [present immigration] bill adds by specific language an exclusion which the authors of the present act thought had been excluded. Until the court ruled otherwise, it was intended that the term 'psychopathic personality' should embrace 'sexual deviation.' By using the precise term the bill makes it plain that Congress intends that aliens afflicted with this *disgraceful disability* be excluded from our shores."[59]

Fourteen years later, the Congress heard speakers calling for reform. The president of the American Psychiatric Association expressed the association's concern about the use of the diagnosis of homosexuality as a means of "social control" rather than for the "treatment of mental illness." The law remained the same.[60]

Not until 1990 was immigration law changed to allow homosexuals entry into the United States. What was described as the "most comprehensive reform of U.S. immigration laws in 25 years . . . wipe[d] from the statute books decades old restrictions barring entry to people on the basis of . . . homosexuality."[61]

# · 6 ·

# Transsexualism

Because a transsexual's psychological identity as male or female contradicts anatomy, transsexuals demand sex hormones and genital-altering surgery to bring their body into conformity with their self-concept. For transsexuals, sexual science implicates the law in several areas, including employment discrimination, use of public restrooms before surgery, legal sex after surgery, marriage and parenting, treatment in prison, and insurance reimbursement for sex-change procedures.

## Male-to-Female Transsexuals

The transsexual's fundamental dilemma before sex reassignment or "sex-change" surgery is illustrated by the following brief vignettes of persons who want to "change sex."[1]

This preoperative male-to-female transsexual is just beginning to live as a woman.

> Male-to-Female Transsexual (M-F TS): Well, my problem to begin with is of very long standing. In fact, all my conscious life, I have been aware that I was of the wrong sex, and I can remember quite clearly back as far as my third birthday. I have scattered little memories of this and that, beginning with my parents. They were sort of expecting a girl when I arrived.
>
> Green: How do you know this?
>
> M-F TS: They had the name picked out. I was to be named Mary Joan after my two grandmothers. The only time I can ever recall as

a child having been involuntarily dressed as a girl was a very, very dim little memory when I was either three or four, and my sister just played one afternoon, and she put one of her dresses on me and started playing around, saying, "This is my little sister." I believed her. It was just right for me, because it happened to be a dress that I had seen her wear and I had wished I could have one like it, so without my even asking her she put it on me and played with me like a doll. Then she said, "Okay," and took it off me. I was frankly a little disappointed.

Green: What other early memories do you have?

M-F TS: There was a place way up in the branches of a tree where I grew up that branched out close enough so I could lie in it like a hammock. I would lie there and look up through the leaves to the sky and pray. I would promise, and I would offer anything if God would do a miracle for me and make me a girl some day. Any day.

Green: Why?

M-F TS: I wanted to be a girl so bad, just like now, if I still felt the same way now as I did then about God, I would be doing the same thing regularly now. I was called a sissy.

Green: What do you remember about your mother?

M-F TS: You know how mothers are about little boys handling themselves where they shouldn't? Well, my mother was no exception. She threatened to cut it off if I didn't stop playing with it. Well, I thought that was a peachy keen idea!

Green: Do you remember what she would say?

M-F TS: "If you don't stop playing with it—your thing—I'm going to cut it off."

Green: Did she say "with your thing"?

M-F TS: She called it a "dirty thing." "If I see you handling that I'm going to cut it off." Of course, my mind as young as it was was able to figure out that this would hurt, but I knew that there were other things that hurt. My other brother and sister were having teeth pulled, and they cried, and they got well, and people got sick and well, so I figured "Okay, I'll get well," . . . I thought that was a very good idea. And when I found out she wasn't going to do that, then I got punished a lot less.

This male-to-female transsexual has lived as a woman for ten years and is married to a man, although genital surgery has yet to be performed.

M-F TS: I remember that as a little girl [sic] I used to lie in bed at night with my penis between my legs and my ankles crossed real tight and play a silly game and say if I did this, in the morning when I'd wake up, it would be gone. This is very, very long ago.

Green: How long ago?

M-F TS: Definitely preschool. I don't know where I got this notion, but I just felt that it would go away by morning, and I was so disappointed because every morning I'd reach down there and there it was . . . In kindergarten the kids used to make fun of me because I was girlish.

Green: How?

M-F TS: I used to like to play with girls. I never did like to play with boys. I wanted to play jacks. I wanted to jump rope and all those things. The lady in the schoolyard used to always tell me to go play with the boys. I found it distasteful. I wanted to play with the girls. I wanted to play the girl games. I remember one day the teacher said, "If you play with the girls one more day, I am going to bring a dress to school and make you wear it all day long. How would you like that?" Well, I *would* have liked it.

## Female-to-Male Transsexuals

This preoperative female-to-male transsexual is beginning a course of sex reassignment.

Female-to-Male Transsexual (F-M TS): I want to be a man very much because I feel like it, and I think most of the time I think more like a man than a woman. It is possible to do it, which I didn't know until one month ago. I understand you can give hormones and perform surgery when someone wants to change their sex.

Green: You say you've never spoken to anyone about this before?

F-M TS: No.

Green: How have you managed to keep it to yourself so long?

F-M TS: Partly it's something you don't go around talking about, and also some people are kind of narrow-minded about it. I don't consider myself homosexual. I think that's one thing people would think of automatically. I just feel like the opposite sex.

Green: To what extent?

F-M TS: Everything I do I feel very unnatural. I don't know how to explain it. I have wanted to be a boy ever since I can remember, but there are no logical reasons for what I feel inside.

Green: When you were a kid you felt like this?

F-M TS: Yes. Part of the time it used to be if you were a boy you could do more things. It was just sort of the way I felt. I used to like playing football. I didn't like being a girl and doing things girls do, and lately, it's gotten more so. I feel very awkward being dressed up and going places as a girl.

Green: To what extent is your family aware of your feelings?

F-M TS: They always considered me a tomboy. My mother used to always try to get me to play with dolls and everything, and I wouldn't do it. I played cowboys and Indians with the boys, climbed trees and rode horses, went hunting and fishing with my brothers. I was always out wrestling with the boys. I wasn't doing what she thought I should be doing, but she kind of got used to it, I guess. I never really did change much . . . I just don't feel like the body and I fit together.

This female-to-male transsexual lived through seventeen years of marriage to a man and raised three daughters while feeling she was a man.

F-M TS: I'm interested in sex reassignment. I have never spoken to a doctor or a psychiatrist about it. I'm forty-one now.

Green: How is it that you haven't spoken to any doctor before now?

F-M TS: I was raising some daughters. I think that's one reason. Although I dress this way [mannishly] all the time, I'm no different when I'm with them. When I was raising them, I just didn't follow this desire through . . . I cannot believe that this is all psychological. I just feel that it is part biological. You can't just feel this way all your life—just something in your mind. Just can't feel this. How does the mind of a *child* perceive something like this?

Green: How far back are you talking about?

F-M TS: As far as I can remember. Three years old. I remember wanting to be a boy. Wearing boy's clothes and wanting to do all the things boys do. I remember my mother as I was growing up saying, "Are you ever going to be a lady? Are you ever going to wear women's clothing?" These kind of things as far back as I can remember. I can remember as I got a little older always looking at women, always wanting a woman . . . I feel like a man, and I feel like my loving a woman is perfectly normal.

## Development of Transsexualism

It remains a sexual science mystery why some males and females are transsexual. No psychological or physiological explanation has proven satisfactory. A psychodynamic explanation is provocative but has not been consistently supported in studies. In one series of male-to-female transsexuals, mothers reported an extraordinary amount of skin-to-skin contact during their son's infancy. This was seen as preventing the psychological separation of the male infant from the female parent.[2] My co-authored study of the role of religious ideology also falls short of a universal explanation. We found that being raised in a religious Catholic family where homosexuality was condemned, coupled with cross-gender behavior in boyhood, was related to a transsexual rather than a homosexual outcome. The posited explanation was that transsexualism becomes a way of engaging in nonhomosexual sexual contact with males, since the male becomes a female.[3] However, not only does the finding not fully explain the development of transsexualism in nonreligious families, it also fails to explain its development in males who are sexually interested in females (and become lesbians after sex-reassignment).

Physiological findings in relation to transsexualism are scattered across several research strategies, but none has been sufficiently replicated to provide causal certainty. The controversial and inconsistently found estrogen feedback response reported for male homosexuals (see Chapter 4) has also been reported for male transsexuals. In a study that has yet to be replicated, of twelve male-to-female transsexuals who were sexually attracted to males, nine showed a positive (female pattern) response. By contrast, of sixteen male-to-female transsexuals who were sexually attracted to females, or both females and males, none showed the positive response.[4] The investigator concluded that a deficiency in the hormonal organization of the male brain before birth results in a female sexual identity.

That an area in the hypothalamic region of the brain may differ in male-to-female transsexuals is suggested by an autopsy report of two transsexuals. Their suprachiasmatic nucleus was found to be twice the normal size. But this area of the brain does not show a male-female difference, although it may be related to the production of sex hormones.[5]

An EEG (brain wave) study reported that nearly half of the transsexuals examined had nonspecific abnormalities.[6] Another study, of right- or left-handedness in male transsexuals, suggests the possibility of a nonspecific developmental brain defect. Compared to 160 nontranssexuals, of whom only 26 percent were non-right-handed (either ambidextrous or left-handed), 72 percent of 32 transsexuals were non-right-handed.[7]

Among female-to-male transsexuals, one-third of a series of forty showed evidence of a sex hormone abnormality. Polycystic ovarian disease (PCOD) is associated with excessive male hormone production. Five of the forty had a proven diagnosis and nine others a probable diagnosis of PCOD.[8]

Whatever the "cause" or "causes" of transsexualism, the "cure" does not often (if at all) come through psychotherapy. A classic example is that of Dr. Richard Raskind, who unsuccessfully underwent eight years of psychoanalytic therapy to change sexual identity before becoming Dr. Renee Richards.[9] But sex-reassignment surgery is not granted upon demand. Patients must demonstrate their capacity to live more comfortably in the aspired-to sex role.

## Employment Discrimination

The foundation on which patient management of preoperative transsexuals stands is the "real-life test." This test requires at least one year of full trial living in the new gender role prior to genital surgery.[10] The basic principle of preoperative care is to do the reversible before the irreversible. The most reversible part of "sex-change" is dressing. The next most reversible intervention is hormonal regulation, followed by nongenital surgery (nose or breast reconstruction, for example). For those who successfully negotiate these components of the "real-life test," irreversible genitalia-alteration can be effected.

One mandate of the "real-life test" is employment in the new gender role. The patient must demonstrate, to self and others, the capacity to negotiate the world successfully in the desired role. But this rite of passage presents the patient with a major dilemma: Should transsexual status be revealed to the prospective employer? If no such announcement is made, and during employment the person commences cross-dressing or otherwise appears in gender transition, it is likely that employment will be terminated. On the other hand, if the patient reveals transsexual status to the prospective employer, including anticipated cross-dressing, or that he or she is a transsexual now cross-dressed, the employer may refuse to hire.

If not hired, or if fired, what legal recourse does the transsexual have? One potential remedy is Title VII of the Civil Rights Act.[11] This Act prohibits discrimination in employment based on race and gender. The manner by which the gender aspect of employment discrimination was added is unique. The Act was originally designed to prohibit employment discrimination based only on race. After much debate, when it appeared that the anti-race discrimination statute would pass, one senator, in a final effort to sabotage the legislation, added gender as another criterion on which employers could not discriminate. Unhappily for the senator, the bill passed. The United States thus has a law that not only prohibits employment discrimination based on race, but also discrimination based on gender.

Several transsexuals have attempted to utilize Title VII for legal protection. One was Karen Ulane. Ulane had been a male pilot for Eastern Airlines for a decade before undergoing sex reassignment and attempting to return to work as a woman pilot. Eastern refused. Ulane sued Eastern claiming that were it not for her present status as a woman, the airline would have no objection. Therefore, to Ulane, there was discrimination based on gender. Alternatively, Ulane claimed that she was being discriminated against because of her status as a transsexual and that such discrimination should also be prohibited under Title VII.[12]

I was an expert psychiatric witness for Ulane. In the following transcript excerpts I testify to the nature of transsexualism and to Ulane's current gender.

Attorney: Would you tell us what is a transsexual?

Green: Transsexualism is a pervasive, severe, and long-standing discontent, discomfort, belonging to the sex to which one was born. It is accompanied by a long-standing wish for a variety of hormonal, surgical, and civil procedures which would allow one to live in the sex role opposite to that to which one was born. This long-term discontent, dysphoria, if you will, with being male or female, is not a product of some significant type of mental disorder . . .

Attorney: Will you describe for me what you meant when you said that transsexualism was not a product of a significant mental disorder?

Green: Sometimes in schizophrenia, which is a significant mental disorder, one sees in a patient delusions of changing sex, delusions which are somewhat transient, are a product of that psychotic state, of being schizophrenic. Quite often they fade as the person recovers from a schizophrenic episode. By contrast, this long-standing, generally lifelong wish or discontent about being of the sex to which one was born [in transsexuals] is not a product of delusional thinking.

Attorney: Now doctor, I have also heard from time to time a word raised in this context, and that is "transvestism" or "transvestites" . . . Can you tell us what, if anything, is different between these two terms?

Green: A transvestite is an individual who is content being the sex to which he was born, does not wish to undergo sex-change surgery. It is an individual whose primary gratification from cross-dressing or dressing in women's clothes is one of sexual arousal rather than a feeling of social comfort . . .[13]

Attorney: To what extent, Doctor, are these people [transsexuals] now females after the surgery as opposed to males as they were before the surgery?

Green: That depends on one's definition of sex. If you are talking to a legal definition of sex, in certain states, as I understand it, post-operative transsexuals do have legal sex change . . .

Attorney: Let's talk about just from a medical point of view.

Green: If you are looking to the medical definitions of sex or gender, there are a number of criteria that are used. These include psychological sex. They include chromosomal sex. They include hormonal sex. They include the anatomical structure of the internal reproductive organs, and they include the appearance of the external genitalia.

Attorney: As far as post-surgically speaking, are these people anatomically male, or are they anatomically female?

Green: It would depend on which criterion you use. If you look to chromosomes, they would still be male. If you look to the appearance of the external genitalia, they would be female. If you look to the psychological sex, they would be women. If you look to the hormonal sex, if they were on replacement hormones, they would be women.

Attorney: What is Karen Ulane's gender?

Green: Karen Ulane is a woman.

Attorney: Would you explain that?

Green: Karen Ulane psychologically has a sexual identity of female and behaves socially and feels psychologically as a woman. She is legally, as I understand it, a female and, additionally, psychologically a woman.[14]

Psychiatric experts for Eastern testified that Ulane was not a transsexual, but a transvestite. They argued that since surgery is not an appropriate treatment for transvestism, a poor psychiatric outcome would follow. Thus, the pilot would be emotionally unstable, and airline passengers would be endangered. Eastern's experts also maintained that, even if Ulane had been a transsexual, sex reassignment surgery is palliative at best, and the long-term psychiatric results are uncertain. Therefore, they contended, Ulane, the transsexual, was too much of a psychiatric risk to vest with the responsibility of piloting a commercial aircraft.

The trial court wrestled with the issues of Ulane's gender status as a male or a female and Ulane's status as a transsexual. Whether Ulane was now "legally" male or female was not clear to the court, even though Illinois, the state in which Ulane had been born, had issued a sex-revised birth certificate.

In a temporary victory for Ulane, the district court ruled that Title VII would apply to protect her, either for discrimination based on gender or for discrimination based on transsexualism.[15] The Seventh Circuit Court of Appeals, however, reversed the ruling. It held that Title VII was meant to prevent discrimination against women and men only, not transsexuals, and that insufficient evidence had been presented to prove that Ulane was discriminated against based on her status as a woman.[16]

In another Title VII case, the court, focusing narrowly on the clothing worn by preoperative transsexuals, upheld dismissal on the ground that the employee violated dress code regulations. The court held that since the employee was male, no Title VII case could be made on the basis of gender, because to this court, the statute was remedial and designed to protect women.[17] In a similar dress code action, a court held that the employee was "not being refused employment because he is a man or because he [sic] is a woman . . . [Therefore] Title VII and the Constitution do not protect him. The law does not protect males dressed or acting as females and vice versa."[18] The phrase "acting like a female" has been further defined by the Fifth Circuit Court of Appeals to include "effeminacy," a sufficient basis for denial of employment.[19]

"Misrepresentation" was the basis for another employee's dismissal. On a job application, the preoperative male-to-female transsexual had specified sex as "female." After the employee was hired "the company's work routine" was disrupted when "a number of female employees indicated that they would quit if [the anatomically male transsexual] were permitted to use the restroom facilities assigned to female personnel." The district court ordered the plaintiff to submit an amended complaint indicating whether discrimination was based on the person's status as a male, a female, or a transsexual. The employee asserted that discrimination was based on status as a female, "[t]hat is, a female with the anatomical body of a male." The transsexual's claim was dismissed by the court as a "manipulation of semantics."[20]

Courts have denied other transsexuals' Title VII claims on the grounds that discrimination has not been based on the person's sex per se, but rather on the individual's *change* of sex. One court, citing congressional intent, difficult as that is to determine considering the Act's "legislative history," noted that "Title VII speaks of discrimination on the basis of one's 'sex' . . . no mention is made of change of sex."[21]

One rationale courts have used in arguing that transsexuals are not covered under Title VII is that neither homosexuals nor transvestites are covered by Title VII.[22] The major distinctions between transsexualism and either homosexuality or transvestism, however, show that rationale to be a nonsequitur.[23] Transsexualism is a statement of one's gender, not of the gender of one's sexual partner, nor is it merely the practice of periodic cross-dressing.

Another federal law under which transsexuals might find protection is the Rehabilitation Act of 1973.[24] This Act prohibits discrimination against any "otherwise qualified, handicapped individual." For the purposes of the Act, a handicapped individual is defined as "any person who (A) has a physical or mental impairment which substantially limits one or more such person's major life activities, . . . or (C) is regarded as having an impairment."[25] The Act is designed to protect persons with handicaps in the employment setting where the handicap does not interfere with a person's ability to carry out employment responsibilities. According to the statute, one way in which a person can be handicapped is through the perception of handicap by others.

The American Psychiatric Association (APA) description of transsexualism provides support for the inclusion of transsexuals within this Act. In its discussion of features associated with transsexualism, the APA *Diagnostic and Statistical Manual* (DSM IIIR) stated: "Frequently the person experiences considerable anxiety and depression, which he or she may attribute to the inability to live in the role of the desired sex." The section describing impairments and complications stated: "[S]ocial and occupational functioning are markedly impaired, partly because of associated psychopathology and partly because of problems encountered in attempting to live in the desired gender role."[26]

The courts have recognized a broad range of psychiatric conditions under the Act, including alcoholism and personality disorders,[27] aggressive and self-destructive behavior,[28] and suicidal behavior.[29] The Department of Health and Human Services has defined impairment to include "any mental or psychological disorder, such as . . . emotional or mental illness."[30] But protection under this Act cuts both ways for the transsexual. The self-image of preoperative transsexual patients is not enhanced by the designation "handicapped." In addition, while the inclusion of this condition in the APA's DSM IIIR may permit third party reimbursement for psychiatric treatment, many transsexuals object to the depiction of their condition as a "mental illness."

The psychiatric status of the postoperative transsexual is an additional dilemma. The DSM IIIR criteria for the diagnosis of transsexualism stated that it is the "persistent discomfort and sense of inappropriateness about one's assigned sex." If this criterion is interpreted literally, the diagnosis would no longer apply to the postoperative person, who would therefore not qualify for protection under the Act. An additional complication is the Americans with Disabilities Act of 1990, which specifically bars transsexuals, along with pedophiles, kleptomaniacs, and pyromaniacs, from protection against discrimination.[31]

These cases demonstrate that in employment settings where clinicians require preoperative patients to negotiate the "real-life test," employers and courts have posed additional hurdles. These hurdles can undermine an essential step implemented by medicine to assure that only transsexual patients with a good prognosis receive irreversible surgery.

Postoperative transsexuals who are schoolteachers have faced additional employment problems. One case that received considerable publicity was the *Grossman* case in New Jersey, involving

Paul, who became Paula.[32] This teacher of ten-year-old students attempted to return to work as a woman after teaching in the preceding term as a man. The school refused, categorizing the teacher as "disabled" because of an expected negative impact on students.

Conflicting psychiatric testimony was presented in the court challenge to dismissal. On the side of the transsexual teacher were Drs. Charles Ihlenfeld and Robert Laidlaw, both of whom had worked with Dr. Harry Benjamin, the "father of transsexualism."[33] They testified that students would not be harmed by the presence of a transsexual teacher, and that any child upset by that teacher would have already been upset about its own sexual identity. On the other side was Dr. Charles Socarides, who testified: "Looking at it from another point of view . . . the teacher's function as object [sic] for identification and one of the major things in teaching is that we learn through identification with the teacher and very often we learn out of love for the teacher. And, boys not only learn their lessons in school, but they learn how to be men from their teachers . . . and if such sexual change were known, I think it would be very disruptive of that process, if that were known."[34] The court ignored the testimony of Ihlenfeld and Laidlaw and ruled that the teacher was incapacitated on the basis of sex reassignment surgery.

In April 1979 I was an expert witness for a male-to-female transsexual in Philadelphia, where a high school teacher had been summarily dismissed by the school board after undergoing sex reassignment. Although the lower federal court ordered a temporary reinstatement and back pay, to be followed by a full administrative hearing, the teacher settled the case prior to a hearing and ceased teaching. Experts for the school district had testified to the "grave, harmful psychological effects that the presence of plaintiff as a school teacher would have upon the many children who had formerly been plaintiff's student while plaintiff was a male."[35]

In October 1988 I was an expert witness in a case in Denver, in which a teacher of sixteen- and seventeen-year-olds was attempting to return to teaching four years after sex-reassignment. Although the school district argued that *Grossman* provided a precedent, the two cases are distinguishable. First there is student age. The Denver students were six or seven years older than the New Jersey students. If there is potential for a student's confusion over his or her sexual identity, it should be less in the late teen years. In addition, because the Denver teacher had been away from school for four years, there had been a total turnover of students in that school, in contrast to the New Jersey case where students would first have a man, then a woman—the same individual—as teacher in successive terms.

Once more, there was a split in the testimony of psychiatric and psychological experts. The psychologist and psychiatrist for the school district argued that since adolescence is a time of sexual identity conflict, adolescent students would be adversely affected. One testified that there would not be a single student who would not be negatively affected by a transsexual teacher. My testimony argued that the sexual anxieties and conflicts adolescents have— whether to engage in intercourse, whether to employ contraception, or whether to undergo abortion for example—do not engage the core conflict of whether to engage in such sexuality as a man or as a woman. This is because core sexual identity is established in the first few years of life, not in adolescence.[36] At this writing the case remains unresolved.

## Transsexualism and Marriage

In 1945, a Swiss Court concluded that psychological sex or gender identity was the criterion for determining the sex of the postoperative transsexual.[37] A quarter of a century later, an English court disagreed. In *Corbett v. Corbett*,[38] a postoperative male-to-female transsexual married, but the husband, who knew before the ceremony that the bride was a postoperative transsexual, attempted to have the marriage annulled shortly thereafter, contending that the wife was still male. The case provided the English courts with the opportunity to decide the "true sex" of the transsexual. The judge, also a physician, ruled that the ultimate criteria of sex were anatomical. "The [transsexual] has been shown to have XY chromosomes and, therefore, to be of male chromosomal sex; to have had testicles prior to the operation and, therefore, to be of male gonadal sex; to have had male external genitalia without any evidence of any internal or external female organs and, therefore, to be of male genital sex; . . . [t]he law should adopt . . . the . . . three . . . criteria, . . . i.e., the chromosomal, gonadal, and genital tests, and if all three are congruent, determine the sex for the purpose of marriage."[39]

In 1990, the European Court of Human Rights refused to order the British government to alter the birth certificate of another postoperative transsexual, who had been a "James Bond girl" in the film *For Your Eyes Only*. She was also denied the right to marry a man under British law. Her unsuccessful appeal hinged on two articles of the European Convention on Human Rights forbidding interference by a public authority in a person's private life and guaranteeing men and women of marriageable age the right to marry.[40]

The sciences of anatomy and endocrinology teach that relying on anatomic criteria as the ultimate deciders of sex can be misleading.[41] One example is the androgen insensitivity syndrome, formerly called "testicular feminization" (see Chapter 4), in which an individual with the male chromosomal configuration (XY) and testes within the abdomen has a female-appearing body. The person's body develops as female because of a defect in the cells that renders male hormone from the testes inactive. The person is considered female at birth, is raised as a female, and evolves a female sexual identity. Thus, the person is a woman with a male sex chromosomal pattern, male gonads, and male hormone. To rule that the woman is nevertheless a man would be psychologically tragic. Another example is the syndrome of congenital virilizing adrenal hyperplasia (formerly called the adrenogenital syndrome) (see Chapter 4), in which the newborn has a male-appearing body but a female chromosomal configuration (XX) and ovaries. The male appearance is due to the excess of androgenic (male-type) hormone before birth, resulting in male-appearing genitalia. The child, if designated male, evolves a male sexual identity. Thus, the person is a man with a female chromosomal pattern and ovaries. To rule that the man is nevertheless a woman would also be psychologically tragic.

A New Jersey case also involving a postoperative male-to-female transsexual marital partner stands in contrast to *Corbett*. The state's highest court ruled that the marriage was valid because the transsexual was a female for the intent of marriage law. "For marital purposes, [if] the anatomical and genital features . . . are made to conform to the person's gender, psyche or psychological sex, then identity of sex must be governed by congruence of the standards . . . Plaintiff should be considered a member of the female sex for marital purposes . . . Such recognition will promote the individual's quest for inner peace and personal happiness, while in no way disserving any societal interest."[42]

Another question concerning the transsexual's right to marry is at what point in the transsexual's medical/surgical evolution it should be permitted. If transsexuals can marry, should it be only the postoperative transsexual? Should a person be considered a woman who has been living as a woman, cross-dressing for many years, and taking female hormones, but who has elected not to have genital surgery? The "slippery slope" argument here that concerns courts ultimately leads to "gay marriage."[43]

## Child Custody

Family law cases in both the United States and the United Kingdom have involved child custody and child visitation ("child access" in England) with transsexual parents. The concern is whether children will experience sexual identity conflict because of exposure to a parent who is either undergoing metamorphosis to the new sex or has changed sex.

I have collected data on sixteen children whose parents "changed sex." I evaluated nine children of a female-to-male transsexual parent whose ages at evaluation were seven to twenty years. In six households the child was five years or less when the parent began the process of sex reassignment. Seven children were adolescent or young adults at the time of evaluation. For all seven, sexual orientation was heterosexual. There was no gender identity disorder in the younger children. I also evaluated seven children with a male-to-female transsexual parent whose ages were three to thirteen. The erotic fantasies of the two oldest children, thirteen and eleven, were heterosexual. Again there was no evidence of gender identity disorder in the younger children.[44]

In 1981, I was a witness in the first case in England in which the Court of Appeal ruled on whether a preoperative transsexual father could have access to his child. The child was a four-year-old girl who was aware that the person currently dressing in women's clothes was also the person she had known as her father. One pro-

posal before the court suggested that the child have no further contact with the father and that she be told he had died or had moved
too far away to visit. I testified that the child should continue contact with the father during the continuing transition to woman's status. I suggested that counseling could assure the child that her own
identity as a girl was secure. I argued that the child would be appropriately angered when she later learned that she had been deceived
into believing her father was not available to her during her earlier
years. The trial court (High Court) ruled that the father could have
access only when dressed as a man. This requirement was overturned by the Court of Appeal.[45]

If there is a time of potential sexual confusion for children who
witness a transsexual parent undergoing metamorphosis, it should
be in the first years of life—before the attainment of "gender
constancy"[46]—when children are consolidating their sexual identity. At an earlier cognitive level, children believe that things adults
know to be stable are changeable by superficial means; thus, a dog
mask placed over a picture of a cat changes the animal's species.
Beyond these first years of life, however, there is no indication that
parental change is specifically traumatic in terms of the child's sexual identity as male or female.

## Name Change

Even the "simple" request for a change of name prior to surgery
has resulted in court action. In New Jersey, a male-to-female transsexual living the "real-life test" prior to genital surgery encountered
employment difficulties because the woman's name being used on
job applications was not legally documented. A Law Division judge
denied the request for a name change because "it is inherently
fraudulent for a person who is physically a male to assume an
obviously 'female' name for the sole purpose of representing himself to future employers and society as a female." However, the
Appellate Division reminded the lower court that under the common law individuals can change their name providing that the intent
is not fraudulent or criminal, that the transsexual's intent here was
not fraud, and that "a person has a right to a name change whether
he or she has undergone or intends to undergo a sex change . . . is

a transvestite, or simply wants to change from a traditional 'male' name to one traditionally 'female.'"[47]

## Sports Competition

A more esoteric instance in which a person's "correct" sex becomes relevant is in sports. The advent of sex chromosome tests permitted testing of the sex of athletes in Olympic and other competition beginning in 1968. Disqualifications are usually based on a cryptic intersex state. But Renee Richards, born Richard Raskind, the woman tennis player and eye surgeon, presented the United States Tennis Association with a unique dilemma. A couple of years after Raskind's sex-reassignment surgery, the Tennis Association demanded that Richards have a buccal smear test (a scraping from the lining of the cheek), which reveals whether there is a second X (female) chromosome. In its absence, Richards would be barred from entering the U.S. Open Tennis Tournament as a woman.[48]

Richards's surgeon testified that the internal organs of his patient after surgery were "anatomically similar to a biological woman who underwent a total hysterectomy and ovariectomy."[49] Another physician testified that Richards had the "endocrinological makeup and psychological and social development of a female," and so should be "considered a female by any reasonable test of sexuality."[50] A medical psychologist testified that "for all interests and purposes, Dr. Richards functions as a woman."[51] He described the inadequacies of using the chromosome test as the ultimate criterion of sex, citing Klinefelter syndrome (in which the man has testes and a penis but a second X chromosome, and so would "pass" the test as a woman) and Turner syndrome (in which the woman has no testes or penis but lacks a second X chromosome, and thus "fails" to qualify as a woman).

The court ruled that to require Richards to pass the chromosome test violated the New York Human Rights Law. That law declares that "the State has the responsibility to act to assure that every individual within this state is afforded an equal opportunity to enjoy a full and productive life." The court concluded that the "only justification for using a sex determination test in athletic competition is to prevent fraud, i.e., men masquerading as women, competing against women."[52] For a transsexual athlete, the chromosome test "should not be the sole criterion."[53]

## Restroom Facilities

If medicine demands that transsexuals live socially as the other sex in the "real-life test," then the use of public restrooms becomes an issue. In a recent incident at California's Disneyland, a preoperative male-to-female transsexual who carried a certificate from a gender dysphoria treatment facility stating that she was living the "real-life test" was detained by security guards after using a women's restroom and ejected from the amusement park.

In situations like these, the rights of transsexuals must be weighed against the rights of the public. Women's restrooms are constructed in a way that provides more privacy than men's. This argues that it would be better for a transsexual to use the women's room. In addition, a male transsexual dressed as a woman, even if not "passing" effectively, should be less provocative in the women's room. In the men's room, a cross-dressed male might be more vulnerable to physical assault. In terms of safety to the public, if the concern is sexual assault in the women's room, the fact that male-to-female transsexuals are typically not sexually interested in females should be reassuring. From the public's perspective, permitting transsexuals living the "real-life test" to use the women's restroom could invite fraudulent entry by cross-dressed nontranssexuals. Deceptive entry, however, could occur whatever the decision about permitting access to transsexuals.

## Treatment in Prison

Incarceration of those claiming to be transsexuals poses additional hardships, including access to medical and psychological treatment. Prison authorities have not been receptive to these demands. A preoperative male-to-female transsexual was serving a thirty-five-year sentence for murder. She described living as a woman from age fourteen, receiving estrogen for the preceding nine years, and undergoing breast augmentation and other nongenital surgeries. Prison authorities refused her request for estrogens, and her lawsuit was dismissed in federal district court without trial. But the appellate court held that prisoners are entitled to treatment for a "serious" medical condition, and, citing *Ulane v. Eastern Airlines,* it described the nature of transsexualism and concluded that it is a "serious" illness. The lawsuit was ordered reinstated. The court did not hold that estrogen treatment was required, however, only that if the prisoner proved her case, *some* form of treatment was mandated.[54]

In a similar case, another court found no constitutional right for a transsexual prisoner to receive estrogen treatment, wear women's clothes, be transferred to a women's prison, or receive sex-reassignment surgery, providing that some treatment was available.[55] Another prisoner was denied hormone treatment, in part because a prison psychiatrist, who did not examine the prisoner, concluded that transsexualism could not be diagnosed in prison because of the stress of institutionalization. The psychiatrist also pointed out that the prisoner had not lived the "real-life test." However, that hurdle is used as a screen for genital surgery, not for diagnosing transsexualism.[56]

Partial self-castration was effected by one transsexual prisoner after the prison denied estrogen administration. Prison surgeons then completed removal of the testes. In an example of grotesque medical management, the prison finally agreed to administer sex hormone: *replacement testosterone (male hormone).* This treatment was held not to be unconstitutional because there was not a total failure to provide medical attention.[57]

On a happier note, another court ordered a prison to administer female hormones to a prisoner who had received estrogen and lived as a woman for years prior to incarceration, because to permit the return of some masculine physical characteristics (the prisoner's testes had not been removed) constituted deliberate medical indifference. A psychiatrist who had testified for the prison as an expert witness had stated that the prisoner was not a transsexual and had not passed the "real-life test" because there had been no formal name change and because recent work had been in a male profession. The prisoner had been a female impersonator.[58]

## Transsexual Surgery: Experimental or Established?

Should sex reassignment surgery be reimbursed by government subsidies or private insurance carriers for medically indigent transsexuals? The arguments against insurance coverage maintain that transsexual procedures are either elective or experimental, or both.

In the case of the Denver schoolteacher described previously, the school district's attorney argued that transsexual surgery was "elective." Surgery was not seen as life-saving in the way that removing a malignant tumor might be because people could rationally decide not to have the procedure. In response, I offered the model of kidney transplant surgery as opposed to kidney dialysis. Prior to the availability of transplant surgery, it was possible for persons with kidney failure to live for many years through kidney dialysis. This procedure entailed connecting the patient to a dialysis machine for a day, after which the patient was discharged from the hospital and resumed normal functioning for a few days until progressive sickness required a return to the hospital for the next treatment cycle. When transplant surgery became available, a patient could "elect" to have surgery. While the procedure might not be life-saving, the quality of life would be enhanced greatly by surgery. Similarly, while it might be possible for some transsexuals to live without sex reassignment surgery, the quality of life might well be enhanced with it.

It has been a quarter of a century since The Johns Hopkins University and the University of Minnesota instituted formal programs of sex reassignment surgery.[59] Since then, thousands of transsexuals have been operated on, with many follow-up reports in the medical and psychiatric literature in Europe and the United States.

Individual medical center series are variable. A U.S. study of seventeen male transsexuals evaluated on an average of eight years after surgery found no changes in psychological test scores on a standard measure of psychopathology, the Minnesota Multiphasic Personality Inventory (MMPI), and only "modest" gains in economic status and interpersonal relationships. Larger gains were seen, however, in sexual satisfaction and acceptance by family members. No patients reported regretting the surgery.[60] On the other hand, a Danish study that evaluated twenty-nine male patients an average of six years after surgery found that three had committed suicide, the majority were unemployed, and two-thirds lived alone. None, however, had "more severe psychic sufferings or psychosis" postoperatively, and over four-fifths "felt better" than before surgery.[61] A study by the same investigator of eight females an average of five years after surgery found one regretting the surgery and six viewing it as "completely satisfactory."[62] In Sweden, of thirteen male patients, four regretted surgery six to twenty-five years later, and two returned to living as men.[63]

An extensive review of published reports in 1986 found that two-thirds of patients who underwent sex reassignment surgery were improved.[64] Two years earlier, another review that looked at outcome from a different perspective found that reassignment was unsuccessful for only 10 to 15 percent of patients.[65]

In a review of follow-up reports published between 1979 and 1989, which I co-conducted in 1990, we concluded that for 220 male-to-female transsexuals, 87 percent could be considered to have a "satisfactory" outcome, and for 130 female-to-male transsexuals, 97 percent could be considered "satisfactory." Although this classification is gross, and is based principally on whether the patient regrets having undergone sex-reassignment, utilizing this criterion may not be as naive and simplistic as it appears at first glance. Many pivotal life decisions—such as whether to have married a specific individual, whether or not to have had children, and choice of occupation—are evaluated as wise or not according to this standard.[66]

Although the results of surgery are not uniformly favorable and often do not demonstrate substantial objective gains, clinical experience with transsexual patients before surgery shows them to be very poorly adjusted psychosocially and rarely amenable to alternative ways of resolving their extraordinary conflict. In the era before medicine facilitated sex-reassignment surgery, suicide was a commonly sought escape from this profound conflict.[67]

In the face of these data, insurance carriers and federal agencies have refused to reimburse physicians for sex-reassignment procedures. However, a handful of federal and state courts have ruled that Medicaid programs cannot arbitrarily deny a physician's reimbursement for transsexual surgery.[68] For example, "We find that a state plan absolutely excluding the only available treatment known at this stage of the art for a particular condition must be considered an arbitrary denial of benefits."[69] However, another court heard testimony for and against the surgery, where those opposed labeled it "experimental." The court ruled that "the state could reasonably determine that transsexual surgery is experimental."[70] Thus, because the state need not fund experimental programs, transsexual surgery funding could be denied.

The transsexual presents an important research model for understanding sexual identity. If sexual identity is seen to have three components: core identity ("I am male" or "I am female"), gender behavior (culturally "masculine" or "feminine"), and sexual orientation (heterosexual or homosexual), the transsexual is unique. The transsexual is atypical on all three. Thus, for those whose research challenge is to understand the development of sexual identity, as a model of contrast for conventional development the transsexual provides a valuable paradigm.

Transsexualism also provides a model of several sex and gender dilemmas facing the law. Basic legal issues include the definition of a man or a woman, the essence of marriage, the best interests of children, and the extent of protection to be given to those whose sexual identity is dramatically atypical.

# · 7 ·

# Pornography

Pornography is a rich example of the interface between sexual science and law. Extensive research in the community, in the laboratory, and in prisons has attempted to gauge the effects of pornography on sexual attitudes and behavior. The question for the law is whether the data gathered by sexual science can penetrate the protective cloak of the First Amendment.

## Social Science Research: Cross-Cultural Analyses

Does pornography lead to rape? The relationship between the availability of explicit sexual materials and rates of sexual assault may be examined through the crime statistics of countries that have made pornographic materials readily available. Two Western countries that have relaxed laws restricting access to pornography are Denmark and the Federal Republic of Germany. To a lesser degree this has also happened in Great Britain and in some regions of the United States.

### Denmark

Before 1967, Danish laws against pornography were similar to those of other Western nations. *Fanny Hill, or Memoirs of a Woman of Pleasure* was successfully prosecuted in 1958. After 1961, when prosecutions of explicit erotic writing ceased, the production of these materials rapidly increased and peaked in 1967, the year in which the laws against pornographic literature were repealed. By 1967, the illegal production of sexually explicit photographic magazines had begun. It peaked in 1969. In that year, the Danish Parliament legalized the sale of sexually explicit materials to persons over sixteen.[1]

The rate of reported rape in Denmark remained steady between 1966 and 1972 (during that six-year period it increased by eighteen cases for the entire country). This steady rate is noteworthy in that during the same period there was a sharp increase in the rate of nonsexual assault. At the same time, the Danish women's movement was encouraging rape victims to report attacks, whereas many had previously gone unreported, so that the actual rate may have dropped.

As for child pornography, taking pornographic pictures of children remained punishable, but their reproduction and sale were not illegal between 1969 and 1980. Between 1967 and 1972 child molestation, or "physical sexual interference with female children," showed a marked decrease. The drop in the rate of child molestation concurrent with the increased availability of pornography, including child pornography, was 67 percent (from 24 per 100,000 population to 8 per 100,000 population). There is no evidence that the reported drop in the rate resulted from a national acceptance of such conduct or failure to report these offenses to police.[2]

## Federal Republic of Germany

What was then called "West Germany" legalized pornography in 1973. Between 1972 and 1980 the total number of sex crimes reported to the police decreased 11 percent. Sex offenses against minors under fourteen also showed a slight decrease. In the category of sex offenses against victims under age six, the decrease was substantially larger, from 100 per 100,000 population to 40 per 100,000, a drop of 60 percent. For rape, the number of reported cases remained the same. Concurrently, however, nonsexual violent offenses increased sharply, up 127 percent.[3]

## Great Britain

In 1974, England witnessed an upsurge in the number of sexually explicit magazines that peaked in 1976. Although the rate of rape rose during this period, it had begun to increase before pornography became more readily available. At the same time, the rates of other offenses against the person increased by a greater percentage.[4] The British Committee on Obscenity and Film Censorship "unhesitantly reject[ed] the suggestion that the available information for England and Wales lends any support at all to the argument that pornography acts as a stimulus to the commission of sexual violence."[5]

The explanation for the drop in sex-crime rates with the increased availability of pornography has been called the "substitution hypothesis." The common male reaction to pornographic pictures is sexual arousal and masturbation. Thus, the availability of portrayals of nudes and forbidden activities, accompanied by auto-erotic behavior, may provide an outlet for antisocial sexual impulses, permitting vicarious experience of what would otherwise be acted out with a victim. As one sexual scientist testifying before a congressional committee reported: "[P]atients who request treatment in a sex offender clinic commonly disclose that pornography helps them contain their abnormal sexuality within imagination only, as a fantasy, instead of having to act it out in real life with an unconsenting, resenting partner, or by force."[6]

## The United States

Since data from other nations may not be applicable to the situation in the United States, U.S. crime rates, sexual and otherwise, during the period of increased availability of sexual materials must also be studied. It is helpful to look at the United States as a group of regional subcultures, since in some areas explicit materials are much more available than in others.

Between 1970 and 1978, when sexually explicit films became widely available, the reported U.S. rape rate rose from 20 per 100,000 to 30 per 100,000 population. By comparison, the rate of aggravated assault rose from 150 per 100,000 to 230 per 100,000.[7] Thus, the rise in reported rape may have been a nonspecific correlate of the rise in assaultive crimes in general. Furthermore, if, through the feminist movement's raising of women's consciousness during the same period, a higher percentage of rapes were reported, the rape rate may actually have declined.

Regional analyses of the relation between the availability of sexual materials and sex-crime rates do not support a positive relationship between the two. The availability of sexually explicit materials in adult theaters and bookstores does not correlate significantly with rates of reported rape. But other variables do. These include alcohol consumption, the percentage of poor in a region, and the circulation of another type of magazine, "outdoor" publications such as *Field and Stream* and *Guns and Ammo*.[8] Although a preliminary study found that states with a higher circulation of sex magazines also had higher rape rates, three other variables were found to correlate more closely with rape: the number of divorced men, the degree of economic inequality, and urbanization.[9]

The learned critique of these studies is that they are correlational. The results do not prove that the increased availability of pornography reduces sex crimes. While the concordance of findings across cultures argues that the correlations are not spurious, the decrease in sex crime could be related to a third variable. Perhaps the concurrent rise in nonsexual antisocial behavior channels the pernicious energies of a society, or perhaps there is a fixed pool of antisocial potential. Although this is speculation, scientists must nonetheless be prepared to consider the possibility of intervening variables before attributing causality to correlation.

Research into the effects of pornography was galvanized by the reports of two executive commissions. The first, appointed by President Johnson in 1967, sponsored major research studies throughout the United States. In 1970, when the research data were in, seventeen of the nineteen commission members concluded that "empirical research designed to clarify the question has found no evidence to date that exposure to explicit sexual materials plays a significant role in the causation of delinquent or criminal behavior among youth or adults. The Commission cannot conclude that exposure to erotic materials is a factor in the causation of sex crimes."[10]

A minority report issued by two commission members and concurred in by Charles H. Keating, Jr., later to achieve notoriety through his conviction for fraud in the collapse of his Lincoln Savings and Loan empire,[11] found "both conclusions and recommendations [of the majority] fraudulent . . . [It] is a Magna Carta for the pornographer. [The concern must be] prevention of moral corruption." Commissioner Keating condemned the majority report as "shocking and anarchistic . . . [and] advocacy of moral anarchy."[12] Sexual scientists received especially scathing criticism. The majority report was the work of "academicians with ivory tower views, who have little or no responsibility to anyone or anything, excepting their own thought processes which go unhoned by the checks and balances of a competitive, active, real world."[13]

The recommendations of the commission majority were rejected by President Nixon as "morally bankrupt." A psychology professor charged that "several scientists" affiliated with the commission had "suppressed" and "covered up" data. He also proffered an exponential nightmare he believed would result from the availability of erotic materials: "[I]f pornography were a factor in causing only one adolescent or adult into having disturbed sexual feelings, changed sexual orientation, or some manner of antisocial sexual deviancy, and if this person yearly influenced only one other individual who, in turn affected only one other, in 20 years, 1,048,575 sexually or otherwise disturbed people would be the result."[14]

Sixteen years after the Johnson commission report, another commission appointed during the Reagan administration by Attorney General Edwin Meese reached a different conclusion: "Substantial exposure to sexually violent materials . . . bears a causal relationship to antisocial acts of sexual violence."[15] The majority report was authored by, among others, Father Bruce Ritter, who was later to achieve notoriety for charges of having engaged in sexual relations with young men seeking sanctuary from sexual abuse at his Covenant House.[16] The majority concluded that sexually violent material was linked with sexual assault against women, but it was "less confident" about the findings regarding nonviolent sexual materials.

Two women members of the commission dissented: "To say that exposure to pornography in and of itself causes an individual to commit a sexual crime is simplistic, [and] not supported by the social science data."[17]

## Laboratory Research: In Search of the "Real World"

Because sex offenders are not readily available to academic researchers, and because the factors that led them to commit sexual assault are not easily studied, investigators have taken to the experimental laboratory in their search for models of sexual aggression. But laboratory research on sex crimes faces several formidable, if not insurmountable, obstacles.

The first concerns the persons studied. Subjects are typically undergraduate college students who receive either academic credit or a fee for serving as "guinea pigs." As students, they may be aware of the research reputation and experimental approaches of the faculty researchers, and thus may not be naive subjects. In demographic and psychological background they are often different from sex offenders. In addition, they are usually persons who have never committed a sexual offense and will never do so.

A second concerns the experimental setting, which is necessarily artificial. Situations are contrived, with varying levels of credibility. In experiments in which subjects are allowed to "aggress" against a putative "victim" after viewing pornography, they are given permission (if not in fact encouraged) to do so by the authority figure in charge of the experiment. The circumstances of the experiment are often remote from "real world" settings. According to one typical laboratory model, a male student views a sexually explicit film just after a female has attempted to provoke him to anger. He is now permitted to punish her by delivering a shock he believes to be real. The tether to street sexual assault is tenuous.

A third criticism of laboratory research is that assessments are usually performed shortly after exposure to the materials, so that extending these findings to long-term attitudinal change is problematic. Finally, extending attitudinal change to behavioral change is even more problematic.

Some findings from well-conducted studies, however, do suggest that some types of pornography affect men's attitudes toward women. Contrary to expectation, with mildly erotic nonviolent stimuli, aggression against females in laboratory settings may decrease.[18] With highly erotic nonviolent stimuli, the level of aggression, while not decreasing, may not increase beyond what is obtained with nonerotic stimuli.[19] But exposure to more violent pornography, in conjunction with provocations to anger, may increase aggression against the female confederate of the researcher.[20] These materials may also intensify a viewer's condonation of violence against women. Interestingly, the study that demonstrated this finding used R-rated, not X-rated films.[21] Age restrictions for viewing R-rated films are lower than those for X-rated films or the new rating, NC-17. The response of the female in the film to the sexual assault also appears to influence attitudes, at least in the short term. When an initially resistant female is subsequently shown enjoying the sexual interaction, male viewers may be more condoning of rape behavior.[22]

The "real world" concerns of society may not be so much for the occasional viewer of explicit films but for the habitual viewer. In some studies, therefore, subjects have been exposed to heavy doses of pornographic material, up to thirty-five hours. After massive exposure, subjects were less supportive of the feminist movement and less punitive toward a hypothetical rapist.[23] Similarly, after viewing violent sexual films (again, R-rated) on a daily basis, subjects became somewhat attenuated in their attitudes to the violence against women portrayed in the films.[24]

On the other hand, repeated exposure to violent sexual material may reduce sexual arousal to rape depictions. Prior to exposure to the materials, subjects were classified as "force-oriented" or "not force-oriented" depending on their responsiveness to rape stimuli. Thus the study could be considered a model for persons more likely to commit sexual assault. Among the force-oriented subjects, exposure to either violent or nonviolent sexual materials resulted in a reduction in sexual responsiveness to rape portrayals. The authors suggest that repeated exposure to rape stimuli may therefore be therapeutic to rape-prone persons.

## Prison and Clinical Research on Sex Offenders

A study in which I was a co-investigator assessed convicted rapists' and pedophiles' (child molesters) experiences with pornography compared with those of males in the community. The sex offenders' experience with a wide range of pornography, both in adolescence and in the year prior to incarceration, was lower.[26]

The largest study of sex offenders and pornography was conducted at the Kinsey Institute. Over 1,300 imprisoned sex offenders were compared with 900 prisoners not convicted of sex crimes and 500 nonprisoners. The groups did not differ in reported exposure to pornography or reported arousal by pornography. If anything, those convicted of sex crimes may have been less responsive to pornography and less interested in it.[27] Similar findings emerged in a smaller study in which incarcerated sex offenders were compared to prisoners who were not sex offenders. The sex offenders reported less exposure to pornography during childhood.[28] And a 1990 Canadian study again confirmed the inverse relation between a history of exposure to pornography and the commission of sex crimes among incarcerated offenders.[29] A major shortcoming in all these studies, however, is their reliance on reported experience.

Another group whose experience with pornography is often reported consists of individuals who contribute anecdotal reports about the role of pornography in their lives. This material, while genuine, may not be representative of the general population. Unrepresentative reports are a historic difficulty in clinical psychiatric research, where troubled patients typically report earlier life trauma and psychiatrists conclude that those events caused the present difficulty. Clinicians do not see persons for whom the same events did not lead to difficulty. For example, even if one accepts the validity of serial murderer Ted Bundy's death row indictment of pornography for having caused his brutal crimes, this does not account for those who viewed the same pornography and did not become sadistic murderers.

A major obstacle in weighing the significance of anecdotal reports, whether from patients, volunteers at public hearings into the effects of pornography, or apprehended sex offenders, is that the population on the other side of the balance is invisible. On that other side could be placed those persons who flirted with aggressive or deviant sexual acts in fantasy but were repelled by the depiction of these acts in pornography. On that other side could also be placed persons who were able to satisfy their interest in antisocial activity vicariously, by means of pornography, rather than by acting it out.

## Homosexual Orientation and Pornography

A common concern among the general population is that exposure to depictions of deviant sexual behavior will promote deviant sexual behavior. In this connection, because homosexuality is a common focus of societal concern, homosexual pornography is seen by some as promoting this pattern of sexuality. My research does not support this claim. I studied two groups of young boys over fifteen years as they matured into adolescence and young adulthood. At follow-up, over three-fourths of one group was homosexual or bisexual. Only one in the second group emerged as homosexual or bisexual. As previously described, what distinguished these two groups developmentally was their early childhood behavior at ages three through six. One group showed extensive cross-gender behavior. They liked to cross-dress in women's clothes, liked to role-play as females, said they wanted to be girls or women, and preferred the toys and the companionship of girls.[30]

In some families in both groups, heterosexual pornography such as *Playboy* and *Penthouse* was available to the child. As the boys emerged into adolescence, some sought out or were exposed to a wider range of erotic materials. The boys who were already aware of homosexual attractions found erotic depictions of males sexually arousing. Those aware of heterosexual attractions found depictions of females arousing. Patterns of interest in erotic materials followed the emergence of sexual orientation.

## Prosocial Uses of Erotic Materials

Films with heterosexual or homosexual content have been widely utilized in educational settings for adults. The records of the Multi-Media Resource Center in San Francisco show that, as of 1979, four thousand institutions were using graphic sexual materials. Explicit sexual materials are also used in the treatment of sexual dysfunctions (impotency in the male, nonorgasmic response in the female, inhibited sexual desire in both). The records of the Multi-Media Resource Center also show that almost eight thousand practitioners and counselors had rented or purchased explicit sexual material during the late 1970s.[31] There are several reasons for using pornography: to increase knowledge about the range of sexual expression, to facilitate communication about sexuality between partners, and to increase sexual arousal in clinically inhibited persons.

## In Search of the Miller Standard

In his dissenting opinion in a 1968 case, Supreme Court Justice John Harlan observed that "the subject of obscenity has produced a variety of views among the members [of the Court] unmatched in any other course of constitutional adjudication. In the 13 obscenity cases [i]n which signed opinions were written . . . [t]here has been a total of 55 separate opinions among the Justices."[32]

Obscenity was rejected as protected speech under the First Amendment to the Constitution in the 1957 Supreme Court case *Roth v. United States*.[33] According to the decision written by Justice William Brennan, obscenity could be banned because it was "utterly without redeeming social importance." Nine years later, in *Memoirs v. Massachusetts*[34] the Court, in a three justice plurality, held that three elements must be proven before erotic material is obscene: "[I]t must be established that (a) the dominant theme of the material taken as a whole appeals to a prurient interest in sex; (b) the material is patently offensive because it affronts contemporary community standards relating to the description or representation of sexual matters; and (c) the material is utterly without redeeming social value."[35] Thus *Roth* assumed that obscenity was utterly without social redemption, and *Memoirs* required its proof.

Justice Brennan abandoned his *Roth* analysis in 1973. "[A]fter 16 years of experimentation and debate I am reluctantly forced to the conclusion that none of the available formulas, including the one announced today, can reduce the vagueness to a tolerable level . . . Any effort . . . must resort to such indefinite concepts as 'prurient interest,' 'patent offensiveness,' 'serious literary value,' . . . The meaning of these concepts necessarily varies with the experience, outlook, and even idiosyncrasies of the person defining them."[36]

In 1973, the court articulated a new standard in *Miller v.*

*California,* with Justice Brennan dissenting. According to this standard, in addition to the two familiar findings regarding prurience and patent offensiveness the jury or judge must determine the additional finding of "whether the work, taken as a whole lacks serious literary, artistic, political or scientific value."[37] This newer standard presented a lower threshold of proof for the prosecution.

## Sexual Science and Obscenity Trials

The role of sexual science in obscenity prosecutions has been problematic from the outset. Earlier cases argued whether the prosecution had to offer expert sexual science evidence to prove obscenity, and whether the defense must be allowed to offer expert evidence in rebuttal. The Supreme Court held that the defense must be permitted to proffer expert testimony.

> [There is a] right of one charged with obscenity . . . to enlighten the judgement of the tribunal . . . Community standards or the psychological or physiological consequences of questioned literature can as a matter of fact hardly be established except through experts . . . interpretation[s] ought not to depend solely on the necessarily limited, hit-or-miss, subjective view of what they are believed to be by the individual juror or judge . . . Unless we disbelieve that the literary, psychological or moral standards of a community can be made fruitful and illuminating subjects of inquiry by those who give their life to such inquiries, it [is] violative of 'due process' to exclude the constitutionally relevant evidence.[38]

Yet the government need not introduce expert testimony: "[It is not] error . . . to fail to require 'expert' affirmative evidence that the materials were obscene when the materials themselves were actually placed in evidence. The films, obviously, are the best evidence of what they represent."[39]

Sexual scientists have been given short shrift by federal courts: "No amount of testimony by anthropologists, sociologists, psychologists, or psychiatrists could add much to the ability of the jury to apply [the] tests of obscenity."[40] According to another court, "To hold, in effect, that we must turn the application of the obscenity statutes over 'to a collection of randomly chosen Ph.D.s' as expert witnesses . . . is to require abdication of the judicial function of the judge or jury as triers of fact."[41] And in the view of the Supreme Court, "the 'expert witness' practices employed in these cases have often made a mockery out of the otherwise sound concept of expert testimony."[42]

Sexual scientists have difficulty addressing the *Miller* criteria. First, there is the issue of "prurient" interest. In their medical school training, psychiatrists met *pruritis* in dermatology, where it means "itching." In terms of sexuality, *prurient* might mean "a desire that demands relief." As defined by the courts, however, prurience is a "shameful, morbid, [unhealthy] interest in nudity, sex, or excretion."[43] This requirement invokes the question, What is a *healthy* interest in nudity, sex, or excretion? Is it ever healthy to watch filmed depictions of persons engaging in any kind of sexual behavior?

Even more difficult than determining the nature of a prurient interest is the issue of in whom to find it. The jury determination is based on whether the average person would find that the particular material appeals to a prurient interest. Is a juror with a healthy sexual interest to determine which small group of persons in the community with an unhealthy sexual interest would find the material appealing? It would appear not to be that, because an appeal to the weak links of society was no longer to be the test after *Roth* dispensed with the English-derived *Hicklin* test. Under *Hicklin*, courts were concerned with "a tendency" of the material "to deprave or corrupt those whose minds are open to such immoral influences."[44] Prurient appeal, then, should be found in the average person, an "original sin" view of human sexuality. It presumes the presence in everyone of a morbid, shameful interest in sexuality.

Using the interpretation that prurience is to be found in the average person, a defendant in a case involving a film containing bestiality, in which a woman was sexually involved with animals, argued that, since the film was so repulsive as not to be erotic to the average person, it could not be found obscene. The appellate court agreed with the defendant's characterization of the film as "absolutely disgusting" but found that it would "have an appeal to the prurient interest of an otherwise sexually normal person." In a somewhat obscure holding, the Fourth Circuit panel wrote, "[T]he average person comes into the test not as the object of the appeal but as its judge. It is he . . . who, applying contemporary community standards, determines whether or not the work appeals to the prurient interest. There is no explicit requirement that the average person determine that the material appeals to the prurient interest of the average person."[45]

The next obstacle for sexual science is determining patent offensiveness. Can a demographically representative public sampling be obtained to measure contemporary community standards? Can a valid sampling be shown examples of currently available erotic material? Is the availability of comparable material in bookstores an indication of its lack of patent offensiveness? Does availability reflect community tolerance?

In a 1980 case, an Illinois trial court refused to admit a public opinion poll on the issue of a consensus in community standards. The expert witness defined a "consensus" as that agreed to by 75 percent of the population and found that there was no consensus on the acceptability of sexually explicit materials. A survey of over seven hundred people found that 58 percent thought it acceptable for the average adult to see any depiction of actual or pretended sexual activities in movies and publications. But the trial court ruled that the survey and analysis of results invaded the province of the jury.

Because the Illinois Criminal Code permits evidence showing "the degree . . . of public acceptance of the material,"[46] the appellate court reversed. It held that the survey was relevant to the question of whether some explicit sexual depictions are "patently offensive" and appealed to the "prurient interest,"; however it barred the expert's *analysis* of the survey because that might be "confusing" to the jury.[47]

By contrast, jurisdictions have barred polling a community sample because of "the absence of any indication that the willingness, the lack of willingness, or the indifference of a group to the sale of sexually explicit magazines or the showing of sexually explicit films has any relevance . . . [to the question of] whether the particular sexual conduct involved . . . was depicted or described in a patently offensive way."[48] But another court held that a poll assessing community acceptance of "nudity and actual or pretended sexual activity" was relevant to determining whether an explicit film was acceptable.[49]

An "ethnographical" study of community standards has been held inadmissible. In a 1988 case, a social scientist spent a week in a community visiting adult book and video stores and talking with newspaper editors, and owners and customers of sexually oriented businesses. The court pointed out that the expert "did not visit churches, community centers, garden clubs, [or] Rotary Clubs," and characterized the scientist's results as "neither science, nor work requiring expertise."[50]

The third obstacle for sexual science is determining "serious literary, artistic, political, or scientific value." What is *serious* scientific value? Is anatomic depiction of the genitals scientific? "Seriously" scientific? If education is science, how formal must the process be for it to be "serious"? If the material is used by medical professors to "desensitize" students to a range of sexual behaviors so that they can be more comfortable in discussing sex with patients, is that sufficient? If so, what about the general public or a segment of the public that desires visual education in a range of sexual behaviors they have only heard about?

Is sex therapy "science?" If the material is used by professional therapists so that patients may observe a pattern of sexuality they find arousing for application with a consenting partner, is that sufficient? If used by the therapist with both partners as a vehicle to facilitate communication about a sexual behavior that may enhance their relationship, is that sufficient? If so, what about the general public, or a segment of the public, that desires comparable therapeutic advantage but views the material without the supervision of a therapist, whom they cannot afford?

A 1973 California case, the first in which I testified as an expert witness, illustrates the courtroom use of sexual science data.[51] Oral-genital sex was a felony in California in 1973 (Penal Code Section 288a). A film producer was charged with making and distributing an obscene film and with *conspiracy to commit oral copulation* (in the process of making the film). The defense attorney, Anthony Glassman, attempted to establish the normative features of oral-genital sexuality and the consequences of its proscription. The following excerpts are from trial testimony.

*Normative Behavior*

[At the time of the trial, *The Sensuous Man, The Sensuous Woman,* and *Everything You Always Wanted to Know about Sex (but Were Afraid to Ask)* were on the best-seller list.]

Attorney: With respect to each of these books, are there passages running on at some length which describe various oral-genital sexual techniques?

Green: In both *The Sensuous Man,* and particularly in *The Sensuous Woman,* there are passages running several pages describing a variety of procedures with respect to oral-genital sexual contact. *The Sensuous Woman* instructs the woman on the oral techniques which are described as the most exciting to the male.

*Everything You Always Wanted to Know about Sex* is not so much a book on technique, but is designed to dispel people's preconceived notions or prejudices against participating in oral sexuality. Essentially it is instruction in trying to desensitize or disinhibit such people against this behavior, but does not in fact offer a course of instruction as do the other two best-selling books.

Attorney: Does the fact that these books have become best-sellers have any particular meaning to you as a psychiatrist?

Green: It does. These are behaviors which have been widely practiced, if we can believe the data from the Kinsey books, but not publicly acknowledged, and carry with them a certain amount of guilt because of the secrecy clouding such behavior in the past. It is behavior which is not only being practiced, but more openly discussed. I would submit that as an accompaniment of more open acknowledgment and discussion of such behavior the majority of persons who practice such behavior would benefit psychologically because of assuagement of guilt and conflict over what they are practicing.

*Effects of Proscription*

Attorney: Have you, Doctor, had the opportunity to read California Penal Code Section 288(a) which purports to prohibit any kind of oral-genital sexual contact?

Green: Yes, I did.

Attorney: Is the prohibition itself, Penal Code Section 288(a), is its existence, in your opinion, psychologically harmful?

Green: I would have to say yes.

Attorney: And could you indicate why you feel that it is.

The Court: The existence of the Section is psychologically harmful; is that what you're saying, Doctor?

Green: Yes.

The Court: All right.

Green: From the time of the classic writings of Freud, there has been an emphasis on conflict over sexuality. Traditionally this has been seen as one of the cornerstones out of which springs a variety of psychologic conflicts.

    Based on my experience with patients, when one is confronted with a pattern of behavior which is practiced by most, if not all of us, and one is then told either by a religious authority that it is immoral or sinful, or by a penal authority that it is illegal, and one is essentially responding to a biological drive, a normal part of sexuality, then conflict is generated in the person. It can only lead to inner conflict, it can only lead to guilt, it can only lead to anxiety. These are psychological phenomena which are harmful.

### Effects of Viewing the Film

[Testimony was given that sexually explicit films showing oral-genital sexuality are shown to medical students.]

Attorney: Referring to the films you have seen which you have made reference to, those shown in the medical school setting depicting oral-genital sexuality, if those films were to be shown in a metropolitan theatre, do you have an opinion as a psychiatrist whether or not that film would have social value?

Green: Based on clinical interviews of patients who have seen so-called adult films, by and large I would say that these people report, first of all, not being offended by them, and secondly, report that they have been able then to introduce more communication with their spouses regarding their own sexual relationship. In some cases they have been able to introduce new varieties of sexual technique into their marriage.

    In one of the studies reported in the [Pornography] Commission report, in which some 250 people were interviewed after leaving adult film houses in San Francisco or Los Angeles, a majority of people reported to the interviewers that their sexual relationship was more enjoyable and that there was more communication about sexuality following their having seen these films. These were married people who have been frequenters of adult film houses.

Only one percent of all the subjects reported a negative effect on sexual adjustment after seeing the films.

Attorney: Is there anything about the fact that a given type film, namely the type that you have seen and that you are now discussing, is taken outside of a medical classroom and shown in a metropolitan theatre that in any way detracts from the kind of social value and utility that you are discussing? For example, the absence perhaps of a medical lecture by a psychiatrist or a physician to accompany the film, would that detract from it, in your professional judgment?

Green: No. The films which are being shown this year [in the university human sexuality course] will not be accompanied by lectures during those hours. They will merely be the film presentations. That would be comparable to a public viewing in which there would not be an accompanying medical or scientific lecture.

The film was found by the jury not to be obscene, but the producer was convicted of conspiracy to commit oral copulation. His conviction was upheld on appeal.

## Legal Contours

If sexual science data demonstrate that erotic materials currently deemed pornographic and not obscene are related to sex crimes against women because some persons become aroused by the material and model their behavior on it, or because the material affects cultural values, so that women become objects for sexual conquest, will this remove pornography's First Amendment protection? Probably not, so long as *Brandenburg v. Ohio* remains the measure.

In *Brandenburg,* a group of Klansmen held one meeting at which a cross was burned and another at which a hooded figure stated "I believe the nigger should be returned to Africa, the Jew returned to Israel." The Klansmen were convicted under Ohio's Criminal Syndicalism statute for "advocat[ing] the . . . necessity or propriety of . . . violence." The conviction was reversed, the defendants' actions being protected because of the "distinction . . . between mere advocacy and incitement to imminent lawless action."[52]

Whatever the weight given to the correlational studies reporting a relationship between pornography (of some types) and attitudes toward sexual assault, the link is so far too tenuous to meet the test of "incitement to imminent lawless action." Therefore, those who would bar pornography (and not just obscenity) must devise a principled constitutional analysis that would permit the Klan to meet, the Nazis to march, and both groups to disseminate hate literature, but would curb pornography.

As played out so far in the courts, two attempts to impose liability on the media for inducing sexual assault and homicide have failed under the weight of the First Amendment.

In one action, a television drama in which a group of young women raped another young woman with an "artificial instrument" (a "plumber's helper") was alleged to have led to the sexual assault of a nine-year-old girl with a bottle four days after the assailants viewed the show.[53] NBC argued that the test for incitement under *Brandenburg* had not been met. When the plaintiff argued that incitement was not the legal theory for recovery but rather "stimulation, foreseeability, negligence, [and] proximate cause," to the Court, "the chilling effect [on the First Amendment] [was] obvious." The action was dismissed because "if liability were to be imposed on a simple negligence theory . . . the effect of the imposition . . . could reduce the U.S. adult population to viewing only what is fit for children. Incitement is the proper test here."[54]

Another action was brought against three broadcasting companies to recover damages on the theory that television violence, to which the plaintiff had been exposed from age five to fifteen, caused him to become addicted and desensitized to violent behavior, resulting in his killing an eighty-three-year-old woman.[55] The court held that the imposition on the defendant of the duty argued by plaintiff "has no valid basis and would be against public policy."[56] To impose civil responsibility for damages "would have an impact upon and indeed act as a restraint on the defendants' exercise of their asserted First Amendment rights."[57] Although "one day, medical or other sciences . . . may convince the F.C.C. or the Courts that the delicate balance of First Amendment rights should be altered to permit some additional limitations in programming [, t]he complaint before the Court in no way justifies such a pursuit."[58]

By contrast, in a decision bypassing First Amendment speech protection, the Supreme Court in 1991 created a distinction between filmed pornography and live nudity.[59] Whereas obscenity must be proved for a filmed depiction to be barred, nude dancing, as in a striptease, without any determination of obscenity, can be barred. This because a ban on nude dancing is not a proscription of the "erotic message conveyed by the dancers . . . the perceived evil . . . is not erotic dancing, but public nudity."[60] To the Court, the statute reflects "moral disapproval of people appearing in the nude among strangers in a public place" and serves the state's interest in "protecting societal order and morality."[61] To the four-vote dissent, the foregoing analysis is "transparently erroneous," violates the First Amendment, and impermissibly permits a state to regulate "emotions and feelings of eroticism and sensuality."[62]

United States Supreme Court rulings notwithstanding, some states have held that the right to (sexual) privacy found in their state constitution trumps concerns over pornography, whatever the sexual science data show. Hawaii, for example, permits the sale of adult pornography to adult consumers. The Hawaii Constitution "affords greater privacy rights than the federal right to privacy, so we [the Hawaii Supreme Court] are not bound by the United States Supreme Court precedents." Hawaii's Constitution asserts that the "right of the people to privacy is recognized and shall not be infringed without the showing of a compelling state interest."[63]

Oregon protects pornography. "No law shall be passed restraining the right to speak, write, or print freely on any subject whatever." In *State v. Henry,* the court held that "any subject whatever" means what it says and "does not contain any express exceptions for obscene communications."[64]

In states that protect the sale of pornography, the enforcement of federal laws presents a paradox. A person sending pornography through the mail to a bookstore in Hawaii, where it can be sold, is liable to be prosecuted by the federal government for sending it. The paradox is similar to that in *Stanley v. Georgia,*[65] in which the United States Supreme Court ruled that possession of adult pornography in the home is protected, even if its sale by the local bookstore could be prohibited. These paradoxes could be seen as promoting an in-house or in-state cottage industry of pornography.

"Child pornography" is not protected, whether in the home or the "adult" bookstore. Material depicting minors need not meet the *Miller* criteria for adult obscenity to be unprotected. The purpose is "safeguarding the physical and psychological well-being of a minor," a governmental interest "of surpassing importance."[66] The rationale, as explained by the Supreme Court, is that "the materials produced are a permanent record of the children's participation and the harm to the child is exacerbated by their circulation."[67]

Although in-home possession of adult obscenity (not just pornography) is protected under *Stanley v. Georgia,* under *Osborne v. Ohio* possession of child pornography is not.[68] A state law permitting conviction for the possession of four photographs of a nude adolescent male withstood a First Amendment defense, including the argument that it was too sweeping a net to accomplish the State's purpose. The six justice majority cited the importance of stopping pornographic sexual abuse of children, the need to eliminate the permanent record, and the use of child pornography by pedophiles to entice children into forbidden sexual acts.

Criticizing the law's impermissible sweep, the dissent pointed out that it could snare a family friend who was given a nude photo of a child by its parents. Responding to the State's interest in destroying the permanent record of the victim's abuse, the dissent argued that there was "no requirement that the State show that the child was abused in the production of the materials."[69]

Common sense supports a concern about both the short- and the long-term consequences to young children of participating in pornographic productions. Yet, whereas hundreds of commercial child pornography magazines are reportedly produced each month, and in Los Angeles there are allegedly tens of thousands of such sexually exploited children,[70] research reports on the specific sequelae of child pornography have yet to be published. "[T]here is no concrete empirical evidence clearly demonstrating its effects, immediate or long term."[71] A methodological problem for sexual scientists is that of distinguishing the negative effects of the sexual interaction itself from the record of the interaction being memorialized on film.

# 8

# Intergenerational Sexuality

A comprehensive analysis of sexual contact between adults and children or early adolescents must address a range of issues: the legal concept of age of consent, the frequency with which such sexual contact occurs, its short- and long-term psychological significance for the younger person, the impact of societal (including legal) responses to the sexual experience, and the emergent politicalization of this interface between sexual science and the law.

The legal age of consent for participating in sexual activity (generally intercourse) ostensibly reflects the capacity for meaningful psychological consent. Legal consent requires more than willingness. It demands a requisite level of cognitive and emotional understanding (informed consent).

For over seven hundred years England prohibited males from having intercourse with females below a specific age. In 1275 that age was twelve.[1] It was lowered to ten in 1576, during the reign of Elizabeth I and stayed there for another three centuries.[2] In 1876 it was raised to thirteen, and in 1879 it settled at the current age of sixteen. Until 1929, the age at which a female could marry was twelve, four years younger than the age of consent for intercourse.[3]

The age at which two males can sexually engage in England is eighteen, two years older than that for a male and a female or a female and a female. The English Policy Advisory Committee on Sexual Offences voted down a proposal to fix the male-male age of consent at sixteen in order to help young men "avoid homosexual relations while they are immature." Five women members of the Committee dissented, citing the argument of the Royal College of

Psychiatrists that sexual orientation is fixed prior to sixteen.[4] European nations that make no distinction between the age of consent for heterosexual and homosexual behavior include Denmark, France, the Netherlands, Italy, Norway, Poland, and Sweden.[5]

In the United States the youngest age of consent has been seven years (in Delaware into the 1950s). Currently in the fifty states it ranges between eleven and eighteen.[6] Certainly, cognitive and emotional capacities differ considerably at the outer limits of this developmental continuum. Thus considerations other than those of sexual science enter the calculus as state legislatures fix the age at which that state consents to its residents' consenting to sex.

Debate continues not only over the specific age at which consent to sex can be given legally, but also over whether age of consent laws should be abolished. The more radical view sees sex between children and older persons as natural, and not only benign but often psychosexually beneficial. Moderates who urge the repeal of age of consent laws decry setting an arbitrary age limit, arguing that the legitimate purpose of protecting young people from sexual victimization is better served by other laws.

The radical perspective asks whether children have the right to say "yes" as well as "no" to sex with an adult. Tom O'Carroll, a spokesman for the English pedophile movement, proposes several basic requirements for freedom of choice: "full knowledge of all the short- and long-term consequences . . . a developed notion of which sexual activities (and partners) are excitable and desirable . . . [and] control over the situation so that withdrawal from it can be made."[7] He attempts to distinguish "consent" and psychological "willingness," arguing that the latter is sufficient when these elements are assured, and concludes that "there is no need whatever for a child to know 'the consequences' of engaging in harmless sex play, simply because it is exactly that: harmless."[8] He also reminds readers that adults do not always know the full consequences of a sexual interaction, a truism that does not convince those who do not regard child-adult sex play as harmless. Reversing the usually advanced developmental sequence, O'Carroll proclaims that "far from needing to be mature before having a sex life, an unthwarted sexual development helps lead to full sexual maturity, as opposed to the mere attainment of adult years."[9] To O'Carroll, the standard should be "whether we can ensure that children are willing participants."[10]

A more moderate critique by the Australian writer Paul Wilson holds that often "a legal age of consent is an arbitrary point, a line drawn that has no basis in the physiological or psychological development of the child. Furthermore, [it] does not prevent the sexual activity taking place and serves to perpetuate the myth that most, if not all, adults can and always do rationally consent to sexual relations." To Wilson, "offences should be considered on the basis of the use of violence, force, fraud or pressure rather than an arbitrary age limit."[11]

The Canadian psychiatrist Cyril Greenland concedes that "unpopular though it may be, a strong case may still be made for the complete abolition of the age of consent for hetero- and homosexual relationships. [However] [t]his does not mean encouraging or even condoning sexual contacts between children and adults. Instead, one needs to consider whether the criminal law is the best available instrument for regulating sexual conduct."[12]

The English psychiatrist and criminologist Donald West argues that all forms of unwelcome, exploitive, or violent sexuality with minors can remain criminal without age of consent laws. He offers assurances that parents who are concerned about whether the relationship in which their child is engaged is consensual should be able to turn to the appropriate child welfare legislation.[13]

Those who would not abandon a bright line legal age of consent concede the need for periodic revisions "to keep the age consistent with prevailing social trends." Revisions should be based on "practical, psychologic, and cultural considerations." But just how to apply sexual science data in this context is problematic. "If the estimate that nearly 50 percent of females under the age of 18 years have had [premarital] sexual intercourse and . . . many of these acts are statutory rape . . . the age of consent needs to be lowered . . . certainly, at least to an age when relatively few females are likely to have had sexual intercourse . . . [This leads to the question of] what is meant by 'relatively few'?"[14]

Perhaps reference points in other areas of "capacity to consent" law, such as medical procedures, can guide sex law. In England and Canada a bright line age of consent for medical procedures has been rejected. No strict age has been set in England because "capacity to consent depends on the child's intellectual capability." True consent "depends on whether the person is capable of understanding and coming to a decision on what is involved."[15] Canadian cases have held that there is no age below which minors are automatically incapable of giving consent. It is a minor's right to consent if he or she is able to understand fully what is involved for the medical procedure in question.[16]

"Variable competence" for children has been advanced by the medical ethicist Willard Gaylin, who proposes a grid that "sets some limits and identifies some principles" for establishing competence for different types of decision making by minors. In the area of sexuality, emotional and cognitive components of that grid should be marked "before it is concluded, for example, that at age eleven a child should have the right to decide to have an abortion, or indeed, to carry a pregnancy to term . . . or that a thirteen-year-old will be free to consent to sex."[17]

Sexual science data can inform the debate on age of consent law. What is known about the effects on young minors of sexual contact with older minors or adults? Is there an age before which sexual contact with someone of any age is necessarily or usually harmful? Or do other factors, such as the type of sexual interaction or the relationship between the participants (for example, family, nonfamily), override age?

## Historical Perspectives

It is not only radical factions, such as the Rene Guyon Society with its inflammatory slogan "Sex by Eight or Else It's Too Late," or the Gay Liberation Movement's bête noir, NAMBLA (The North American Man-Boy Love Association), that stir up the debate. Mainstream clinicians, educators, and researchers also question whether all of the "sexual" experiences between children and adults are necessarily "abusive," and whether short- and long-term trauma and scarring are inevitable consequences. They see parallels with the earlier sexual science view of homosexuality.

The psychiatric and psychoanalytic literature of the 1950s and 1960s repeatedly documented the clinical problems of homosexual patients. The conclusion drawn from these case histories was inevitable: homosexuals as a class were mentally ill. Obviously, discerning sample bias was not a methodologic strength of psychiatry or the discipline Freud called "our science." The fact that it is sick people who are treated by physicians escaped critical notice. Also apparently escaping notice were the "sick" heterosexual patients who fleshed out the remaining psychiatric treatment hours. Not until behavioral scientists studied nonpatient samples and control groups was this conclusion questioned. By 1973 the data were clear: homosexuals were not all mentally ill by the standard criteria for judging mental illness. As with heterosexuals, some behaved in ways that fit the criteria for mental disorders, but most did not. The axiomatic equation "homosexuality equals mental disorder" was discredited and in 1973 homosexuality per se was dropped from the psychiatric diagnostic manual.[18]

With intergenerational sexuality, early psychiatric patient descriptions of adults reporting childhood sexual experiences with older persons also described a range of mental health problems. The conclusion drawn was that the earlier sexual experiences were responsible for the later problems. For example, a 1972 report described twenty-six women with incestuous experiences who were seen in a psychiatric clinic. Eleven had a character disorder (promiscuity, prostitution, antisocial behavior), five were sexually "frigid," and four had "frank neurosis" (one with anxiety, three with depression), while six had no apparent illness. No control group was studied to determine the incidence of these disorders in women patients without a history of childhood sexual interaction. Causality between the early experience and the later diagnosis was assumed.[19]

With rare dissenting views, the psychiatric community endorsed the conclusion that child-adult sexuality is inevitably traumatic and scarring to the child. Two discordant notes amid this chorus are noteworthy. Over forty years ago Lauretta Bender and Karl Menninger challenged this conclusion. Bender studied ten girls and four boys who, between the ages of five and twelve, had been involved sexually with adults over a "prolonged time."[20] Follow-up evaluations were conducted eleven to sixteen years later. Of the four who had been involved sexually with a parent, three "attained moderately successful adjustments." For six others involved sexually with nonrelatives, all were described as having had "positive" outcomes. The course for the remaining four with "severe limitations in native endowment, including intellectual ability," was "generally unfavorable." Bender commented: "It may be remembered that in contrast to the harsh social taboos surrounding such relationships, there exists no scientific proof that there are any resulting deleterious effects."[21]

Likewise, in *Love against Hate,* Menninger wrote: "The assumption is, of course, that children are irreparably ruined by such [child-adult] experiences. Without intending in the least to justify or excuse such criminal behavior I may nevertheless point out that in the cold light of scientific investigation no such devastating effects usually follow."[22]

The extent to which intergenerational sexual activity occurs underscores medical, legal, and public concerns. In a survey of eight hundred U.S. college students, 19 percent of females and 9 percent of males reported "sexual involvement" with an adult between early childhood and adolescence.[23] In a more representative group, a probability sample of three thousand persons in one city, 7 percent of women and 4 percent of men reported forced sexual contact during childhood.[24] In a sample of nine hundred women, 12 percent reported having been sexually abused by a relative and 20 percent by a nonrelative before age fourteen. Fewer than 5 percent had reported the incident to police.[25]

In a national sample of two thousand men and women in Great Britain, 12 percent of females and 8 percent of males reported "sexual abuse" before age sixteen. Abuse included experiences with a sexually mature peer and "showing pornographic materials or talking about things in an erotic way." Half of the abusive experiences involved no physical contact, and intercourse was reported by only 5 percent.[26] In a Canadian survey, 15 percent of females and 6 percent of males reported experiencing unwanted sexual contact ranging from genital fondling to completed rape prior to age sixteen.[27]

## Recent Reports

### Short-Term Effects on Primarily Female Children

Sixty-one girls, aged three to twelve (with an average age of 6), who had experienced a sexual encounter with a late adolescent or adult within the previous two years, were evaluated at a treatment facility. On a symptom checklist, nearly half had elevated scores showing that they were fearful, inhibited, depressed, and overcontrolled, while about two-fifths were elevated on scores for aggressive, anti-social, and undercontrolled behaviors. Only 2 percent of the normal population should score in this range.[28] Girls reporting more frequent experiences with an emotionally close older person exhibited more problem behaviors. Boys exhibited more symptoms when the experience was with an emotionally close older person and of long duration. Symptoms were greater when the adult was a biological parent (29 percent of the cases). One explanation given by the investigators for this latter finding was that when an incestuous parent is removed from the home there is "subsequent loss of income, family integrity, and possible scapegoating of the victim for her role in the breakdown of the family."[29] In interpreting their findings, the researchers acknowledge that because their subjects were obtained from families in treatment, they "probably display[ed] a more pronounced response to the abuse" than children with sexual experiences who were not seen in therapy.[30]

Over 350 children (80 percent girls) aged four to seventeen (with an average age of 8.8), also at a treatment center for sexually abused children, were compared with children who had no sexual involvement.[31] Symptomatic behaviors included poorer self-esteem, more aggression, and more fearfulness than in the contrast group. Children from homes with significant family problems had more symptoms.

Another sample of 150 children ranging in age from infancy to eighteen, also obtained from a sexual abuse treatment program, revealed that 17 percent of the four- to six-year-olds showed "clinically significant pathology." Although they demonstrated more overall disturbance than the normal population, they demonstrated less pathology than other children their age who were also in treatment but had no history of sexual involvement. The highest levels of psychopathology were found among seven- to thirteen-year-olds, of whom 40 percent had substantial problems. (By contrast, few adolescents were seriously disturbed.) Symptoms included severe fears, hostility, aggression, and antisocial behavior.[32]

The short-term effects of child-older person sexual interaction were summarized in a 1986 review of the science literature. "From studies of clinical and non-clinical populations, the findings concerning the trauma of child sexual abuse appear to be as follows: In the immediate aftermath of sexual abuse, from one-fifth to two-fifths of abused children seen by clinicians manifest pathological disturbance."[33]

A 1991 review of the short-term effects reached conclusions that were not notably different and also pointed out several methodological shortcomings in the research:

> There is still a lack of consensus regarding the proportion of children who have been psychologically harmed by the experience, or the nature of the harm they have sustained. We do not know whether many of the symptoms reported in the literature are specific to sexual abuse or whether they are attributable to other factors such as the child's level of premorbid functioning or a disturbed home environment . . . few studies have addressed the impact of disclosure, and specifically in what instances disclosure, and subsequent intervention on the part of medical, legal, or social agencies can be expected to have an adverse or helpful effect on the sexual abuse victim . . . since the majority of studies . . . were based on samples drawn from child protective services or psychiatric facilities, they may overestimate the prevalence and severity of symptomatology associated with child sexual abuse in the general population.[34]

Regarding the emotional problems shown by the children, "[t]he evidence was also equivocal with regard to whether sexually abused school-age children were substantially more or less disturbed than other children referred for clinical problems."[35] However, the one outcome more likely to be found among the children was "inappropriate sexual behaviors (e.g., excessive masturbation, sexual preoccupation, and sexual aggression)."[36]

## Long-Term Effects on Primarily Female Children

In an American community sample of three thousand, the lifetime and current prevalences of psychological symptoms in adults reporting sex abuse before age sixteen were assessed.[37] Respondents who had had a sexual experience were more likely to have one lifetime psychiatric diagnosis (64 percent vs. 29 percent), a history of substance abuse (37 percent vs. 16 percent), an affective, or mood state disorder (20 percent vs. 7 percent), an anxiety disorder (29 percent vs. 11 percent), a phobia, or marked fear reaction (23 percent vs. 10 percent), a panic disorder (8 percent vs. 1 percent), and an antisocial personality (9 percent vs. 2 percent). Within the prior six months, those who reported abuse were more likely to have had a psychiatric disorder (36 percent vs. 14 percent) and higher rates of affective disorder (13 percent vs. 2 percent), anxiety (21 percent vs. 6 percent), and panic disorder (7 percent vs. <1 percent). With admirable caution, the authors concluded, "[T]his study did not ascertain whether the psychiatric disorders are attributable to the abuse, although the disorders . . . are consistent with symptoms most frequently and persistently attributed to child sexual abuse."[38]

A finding of a modest but statistically significant association between reported early abuse and later symptoms was reported in a community sample of two thousand in New Zealand. A higher percentage of women reporting abuse at age twelve or earlier on a questionnaire had psychiatric symptoms, mostly depressive (20 percent vs. 6 percent). The percentage of this difference explained by childhood sex abuse, however, was only 2.6 compared to 4 percent explained by marital status and 3.3 percent explained by the number of children to whom the women had given birth. With an interviewed subsample, sex abuse accounted for 3.6 percent of the difference, compared with 1.8 percent for marital status and 0.8 percent for the number of children.[39]

Although a sample of one hundred American college women recalling sexual abuse that ranged from exhibitionism to intercourse scored higher on a psychological symptom checklist, the investigators noted that "the clinical significance of this finding is small since sexual abuse accounted for less than 2 percent of the variance" (that is, less than 2 percent of the contribution to the symptoms).[40] Moreover, another scale, the Parental Support Scale, was a better predictor of symptom scores than the history of abuse. "This suggests that the relationship of sexual abuse with later adjustment is not due to the sexual abuse per se, but rather to the confounding of sexual abuse with family background (specifically the lack of parental supportiveness which characterizes the home of the sexually abused)."[41]

Five hundred women reporting sexual experiences up to age fourteen—experiences not always recalled negatively—were compared to a sample without sexual experience. Although adult psychological functioning did not differ for the two groups, particular types of sexual experience did correlate with outcome. Those with specific categories of older participant and those that were forced, guilt-provoking, and abusive were related to poorer functioning except in the area of current sexual satisfaction. The sexual experience was recalled as pleasant by 38 percent of the women, as neutral by 37 percent, and as negative by 25 percent. One quarter of the experiences were recalled as having been initiated by the women and 30 percent as mutually initiated.[42]

Rarely have sexually abused persons seeking therapy been compared with sexually abused persons who consider themselves well adjusted and who have not sought therapy, as well as a nonabused control group.[43] In one such study, the great majority of the sexual experiences were between the daughter and the father, stepfather, or grandfather. The age at the first experience was comparable between groups, as was the time that had elapsed before the event was reported; at least one-third waited over a decade. Differences between groups were apparent in the age at the last event (twelve for the clinical, eight for the nonclinical), and the duration of the experience (4.7 years vs. 2.5 years). The women in therapy more often reported that the experience involved attempted intercourse, although whether it was completed did not differ between groups. Experiences of oral-genital contact also did not differ. The clinical group reported feeling more guilty at the time of the event and more pressure not to report it (possibly because they were older). Women in treatment were less sexually responsive and had poorer relationships with men.

A comprehensive review in 1986 summarized these long-term effects and concluded that "[a]dult women victimized as children are more likely to manifest depression, self-destructive behavior, anxiety, feelings of isolation and stigma, poor self-esteem, a tendency to revictimization, and substance abuse . . . When studied as adults, victims as a group demonstrate impairment when compared with their nonvictimized counterparts, but under one-fifth evidence serious psychopathology."[44]

Individual factors have been scrutinized to determine whether they specifically influence outcome. The 1986 review found that *force* was one of the few variables associated with children's symptoms. In some research those subjected to coercive experiences showed greater hostility and were more fearful of aggressive behavior in others. Other research, however, found no relation between the degree of force and psychosocial sequelae in children who were followed up as adolescents.[45] *Age at the onset* of the sexual experience did not relate to later sequelae in four studies, but two found prepubertal experiences to be more traumatic.[46] Low correlations have been found between the *duration* of experiences and the level of psychological trauma.[47] A 1991 review concludes, "findings concerning age of onset, sex of child, duration and frequency are still equivocal."[48]

More trauma has not been consistently associated with whether the experiences were with a *relative* or a *nonrelative*. But there is some relationship between sexual involvement with the father and increased trauma.[49] One study found that *penetration* of the child was "the single most powerful variable explaining severity of mental health impairment."[50] Yet another study, using measures of children's anxiety, found that children who had been fondled without penetration were more anxious than those who experienced penetration, while three other studies showed no relation.[51] Two studies of the *age of the older person* have found that experiences were rated years later as more traumatic when the older person was an adult rather than an adolescent.[52] When *parents reacted more negatively* to the child's experiences, that is, with anger and punishment, children have shown more behavioral disturbances.[53] In a 1988 study, longer periods of abuse, co-existing physical abuse, multiple perpetrators, and bizarre sexual abuse (insertions of foreign objects, sexual torture, gang rape, use of animals) were associated with sexual problems, alcoholism, drug addiction, suicidality, and the recurrence of rape or sexual assault.[54]

There are methodological problems with many of these studies, however. As the psychiatrist Arthur Green concluded in 1988,

A critical review of the literature reveals: 1) failure to employ comparison or control groups; 2) exceedingly small samples; 3) lack of control for psychological impairment antedating any known sexual abuse; 4) confounding independent variables, e.g., physical abuse in addition to sexual abuse; 5) failure to match for the child's age or level of development; 6) use of unstandardized assessment instruments; and 7) lack of discrimination between acute and long-term psychological sequelae.[55]

A detailed review by Angela Browne and David Finkelhor in 1986 criticizes both research sampling and study instruments:

> The empirical literature on child sexual abuse . . . suggest[s] the presence—in some portion of the victim population—of many of the initial effects reported in the clinical literature, especially reactions of fear, anxiety, depression, anger and hostility, and inappropriate sexual behavior. However, because many of the studies [lack] standardized outcome measures and adequate comparison groups, it is not clear that these findings reflect the experience of all child victims of sexual abuse or are even representative of those children currently being seen in clinical settings.[56]

Regarding long-term effects, the review concluded that "most sexual abuse victims in the community, when evaluated in surveys, show up as slightly impaired or normal."[57] Commenting on the questionable representativeness of the samples studied, it continued:

> Many of the available studies are based on samples of either adult women seeking treatment or children whose molestation has been reported. These subjects may be very self-selected. Especially if sexual abuse is so stigmatizing that only the most serious cases are discovered and only the most seriously affected victims seek help, such samples could distort our sense of the pathology most victims experience as a result of this abuse.[58]

Another review, in 1992, concludes that the specific effects of the early sexual experience, independent of the use or threat of force, or parental psychopathology, remain to be clarified. Greater long-term sequelae appear to be associated with contact with the father or stepfather and an experience involving penetration.[59] Although suicidality is reported to be more common in women with a history of sexual abuse in conjunction with physical abuse,[60] "[f]rom these data, it is difficult to assess the relation between child sexual abuse and suicidality independent of physical abuse."[61]

In the literature on sexual abuse, correlation and causality are often not distinguished. "Few non-clinical studies attempt to probe the causality of any abuse-effects association uncovered; instead they tend to interpret any statistically significant relationship as de facto evidence of the traumagenic impact of sexual victimization."[62]

The need for caution in order to avoid confusing family problems and their effects with the effects of the sexual behavior has also been stressed: "Since negative family variables are often associated with sexual abuse and since family problems and sexual abuse are each associated with later psychological difficulties, there is no easy way to determine how much of adult symptomatology is 'due' to abuse as opposed to family influences."[63]

One example of methodological weakness (among many other similar studies) is a 1988 report of 152 women seen in a crisis unit.[64] Forty-four percent had a history of "sexual abuse," defined as fondling to intercourse before age fifteen with a person five years older. Compared to nonabused women, these women were more likely to be taking psychiatric medication, to have a history of substance addiction, to have been victimized in a more recent adult relationship, and to have made at least one suicide attempt. Women reporting a history of abuse also reported more dissociative feelings, sleep problems, feelings of isolation, anxiety and fearfulness, problems with anger, and sexual difficulties.

The researchers treat sexual abuse as a nominal variable— it either happened or it did not. Thus, one experience at fourteen of fondling by a nineteen-year-old is treated in the same way as repeated acts of intercourse by a father with a prepubescent child. They then compare the occurrence of a wide range of psychiatric symptoms in adulthood in those with and without this history.

A further methodological problem is the possible confounding effects of many other early and later life variables that may influence current psychological functioning. What is known of the antecedent variables in both groups of families while the children were growing up? Was the sexual experience a reflection of other factors that could disturb development? Was there physical, nonsexual abuse? What else happened to the two groups of women in the decade or so since the sexual experience or experiences that could have influenced their psychological status? In addition, some types of psychopathology, such as suicide attempts and substance addiction, are known to have some genetic basis or to run in families. Without data on the psychiatric history of the parents (and psychological comparisons of the sexually involved children with their noninvolved siblings), and answers to the foregoing questions, it is scientifically unwarranted to reach the authors' conclusion that the results "[link] childhood sexual victimization to adult [current] psychosocial disturbance."[65]

## Male Children

Among the "Sambia" of New Guinea, oral-genital sex between prepubertal and young adult males is normative. All males pass through the stages of being first fellators, then fellateds before moving on to heterosexual behaviors. In this culture, boys must drink semen to grow strong.[66]

In Western society the commonly reported consequences for boys who have had sexual experiences with older persons (usually male) are fears of homosexuality, increased drug abuse, and the abuse of other children.[67] Other reported behavioral problems include aggression, destructive behavior, peer difficulties, and argumentativeness.[68] One study reports depression and suicidality as more common,[69] and an association with sex offender behavior in adulthood is also found. Three-quarters of a group of rapists reported being sexually assaulted by a family member, as did one-quarter of a sample of child molesters.[70]

But some reports contrast with these typically negative reports of minor-adult male sexuality. One was a questionnaire study of 215 pederasts (most of whom had never been arrested) and interviews with 300 boys who were sexually involved with them.[71] Many of the boys were characterized as seeking affection and friendship. "One repeatedly discovers . . . that a [relationship that is paternal or platonic but allows erotic overtones] frequently salvages boys from sexual and other delinquency."[72] Most of the sexual relationships studied were "episodic, an occasional experience as a part of a meaningful relationship which essentially is not sexual at all."[73]

In the Netherlands, twenty-five boys aged ten to sixteen who were sexually involved with men aged twenty-six to sixty-six were interviewed.[74] They were found with the help of their adult partners, who were located through "pedophile and young emancipation" groups. While no long-term follow-ups are given, short-term reports by most of the boys were positive: "The boys overwhelmingly experienced their sexual contact with the older partner as pleasant . . . The friendships and the sex which occurred between them had no negative influence upon the boys' general sense of well-being . . . The boys felt they received affection, love, attention, companionship, a sense of freedom and support from their older partners."[75]

A study designed to find persons who recalled some positive feelings associated with sexual experiences with an adult or older child before age sixteen analyzed the experiences of thirty-seven males and twenty-six females. The average age at the start of the experience(s) was eleven. For males, 66 percent of the experiences were with other males, while for females 12 percent of the experiences were with other females. The average number of sexual contacts was fifty-five. No force or violence was reported. Ongoing relationships were usually terminated when one participant moved to another area for reasons not associated with the sexual contact. Positive reactions were described as "pleasurable" and a "learning experience."[76]

Although these reports also suffer from problems of subject representativeness, they demonstrate that not all experiences, including those of a homosexual nature, are necessarily viewed by the younger person as traumatic. From the sexual science perspective, studies of boys who report early sexual experiences are methodologically no better than those of girls. A 1988 review concludes that "the bulk of the research on male sexual victimization suffers from some or all of the following: samples severely limited in size, convenience samples, analyses dependent upon post factum victim reports . . . and lack of replication."[77] A 1990 review concludes that "most current studies of males have relied on small samples . . . [that] are often biased, as the participants are recruited from clinic or therapy-referred boys or men . . . few of the studies . . . have included comparison or control groups."[78]

## Incest

The incest taboo springs from two main roots, one related to genetics, the other to family dynamics. The biological concern about "inbreeding" is that harmful recessive genes "running in families" do not cause medical problems until linked up with their counterparts, an occurrence more likely in incestual unions.

Although studies do report more birth defects or lessened vitality in the children born of father-daughter incest, some of these findings may be confounded by the fact that these mothers are usually very young, another source of infant morbidity.[79] The family dynamic fear is more realistic, at least in the United States. When a child is available to a parent (or sibling) as a potential "lover," the resultant jealousy of other family members may well disrupt family unity.[80] Other theories about the incest taboo look to the functional status of the family. Incest is seen as drawing family members away from their obligation to contribute to the larger society.[81]

Historically, brother-sister and father-daughter marriage was common in ancient Egypt,[82] Cleopatra's marriage to her brother being an example.[83] Incest was also found among the royalty of the Incas of Peru, among the ancient Hawaiians, and in Ireland, where princes married their sisters and kings their daughters.[84] More recently, incest was relatively common in Utah before statehood[85] and "was clearly functional for Mormon Society."[86] In Sweden, father-daughter incest was not uncommon in pre–World War II agricultural society.[87] In Japan, a report of thirty-six incest cases in Hiroshima was published in 1959 where father-daughter incest followed loss of the wife, and brother-sister incest occurred when the father was unable to fulfill his family role.[88]

## Clinical Studies: Negative Effects on Female Children

A sample of 53 female psychiatric patients with a history of incest and 152 women with a history of incest who were not in treatment provides support for the negative effects of specific incest factors. With the nonpatient sample, half reported either no effects or only slight residual effects, one quarter perceived substantial negative effects, and another quarter perceived major negative effects, including negative feelings about men, sexual behavior, or themselves. For the women who were not in treatment, the effects were more negative if the incest was forced or violent, involved penetration, continued over a prolonged period, and was with a person substantially older, usually a father or stepfather. The effects of incest on the patient sample paralleled those of the nonpatients, although far more of the patients experienced the specifically negative factors. Thus 75 percent of the patients' experiences were with father or stepfather compared to 28 percent of the nonpatients, 21 percent of the experiences were forced or violent compared to 3 percent, and 51 percent were of long duration compared to 19 percent.[89]

Twenty-two women students reporting sexual contact when they were under eighteen with a family member who was five years older were compared with students who had not had an incest experience. Fathers were the older family member for 41 percent of the women, and brothers for 32 percent. Intercourse was experienced by 27 percent, and oral-genital contact by 32 percent. The average age at the onset of the incestual experience was 7.8 years. For one-third of the women, it continued for six to ten years.

Incest women had higher test scores for depression, lower self-esteem, poorer body image, and less sexual satisfaction. They also reported more problems in social adjustment. Family variables differed for the two groups. Incest women reported less family cohesion and less involvement with parents "in the more abstract aspects of their upbringing."[90] But physical abuse may have confounded these findings, since it was reported by 28 percent of the incest women compared with none in the comparison group.[91]

A 1992 report found that fifty-two women in treatment who reported a history of incest were more likely than twenty-three psychiatric patients not reporting incest to be diagnosed with agoraphobia (fear of being outside the home alone), alcohol abuse, depression, panic disorder, post-traumatic stress disorder, and simple and social phobia. Incest had included fondling for 96 percent, oral sex for 35 percent, and sexual intercourse for 36 percent. Again, physical, nonsexual abuse was high in the incest group (60 percent) but absent in the contrast group. The authors acknowledge that persons for whom the experience was damaging may be over-represented in their sample: "This was a treatment population, not a random sample of incest victims."[92]

### Clinical Studies: Negative Effects on Male Children
Studies of males involved in childhood incest are less common. In a clinical sample of eight men incest with the mother was found to be associated with later problems in maintaining intimate, heterosexual relationships.[93] When the Minnesota Multiphasic Personality

Inventory (MMPI) psychological test was taken by forty-four male psychotherapy patients with a history of sexual contact before age sixteen (three-fourths of whom experienced incest, and three-fifths of these with their mothers), and by twenty-five male patients without early sexual contact, the men with a sexual contact history showed more rebelliousness, more thinking disturbance, more suspiciousness, and more anxiety. They also more often had histories of substance abuse, compulsive sexual behavior, and self-mutilation. Scores are not provided separately for the men with a history of incest.[94]

## Mixed Effects

Not all reports of incest document harm deriving from the experience. While suffering from some of the same limitations as the clinical reports, particularly in sampling, they challenge the universality of enduring trauma to the child.

In one report of mother-son and father-daughter incest that included prolonged sexual contact, subjects "were not seriously or permanently impaired psychologically; [this was] by virtue of having developed healthy ego functioning prior to the incestuous episodes."[95] And another investigator reported, "Whereas incestuous involvement with a parent is psychologically crippling for some children, others are found not to have suffered any pronounced adverse effects from such an experience."[96]

The evidence documenting the harmfulness of incest is "inconsistent," according to another psychiatrist.[97] He sees a blurring of the effects of a dysfunctional family and the incestual experience.

> It is at least a possibility that the all-pervasive anguish to which incestuous behavior is a dysfunctional solution [in the child's home] is the same anguish which we later identify in the subsequent adult life of the little girl who was the alleged victim of this interaction—that the intense personal pain preceded the incestuous interaction and was in part its motive rather than its consequence . . . In truth the effect of incest on the lives of children is, at present, unknown. Many children do not seem to regard the experience of incest as highly unpleasant or traumatic, but describe it rather in a benign and matter-of-fact way.[98]

A child psychiatrist also looks to family pathology, rather than the sexual relationship, as critical. She reports that "the consensus among child psychiatrists is that factors related to the makeup of the incestuous family rather than the sexual behavior are the most pathogenic."[99]

## Psychiatric and Legal Responses

Forty years ago, the author of a major text on psychiatry and law wrote: "The exposure to sexual experience represents a real threat to the life of a child. Anyone who tampers sexually with a young child is potentially a killer and hence a dangerous individual outside prison walls."[100] When incest is discovered, the goals of psychiatry and the law include preventing further trauma to the child, deterring future child-parent sex, and punishing illegal conduct. The best means toward these ends vary from family to family.

Traditionally, children were removed from the home. In flexible programs, however, the nature of the home environment, its amenability to change, and the availability of alternate resources dictate whether removal is in the child's best interest. Traditionally also, offending parents were nearly always removed from the home and often imprisoned for long periods. Thus, the family was physically disrupted, and one consequence was less income. This approach, too, may be modified.

A community-based treatment program offers hope that additional family trauma in incest families can be avoided.[101] Jail sentences are directed at reconstituting the family. Incarceration time is short, there is a work-release program, and family therapy is instituted. Reported rates of repeated incarceration for those completing the program are about 1 percent, compared with up to 20 percent in other studies.

Another program for reuniting fathers and their families over a one- to three-year period has provided treatment for over three hundred families.[102] The treatment has five phases. Phase I involves individual, group, and family therapy (without the offender), and marital therapy for both parents. Phase II permits visitation with the offender outside of the home. Phase III includes home visitation. Phase IV permits overnight visitation. Phase V is a completion of the reunification process. There is not equal parenting, however. The mother makes all child welfare decisions, and the father is not alone with the children, nor does he discipline them. This program has been operating for eight years. One-third of the families have been reunited, but recidivism rates remain to be reported.

Other research suggests that cases leading to official legal action—rather than being dealt with informally—produce more severe and lasting ill effects on children.[103] An American report concluded: "Most of the psychological damage, if any, stems not from the abuse but the interpretation of the abuse and the handling of the situation by parents, medical personnel, law enforcement and school officials, and social workers."[104] Similarly, an English report concluded: "The degree of lasting harm suffered by victims . . . seems to flow predominantly not from the sexual nature of the experience, but rather from other sources of shock associated with it, notably the use of violence or intimidation or the abuse of parental powers. The subsequent intervention of parents, or other authorities, in order to bring the offender to justice often seems to aggravate the damage caused by the offence itself."[105]

The strongly negative American attitude toward adult-child sexuality is not universally shared by other Western nations. A review of cases reported to the Netherlands State Police found that "most Dutch parents reacted rather calmly to sexual offenses committed against their children . . . [a]s long as no danger is involved, people react less emotionally . . . [t]he same trend can be traced in the efforts of the police officers to help not only the victims but also the perpetrators . . . the majority of sexual offenders are not severe criminals, but people who are maladjusted and very shy . . . [S]ome of them show a genuine interest in children."[106]

## Reporting Laws

In the United States, all fifty states mandate reporting suspected child sex abuse. Reporting is required of any health practitioner, including optometrists and dental hygienists. In California, anyone who fails to make a child abuse report when he or she knows or reasonably should know of an instance of child abuse is guilty of a misdemeanor punishable by up to six months in jail.[107]

The California statute mandating reporting withstood constitutional challenge. A father's argument that being reported by his clinician infringed on his interest in psychiatric care failed when the court ruled that the state's interest in protecting children from abuse outweighed the father's interest in seeking a cure.[108] But in Michigan, the circumstances surrounding an instance of reporting were held to be a violation of a patient's rights. In that case, a man who wanted psychological help for a homosexual relationship with a minor contacted a counseling service several times to inquire about confidentiality, and each time he was assured that his statements would be strictly protected. Yet he was reported to the state's Department of Social Services, who notified police. At his trial, the court dismissed charges on the grounds that prosecution would frustrate the purposes of the state's Child Protection Law, and that prosecution in this case violated due process guarantees. The decision was upheld on appeal.[109]

To what extent are reporting laws followed? A survey of Washington State physicians in 1978 found that 58 percent would not report the sexual abuse of children. Among the reasons given were that reporting would be harmful to the family, that the problem could be handled more easily privately (two-thirds of the physicians), or (for the remainder) dissatisfaction with the way state social agencies handled cases.[110] A national survey of psychologists in 1981 found that one-quarter had never broken confidentiality and reported suspected child abuse, and a third had done so only "sometimes."[111]

Are reporting laws effective in protecting children? In Maryland, changes in reporting laws permitted researchers to review the number of self-referrals by adults who were sexually involved with children and the number of such children being identified at The Johns Hopkins Hospital under three levels of reporting.[112] From 1964 to 1988 sexual abuse by adult patients did not have to be reported. In 1988, disclosures by adult patients of sexual abuse that occurred while they were in therapy did have to be reported. In 1988, the disclosure rate by patients dropped from 21 per year to zero. In 1989, when even disclosures of abuse that occurred before entering treatment were to be reported, the rate of self-referrals dropped from 7 per year to zero. At the same time, there was no increase in the number of abused children who were identified. As the researchers point out, mandatory reporting of disclosures "deterred unidentified potential patients from entering treatment."[113]

## Trial Procedures

Balancing the goals of the criminal justice system in punishing perpetrators of child sexual abuse with the rights of defendants to a fair trial and the rights of children to be protected from additional or initial trauma has yet to find resolution.

The Sixth Amendment to the U.S. Constitution guarantees the defendant in a criminal trial the right to confront adversarial witnesses. Because some children may be traumatized by having to face the defendant and/or repeat the description of the sexual event in court, videotaped testimony is an alternative, and some states permit the use of a child's previously videotaped testimony at trial. Others have permitted an in-court screen that separates the child and the accused adult. In a recent case in Iowa, the one-way courtroom screen that blocked the defendant's view of the child was found to violate the Sixth Amendment.[114] In a case in Maryland, however, the use of one-way television for the child's live testimony, which allows the defendant to communicate with counsel electronically, after a showing of necessity for the child's welfare, was upheld (5–4).[115] However, the dissent was scathing. Justice Scalia, joined by Justices Brennan, Marshall, and Stevens, began: "Seldom has this court failed so conspicuously to sustain a categorical guarantee of the Constitution against the tide of prevailing current opinion."[116]

A child of any age may testify. In 1895, the Supreme Court ruled that no minimum age is required for a child to be a competent witness. Capacity to testify depends on "the intelligence of the child, his appreciation of the difference between the truth and falsehood, as well as his duty to tell the former."[117] Thus, the California Evidence Code provides that "except as otherwise provided by statute, every person, irrespective of age, is qualified to be a witness and no person is disqualified to testify to any matter."[118] The age at which children have been ruled competent to testify has been as young as three-and-a-half, this in a case where that testimony resulted in a life sentence for a father.[119]

The use of "anatomically correct dolls" in diagnosing sexual abuse and in helping children testify has provoked an as yet unresolved controversy. Children are presented with child and adult dolls that have genitalia and use them in play to act out sexual interactions. In some states, the use of such dolls has been codified. Thus, Michigan provides that "if pertinent, the witness shall be permitted the use of dolls . . . including . . . anatomically correct dolls . . . to assist . . . in testifying."[120]

Research to validate the use of anatomically correct dolls is under way. One study found that with young children referred for evaluation of possible sexual abuse, compared to those not referred for abuse, doll play elicited more "unusual" sexualized behaviors. The findings are somewhat tautological, however, since these children were suspected of having been sexually abused in part because they displayed "inappropriate" sexual behaviors.[121] Another study compared ten children who had a history of sexual abuse with ten other children, some of whom had been evaluated for physical abuse. The children were not matched for socioeconomic status. Nine children in the first group demonstrated sexual behaviors with the dolls, as did two children in the contrast group. These findings are suggestive of the test's usefulness, although in this small sample there were two false positives and one false negative. The presumably false positive children, eight and four years old, simulated oral and genital intercourse between the doll representing themselves and an adult doll.[122]

Reactions by courts to anatomically correct dolls have been mixed. After a father was convicted of sexually abusing his young daughter in a trial during which the child placed her index finger on the vaginal and anal openings of the doll and twisted it, the California Court of Appeal reversed on the ground that the significance of such doll play is not sufficiently accepted by the relevant scientific community. The evidence was held inadmissible in order to protect the jury against the "aura of infallibility" that may surround unproven methods.[123] By contrast, a North Carolina court upheld the conviction of a father after a four-year-old, who had told relatives and authorities that her father had put his "ding dong" into her "po po," pointed to a doll vagina and a doll penis and used the same terms to describe the alleged event.[124]

Also controversial is whether there is a valid psychological profile of a sexually abused child that is admissible at trial. A Utah court was not impressed: "The child abuse profile consists of a long list of vague and sometimes conflicting psychological characteristics that are relied upon . . . contrasting traits [include] 'regressive behavior' and 'pseudomature behavior,' 'acting out' or with-drawal' . . . [they] may also describe persons suffering from a wide range of emotional problems unrelated to sexual abuse."[125]

A series of Maine cases also rejected admissibility. In one, after an expert described the "indicators" frequently encountered with sexually abused children and concluded that a boy had been anally sodomized, the court held that "the validity of the summary of symptoms encountered in the population of [the expert's] patients is seriously impaired by selection bias. No comparison testing was done with children who were not victims of sexual abuse."[126] In another, after two therapists had testified that two children "exhibited behavior patterns symptomatic of sexual abuse . . . including non-compliance, inattention, regressive and hyperactive behavior,"[127] the court held that the basis of the testimony did not have "*sufficient reliability* to satisfy the requirements of relevance and helpfulness, and of avoidance of unfair prejudice."[128] In addition, the testimony that these diagnostic behaviors are "generally accepted in [the expert's] profession [did] not establish the scientific reliability of [the] conclusions."[129]

An expert's testimony that a child had been sexually abused, based partly on an unusual picture the child drew and partly on her showing two nonspecific behaviors,[130] was thrown out on appeal in Wisconsin. The picture was of a person with large triangular points on the center of the body that split the legs apart.[131] The expert admitted that she had never seen such a picture before. She also described the array of symptoms that are found in sexually abused children, including poor concentration, bed-wetting, low self-esteem, anger, fear, and either avoidance of sexual topics in conversation or a preoccupation with sex. The child had exhibited anger and fear with her father.

Although a "molested child syndrome" was also rejected in California as evidence that the child witness had been molested,[132] it was admitted in an early case in Hawaii and in another in Florida. The Hawaii court had concluded that the testimony "provided the jury with specific characteristics [the expert] had observed to be shared among children who had been raped by family members" and that the testimony linking the syndrome to the child and the implicit opinion that the child's testimony was believable, "would not otherwise have been available to the jury."[133] In a subsequent case, however, Hawaii agreed that, while an expert can explain the "seemingly bizarre" or contradictory behavior of sexually abused children, testimony that the behavior shown by the child witness is consistent with the crime is not admissible. The expert cannot testify that the child's testimony is believable. "It has not been demonstrated that the art of psychiatry has yet developed into a science so exact as to warrant such a basic intrusion into the jury process."[134] But Florida did admit such testimony because it was beyond the ordinary understanding of the jury.[135]

The "child sex abuse accommodation syndrome" (CSAAS) purports to describe a pattern of reactions among sexually abused children that could mislead some, including jurors, to conclude that abuse never occurred.[136] CSAAS includes delay in reporting the events and, most important, a retraction of earlier statements describing abuse. The "syndrome" has been introduced in courts to strengthen the prosecution's case when these behaviors are used by the defense to attack a child's credibility. Minnesota has permitted its use because the related testimony might help jurors who "are often faced with determining the veracity of a young child . . . who appears an uncertain or ambivalent accuser and who may even recant."[137] A Georgia trial court was convinced that "[such] information is not known to the average juror"[138] and permitted expert testimony that a child's behavior fit the clinical picture of an assaulted child. On appeal, however, the expert's testimony was held inadmissible because an opinion on this ultimate fact in the case, whether the child had been assaulted, could not be rendered unless the jurors were incapable of drawing their own conclusion.[139] California refused to admit CSAAS testimony intended to show that abuse occurred, because the testimony did not meet the test of scientific credibility, although the state did allow expert testimony on the significance of the child's reactions that was based on the expert's clinical experience.[140] In a later case, California permitted CSAAS testimony to "demystify" certain preconceptions jurors might have had about children's reactions that appeared inconsistent with a history of sex abuse.[141]

## Widely Publicized Cases of Alleged Sex Abuse

The McMartin Preschool molestation case in California presented a caricature of the current legal system. Charges were filed against seven defendants on three hundred counts of sexual abuse in 1984.

After two years of investigation, charges against five were dropped. The two remaining defendants were jailed without bail. Three more years passed before the trial began. It evolved into the lengthiest and costliest criminal trial in American history: two-and-a-half years and $15 million. The jury deliberated for over two months. It acquitted one defendant on all counts and the other on forty counts, but remained deadlocked on thirteen counts. The second defendant was retried on five of the remaining and strongest counts. The jury deadlocked on all five. By then, the two defendants had spent a total of seven years in jail without ever having been convicted on a single count, and the children had been subjected to years of repeated interrogation and testimony. One ten-year-old had spent sixteen days on the witness stand under cross-examination.[142]

The jurors' principal reason for not finding the defendants guilty was their perception that the children had been coaxed by professionals into reporting sexual abuse. The transcript of a therapist-investigator interviewing a little boy provides some basis for jurors' skepticism. The discussion involves the "naked movie star game," which the defendants were alleged to have played with the preschoolers.

> Interviewer (Int.): I thought that was a naked game.
> Boy: Not exactly.
> Int.: Did somebody take their clothes off?
> Boy: When I was there no one was naked.
> Int.: Some of the kids were told they might be killed. It was a trick. All right . . . are you going to be stupid, or are you smart and can tell? Some think you're smart.
> Boy: I'll be smart.
> Int.: [The puppet you used earlier in the play interview] is chicken. He can't remember the games, but you know the naked movie star game, or is your memory bad?
> Boy: I haven't seen the naked movie star game.
> Int.: You must be dumb.[143]

When the criminal (not civil) proceedings were finally over, the *Los Angeles Times* concluded, "Surely the longest criminal trial in history will yield the longest list of the right ways and wrong ways to approach such cases so that justice can be done without repeating the grotesqueries of this case. We owe at least that to our children."[144]

Another investigation run amok is described in the Supreme Court dissent in *Maryland v. Craig*.[145] In Jordan, Minnesota, an allegation of child sex abuse escalated into charges involving twenty-four adults and thirty-seven children and included allegations by eight children of multiple murders. Two dozen children were placed in foster homes.

The State Attorney General's report concluded that the children's testimony was "distorted" and in some cases "coerced" and resulted from "children [being] interrogated repeatedly, in some cases as many as 50 times."[146] As a result, "children [who did not at first complain of abuse] were separated from their parents for months." Quoting from the state report, the Court Justices wrote, "It was only after weeks or months of questioning that children would 'admit' that their parents abused them . . . In some instances, over a period of time, the allegations of sexual abuse turned to stories of mutilations, and eventually homicide."[147] Ultimately, three adults were tried for sexual abuse, one pleaded guilty, two were acquitted, and charges against twenty-one were dismissed. The Minnesota Attorney General's office concluded that there was "no credible evidence of murders."[148]

A third unhappy investigation commenced in England in 1987, when a pediatrician became convinced that the medical sign of "reflex anal relaxation and dilation" in children was indicative of sexual abuse. With that alleged sign, eleven children were sent to foster homes, even though none had complained of abuse. Other children seen in the hospital for a variety of medical, nonsexual problems were also given the test. If the alleged sign was present, their parents were denied access to them. In one month, 52 children from seventeen families were removed from their homes. In six months, 121 children from fifty-seven families were diagnosed as sexually abused. Sixty-seven children became wards of the court, and another 27 were removed from their homes. A major uproar resulted in a government investigation, and one year later 90 percent of the children were reunited with parents while review of the remaining cases continued. A Blue Ribbon English Inquiry Report concluded that "an honest attempt was made to address these problems [of sexual abuse] by the agencies. In spring 1987, it went wrong."[149]

## False Allegations during Divorce

The cry of "Sexual abuse!" has become the doomsday weapon in bitterly contested child custody disputes. One study of the validity of allegations of child sex abuse found that the average rate of substantiated claims was only 56 percent. Unequivocally false allegations ranged from 5 percent to 8 percent.[150] Other studies have found that allegations are false over 50 percent of the time.[151]

Our concern here is the extent to which the investigation of a false or unsubstantiated allegation harms the child. A further concern is that false or unsubstantiated allegations will invoke a cynical "cry wolf" attitude in the public that may ultimately dissuade the pursuit of genuine parental abuse.

A dramatic example of a child custody dispute in which one parent accused the other of sexual abuse is described in *Hilary's Trial*.[152] The child was spirited away from the accused father by the mother's mother and hidden on three continents while the mother remained jailed for refusing to divulge the child's location.

## Delayed Discovery

Delayed discovery is a civil law concept whereby the statute of limitations barring litigation is tolled or suspended for the time during which the victim may not be aware of having been wronged. One rationale is that otherwise, effective concealment of harm by the perpetrator would prevent redress by the victim. Because of the view held by many clinicians that victims of sexual abuse, notably incest, "may not recognize incest-related injuries because the symptoms may emerge long after the abusive relationship ended" and because "research indicates that for some victims the negative aftereffects of incest have a 'time bomb' quality,"[153] this concept has been extended to sexual abuse.

In one application of delayed discovery, a victim so traumatized by an event that it is repressed from memory could institute action many years later when the memory is recovered during the course of psychotherapy. In another, the victim may have recalled the event all along but not recognized its harmful effect until the recent psychotherapy.

Court decisions on delayed discovery have varied between

states. The Washington State Supreme Court held that it would not apply in sexual abuse because of the questionable validity of events recalled in psychotherapy. In *Tyson v. Tyson*,[154] the court was concerned not only with the problems inherent in stale claims, such as the absence of evidence and the unavailability of witnesses. It was also concerned because "[p]sychology and psychiatry are imprecise disciplines . . . unlike the biological sciences, their methods of investigation are primarily subjective and most of their findings are not based on physically observable evidence." The *Tyson* court quoted extensively from an article underscoring the questionable validity of "forgotten memories":

> . . . the psychoanalytic process can even lead to a distortion of the truth of events in the subject's past life. The analyst's reactions and interpretations may influence the subject's memories or statements about them. The analyst's interpretations of the subject's statements may also be altered by the analyst's own predisposition, expectations, and intention to use them to explain the subject's problems . . . The distance between historical truth and psychoanalytic truth is quite a gulf. From what "really happened" to what the subject or patient remembers is one transformation; from what he remembers to what he articulates is another; from what he says to what the analyst hears is another; and from what the analyst hears to what she concludes is another.[155]

*Tyson* was essentially overturned when the Washington legislature enacted a delayed discovery statute.[156]

In 1987 California refused to apply delayed discovery when the adult plaintiff had not suppressed all awareness of the sexual contact and knew that it was wrong. To the court, she suffered immediate harm even though alleging as an adult the prior failure to understand the nature and extent of her injuries and what had caused her emotional harm.[157] A 1989 California case, however, held that the time period for filing suit was suspended when it was proved that the sexual acts had been completely repressed from memory.[158] There, a woman alleged that she had been sexually assaulted by her father from infancy to the age of five, having recalled in group therapy memories of being manually penetrated and masturbated by him as an infant. Her therapist informed her that many of her current problems, which included sexual promiscuity, low self-esteem, alcohol and drug abuse, and suicidality were causally connected to these recalled events. A 1990 case held that the period for filing suit was also extended if the person had repressed understanding of the wrongfulness of the sexual acts.[159]

Montana held that delayed discovery did not apply when the person was aware of the sexual contact but did not know the extent of the resulting injuries and had not associated psychological problems with the abuse.[160] Wisconsin applied delayed discovery when, although aware of the abuse, the person did not discover until later the cause and extent of injuries. There, the plaintiff had argued that because of psychological coping mechanisms she could not perceive the existence or nature of her injury. A psychologist had concluded that because the behavior was of such long duration and frequency the victim had perceived it as natural behavior.[161] A federal court applying Illinois law initially extended the limitation period for filing suit for a thirty-six-year-old woman, where the events themselves had been repressed as a self-protecting psychological measure, but when that state later barred suits by persons over thirty, it dismissed the action.[162] Michigan applied the delayed discovery concept to sexual abuse in a case in which a woman allegedly recalled childhood sexual abuse after watching a television program.[163]

Under a 1991 California law, a person may bring an action for childhood sexual abuse within eight years after becoming an adult or three years after discovering that an injury or illness suffered as an adult was caused by childhood sexual abuse.[164] If the person bringing the action is twenty-six or older, he or she must file a supporting document before naming each defendant in the complaint. The document must show that in the opinion of both the person's attorney and a qualified mental health practitioner, there is reason to believe that the person was subjected to the abuse. The court must review these documents *in camera* (in private chambers) and find "reasonable cause" for filing the action. The safeguards introduced in California may help prevent outright fraud by the alleged victim, but they do not answer the criticisms that some therapists proclaim that nearly all of their patients eventually recall childhood sexual abuse and that an attorney, presented with a mental health professional's judgment that abuse did occur and the prospect of a major civil award for damages, may see no obstacle to going forward.

Here behavioral science can contribute valuable data. What is known about the validity of memories of early childhood that are recalled for the first time in the course of psychotherapy? To what extent are they "screen memories," which serve to protect the patient against associated painful memories that did not involve sexual behavior? To what extent can they be induced by the overt or covert suggestions of an authority figure or of others who expect to find them?

A report on group therapy for women who were suspected of having been sexually abused but who could not fully remember it, suggests that memories of sexual abuse in childhood may be recalled in therapy but does not resolve all doubt about their authenticity.[165]

> Patients with mild to moderate memory deficits were often not aware of these deficits prior to participation in group. However, in regard to the intense stimulation of hearing other group members' stories, these patients reported recovery of additional memories . . . Almost all of the women who entered the group complaining of major memory deficits and who defined a goal of recovering childhood memories were able to retrieve previously repressed memories during group treatment.[166]

External validation of some group members' memories was not forthcoming, however, and support for those of some others falls short of convincing proof.

## Political Controversy

Although the scientific evidence leaves many questions about the effects of adult-child or adult-young adolescent sexual interaction unanswered, the topic evokes strong emotion that has led to politicalization.

Citizen groups such as VOCAL (Victims of Child Abuse Legislation) argue that community anxiety over child sex abuse does more harm than good. The organization, which is described as "a support group consisting primarily of persons falsely accused of child abuse,"[167] points to the high rate of unsubstantiated reports of child abuse and the fact that even an investigation with negative findings stigmatizes innocent adults. But not everyone agrees. One writer states that "Overreporting is *necessary* in order to net a high enough proportion of actual cases to reduce morbidity and mortality."[168] The value judgment here appears to be that innocent adults and children should be traumatized in order to snare cases of actual sexual contact, of whatever consequence.

Another group organized more recently is the False Memory Syndrome Foundation. It consists of hundreds of parents of adult children who contend that they and their children have been victimized by therapists who have induced invalid memories of childhood sex abuse that were allegedly repressed for decades.

Researchers and health care workers are beginning to be concerned that the politics of child sexual abuse are compromising efforts to protect children from genuine victimization. This politicization is stressed by a psychologist and lawyer in a 1991 review of child abuse investigation and litigation.

> Differences in expert opinion are sometimes construed as if . . . they were political or ideological schisms rather than merely differences in professional judgments. Experts who sometimes fail to confirm an allegation of . . . abuse may be subject to an insinuation that they condone child sexual abuse. The acrimony that such insinuations carry has the risk of producing a "Gresham's Law" of expertise in which weak expertise drives out good expertise . . . Clinicians who do not routinely confirm allegations of sexual abuse may experience a subtle intimidation . . . The pressures . . . come from some evaluators who specialize in [such] assessment . . . and from "child protection" groups.[169]

Consistent with this critique, at a scientific congress when I quoted the psychiatrist Arthur Green's critique of the sex abuse research methodology mentioned earlier, a prominent sex abuse researcher dismissed it because "he testifies for the perpetrators." Commenting on the politicization of research on child sexual abuse, another reviewer observes, "Researchers and writers who favor descriptive, empirical, or phenomenological models and who may wish to establish a relative degree of objectivity in this difficult field and avoid the rhetorical excesses typical of much of the new research often are attacked by victimologists for 'contributing to the disinhibition of child molesters' [and] 'condoning adult-child sex.' "[170]

## Future Research

This emotional, political interface between sexual behavior and law will be informed by more sophisticated sexual science research. Representative samples of children who have experienced sexual interaction must be obtained, and they should be periodically reevaluated. Standardized clinical interviews must be used, along with valid objective instruments.

Variables that should be analyzed to assess the potential impact of the sexual experience should include the age and gender of the child, the age and gender of the older person, the relationship between the parties, the specific sexual interaction, the frequency and duration of the interaction, the level of preexisting family discord or accord, the preexisting psychological or psychosocial status of the child, and any psychiatric intervention for the child.

Control groups of demographically matched children and adults (perhaps from the same family) without histories of childhood sexual interaction or with histories of other traumatic experiences, including nonsexual physical abuse or parental loss, must be used so that the specific effects of the sexual experience can be identified.

The influence of parents' response to the sexual event and of intervention by the criminal justice system, independent of the actual sexual experience, should also be studied, as should children who are the subjects of false allegations of abuse that lead to extensive investigation.

Researchers must be careful in recruiting subjects. Assuming *arguendo* that not all experiences of incest are recalled as traumatic and damaging, how likely is it that persons with neutral or positive experiences will come forward in response to an announcement like this: "Female nurse-researcher seeks women aged 18 or older who had an incestuous experience . . . to participate in a study of *victims* of incest."[171]

In assessing the effects of child-adult sexual interaction, researchers must use methods that are objective and do not load the dice. A widely cited study of females with a history of incest, for example, trained interviewers to ask, "Overall, how upset were you by this experience—extremely upset, somewhat upset, or not very upset." Presenting the option "not at all upset" was left to the discretion of the interviewer.[172] There was no option for the experience being recalled as positive. Another widely quoted study coded sexual experiences as negative if there was an age discrepancy of more than five years between the parties, even if subjects reported their reactions as neutral.[173]

An additional research problem arises with "high-risk" populations that are studied retrospectively. A frequently cited study linking childhood sexual abuse in girls to later prostitution found that 55 percent of prostitutes reported abuse.[174] Apart from the fact that socially deviant adults may self-servingly report traumatic childhood experiences, correlates of the outcome behavior, in this case prostitution, must also be controlled for. Thus, in a study using prostitutes and a nonprostitute control group matched for age, race, and education, although 45 percent of prostitutes did report sex abuse, this percentage was not significantly different from that of the control group.[175]

Sexual scientists and legal scholars need to do more research on the effectiveness of laws designed to protect children. Are mandatory reporting laws for health care workers bringing more cases of damaging sexual interaction to the notice of those who can ameliorate the harm? Or are they resulting in greater secrecy by perpetrators and the avoidance of health care workers who might effectively intervene?

Are extensive penalties after conviction facilitating or inhibiting disclosure, or testimony, or conviction? Will juries be less likely to find guilt "beyond a reasonable doubt" when the sentence is severe? Do criminal laws deter the commission of intrafamily sexual interaction with children, or are the family dynamics behind incest not amenable to control by the threat of imprisonment? Are the constitutional safeguards of a fair trial for defendants charged with sex abuse invoking more damage to the child than some instances of the sexual interaction itself? Is the public condemnation of adults suspected of sex abuse so severe that no defendant is ever acquitted of the charge, even if found "not guilty" by a court?

Clearly, children and adolescents are sexually abused by older persons, including their parents. Although some reports are false, scientists need not revert to Freud's skepticism over whether fathers were ever sexually involved with their children or his assertion that his female patients were invoking fanciful experiences to question whether all reports are genuine. And membership in the Rene Guyon Society or the North American Man-Boy Love Association is not required in order to question whether every instance of intergenerational sexuality is damaging.

Ultimately, scientists, if no one else, must be objective in their approach to this emotional issue. Judgmental terminology regarding intergenerational sexuality is more dramatic than that in the earlier psychiatric literature on homosexuality. There, patients were labelled perverts and psychopaths. Here, the experience is always *abuse*, the children are invariably *victims*, the adults are *perpetrators*, and those who later report childhood sexual experiences are, without apology to victims of the Nazi Holocaust, *survivors*.

# 9

# Sex Education

Sex education for children in the public schools is an incendiary topic. It is also an ambiguous term. What is sex education? What age are the children?

A group called the Christian Crusade exemplifies the organized opposition to sex education. One of their publications states that "[s]ex educators are in league with sexologists who represent every shade of muddy gray morality, ministers colored atheistic pink, and camp followers of every persuasion, off-beat psychiatrists to ruthless publishers of pornography."[1] "What the sex educators have in mind is simply this. Sex should be as easily discussed as any other subjects in the curriculum, and any inhibitions or moral and religious taboos should be eliminated. . . . If this is accomplished, and the new morality is affirmed, our children will become easy targets for Marxism."[2]

Advocates of sex education rank its importance with the "three R's"; thus, failure to receive education in this area significantly handicaps a person in later life. But parents opposed to sex education in the public schools do not argue against education per se. Rather, they demand that they control the timing of such training and its content. In response, professional sex educators point out that parents often neglect to inform their children about relevant matters during the years when it would be effective in guiding them toward positive experiences. They also point out that two generations ago more than half of the boys questioned reported that neither parent contributed anything to their sexual education. Four-fifths of the boys received no information from their fathers,[3] and when information was provided, it was often erroneous or misinterpreted.[4] Educators argue further that some parents impart a view of sexuality that is ultimately both socially limiting and psychologically damaging.

Reason may be injected into this dispute by calling on the data of sexual science and the principles of law. Can a legal analysis derived from the rights of parents to guide the education of their children, the rights of children, the rights of teachers, and the power of the state to educate fashion a coherent response to those who would challenge school programs? What does research reveal about the effects of formally providing children, at various ages, with information of varying sexual content?

# Rights

## Parents

In the nineteenth century, parents challenged a variety of prescribed school courses, including music,[5] rhetoric,[6] debating, and composition writing.[7] The challenges failed. Because these subjects are closer to the three R's than is sex education, however, their precedential value is limited. Rulings in a number of twentieth-century cases, by contrast, allowed parents substantial latitude in educating and raising children. Thus, although the state has considerable authority in mandating the type and duration of education, the Supreme Court upheld, for example, the demand of Amish parents to withdraw their children from school after the eighth grade so that they could indoctrinate them into their way of life and preserve their unique tradition.[8]

Parents' authority to control their children's education was also underscored in Nebraska's unsuccessful challenge to private schools teaching children a foreign language.[9] In that case, the Supreme Court found a Fourteenth Amendment right to "marry, establish a home and bring up children" and held that the "power of parents to control the education of their own [children]" was within the ambit of the due process clause.[10] The Court has also upheld the parental right to have children educated in a parochial school.[11]

Parents most frequently object to sex education in the public schools for religious reasons. But the compelling state interest in children's welfare, in one instance against child labor, trumped parental religious doctrine. A state law prohibiting children from selling magazines was held applicable to a nine-year-old member of the Jehovah's Witness faith, whose religious duty it was to sell religious tracts.[12]

### Children

When the Supreme Court held that a minor defendant was entitled to counsel and other constitutional rights in a criminal case, children's rights in general took a large step forward.[13] In a later case involving a student protest against the Vietnam war, students were held to be "persons" under the Constitution: "They are possessed of fundamental rights which the state must respect."[14] Children have the right "to inquire, to study, to evaluate, to gain new maturity and understanding."[15]

### Teachers

Although teachers, too, have rights, the courts have not recognized their primary authority in decision making over course content. They do, however, have a right to teach, and "academic freedom" has gained limited court protection.[16]

## Cases

### School Curricula

Early court challenges to sex education in grade school involved mandatory class attendance. In 1971, complaining New Jersey parents charged that compulsory course attendance violated several amendments to the U.S. Constitution (the First, Ninth, Tenth, and Fourteenth) and sections of the New Jersey constitution.[17] The results of a house-to-house canvass, which found that a majority of persons agreed that sex education courses are "necessary and beneficial for the students," were advanced by the state as an argument for instituting the program. Course topics included masturbation, intercourse, and contraception. The parents contended that the teachings were contrary to their religious beliefs and were establishing a *de facto* religion. Although the New Jersey legislature had recommended to the Board of Education that there be a system for excusing children if a parent filed a written objection, the Board rejected this option as having a potentially "far-reaching impact" on the school system. It would "open the door for demands for exclusion, *on grounds of conscience,* for . . . health and physical education, biology, [and] history."[18] Paradoxically, local boards of education had the option of "refrain[ing] from approving any sex education in the schools under their control."[19] Thus *all* students could be denied access to sex education but not *selected* students.

In deciding whether course attendance could be mandated, the New Jersey court asked: "[C]an it readily be said that all parents are neglectful and unfit to explain sexual relations or to teach their children a moral way of life? Is the State, through the educational system, permitted to encroach upon the patterns and molding of a child's behavior in personal family religious beliefs?"[20] Applying a balancing test to the interests of family and state, the court concluded, "It may be that the individual's conscience may be fully protected by excusal from the program, or it may be that attendance is required because failure to perform the imposed duty has a [h]armful effect upon society generally and therefore involves a detriment to others."[21] Refusing vaccination against a contagious disease was cited as an example of a case in which an individual's refusal of state-mandated participation could endanger others. Here, however, the negative impact on society of foregoing sex education was not clear. The parents prevailed.

New Jersey had another turn to consider the question, this time because of a Board of Education regulation requiring each local school district to implement a "family life" program,[22] since only 40 percent of the state's pupils were receiving sex education under the prior "recommended but not required" policy. Sociological and medical statistics buttressed the argument for sex education: one in every five births was to a female fifteen to nineteen years old; 60 percent of females giving birth in that age range were unmarried; 80 percent of pregnant teenagers dropped out of school permanently;

teenagers' babies were more likely to be premature; and the rate of venereal disease was increasing. Further, Gallup poll results indicated that 77 percent of the general public and 95 percent of students favored sex education in schools. The Board of Education report pointed out, however, that "no research studies had been found that showed a correlation between teaching about human sexuality and a reduction in teenage pregnancy or venereal disease."[23]

In contrast to the earlier case, these New Jersey parents were permitted to review materials prior to classroom use. A written objection on moral or religious grounds would excuse the child from the objectionable portion of the course. Still, parents argued that requiring students to assert their objection "exerts an intolerable pressure" on them and cited the school prayer case holding that children refusing to pray would suffer social stigma.[24] To the court, however, the prayer case was an Establishment clause case aligning the state with religion, while this was a Free Exercise (of religion) case. The court held that if public schools could *not* offer "offending" curricula, *that* would violate the Establishment clause.

Sexual science presumptions were given legal weight. If the Family Life Committee Report supported the view that a relationship exists between the program and the reduction of teenage pregnancy and venereal disease, "a presumption of reasonableness attaches" and "the burden of proving unreasonableness falls upon those who challenge . . . [Thus] merely assert[ing] that there are no data that prove that the program will have any effect . . . does not satisfy [the parents'] burden."[25]

A sex education program in Honolulu, Hawaii, was the focus of a pioneering lawsuit by parents of fifth- and sixth-grade students.[26] The program consisted of a film series of fifteen "lessons," which were developed for educational television. Parents were given the opportunity to view the "lessons" on public television at 10 P.M. (when presumably, ten- and eleven-year-olds are asleep) and were allowed to withdraw their child from a particular lesson. In court, the parents based their objections on invasion of privacy. They cited cases that permitted parents to have their children learn a foreign language or be taught in a religious school. But the court read those cases as supportive of freedom of speech, rather than the right of privacy. Parents also argued that their free exercise of religion was violated. Some clergymen testified that the series violated their religious beliefs, whereas representatives of other faiths saw no violations. The excusal system defeated this antireligion argument. The court cited the case in which a state sought to prohibit the teaching of Darwinian theory.[27] There, the Supreme Court held that the "First Amendment does not permit the State to require that teaching and learning must be tailored to the principles or prohibitions of any religious sect or dogma."[28]

The California constitution establishing the right of privacy, along with the usual amendments to the U.S. Constitution, was the basis for another suit.[29] California law provides that any written or audiovisual material to be used in class will be made available to parents before the class and that a parent can request that the child not attend. Another part of the Education Code provides that if instruction conflicts with parents' religious training and beliefs, the child can be excused. Prior to the court action, few parents—less than 5 percent—had taken the opportunity to excuse their children.

The curriculum was designed to be "value-free." Teachers were instructed that in discussing "normal" sexual development, they were not to indicate that certain behaviors are "good" or "bad." Intercourse was to be discussed "within the framework of human love of husband and wife and the means of producing new life." Regarding masturbation, contraception, abortion, and divorce, the teacher was to "indicate that there are many different points of view . . . [and] that it is important that each person live within the framework of his religion or moral code of behavior." With masturbation, for example, if "excessive or prolonged," this was thought by psychologists to be "a symptom of other emotional problems [and] some religions regard masturbation . . . as an immoral act."[30]

Based on this curriculum, the court disposed of the parents' contention that the program promoted immoral sexual intercourse. Furthermore, "[t]he Constitution of the United States does not vest in objectors the right to preclude other students who may voluntarily desire to participate in a course of study under the guise that the objector's liberty, personal happiness or parental authority is somehow jeopardized."[31]

*Student Materials*

The sex education of high school students through a research questionnaire conducted by other students ran into substantial opposition in a New York City high school.[32] The students proposed to query their peers about their sexual attitudes, preferences, knowledge, and experience. The anonymous twenty-five-question survey asked about attitudes toward traditional sex roles in dating, premarital intercourse, contraception, homosexuality, masturbation, and abortion. It asked students to record their sexual orientation and sexual experiences. Results were to be tabulated and the responses interpreted in the student newspaper.

The school argued that "serious harm" could result if certain students were confronted with these questions. But the trial court found that for students in the final two years of high school, those "who are sexually immature or who have certain conflicts would be more likely to resolve these problems if they are faced, as a result of peer pressure . . . [and being] made aware of the fact that many other students have similar problems."[33] Thus it permitted the survey for the older students.

The appellate court focused on affidavits and the testimony of behavioral science experts.[34] One expert witness stated that there were "almost certainly some students with a 'brittle' sexual adjustment" and that for them, "the questionnaire might well be the force that pushes them into a panic state or even a psychosis."[35] One psychiatrist argued that with younger students, aged twelve to fourteen, the questions "might well lead to serious emotional difficulties."[36] A psychologist asserted that a "large number" of students would need help dealing with anxiety reactions.[37]

The students also called in experts. One educational psychologist pointed out that students are otherwise "bombarded with sexually explicit materials."[38] Another argued that the topics covered were of normal interest to adolescents and were common subjects of conversation. A clinical psychologist observed that "in the more than 25 years of active experience . . . I have *never* encountered a situation in which a child, adolescent or adult has been adversely affected by a questionnaire!"[39] Yet another expert, with some humor, described the "sexually-laden" environment of the students "walking to and from school, [who] meet prostitutes, are handed advertisements for massage parlors, and witness homosexual court-ships . . . [Thus], any youngster sufficiently fragile to suffer serious anxiety or depression upon reading questions which s[he] may ignore with impunity or respond to anonymously, is a youngster too fragile to have survived the trip from home to school."[40]

These views notwithstanding, the appellate court extended the trial court's ban on giving the questionnaire to the younger students to *all* students.

A strong dissent argued that for the less informed students and those with less access to peer sharing of attitudes and experiences, the questionnaire "may serve as an outlet for private communica-tion, and a reassurance about similar matters . . . [and] may well serve a valuable educational purpose in reducing fantasy and dis-tortion and relieving anxiety."[41] An expert was quoted who argued that "squelching this student proposal can only serve to drive sex-ual feelings further underground,"[42] and another who concluded: "It is much more likely that collection and dissemination of relevant facts and attitudes from peers will prove to be constructive and useful."[43]

Another group of students was more successful. The Fourth Circuit Court of Appeals upheld a trial court decision holding that their rights were violated when a school board attempted to prohibit publication of an article entitled "Sexually Active Students Fail to Use Contraception."[44]

## Innovative Education

What is "sex education" at home? Does it legitimately include parental sexual intercourse in view of the child? The Supreme Court of Florida faced this question.[45] According to a Florida stat-ute, "[a]ny person . . . who shall knowingly commit any lewd or lascivious act in the presence of [a child under fourteen] . . . shall be deemed guilty of a felony."[46] In this case, a mother stated that after her son, who was under fourteen, asked "how babies are made," she and the boy's stepfather showed him in the bedroom. The court held that "sexual intercourse between a husband and wife in the presence of a child under fourteen years of age for the purpose of demonstrating to such child the method of procreation of the human race is a lewd and lascivious act."[47] To the dissent the statute was not "intended to invade the privacy of a family and a private home." The dissent was not particularly enthusiastic about the parental strategy: "True, what they did is shockingly disagreeable and reprehensible to most of us," but it was "willing to give them the benefit of the doubt that they believed (although perhaps mistakenly) they could give their own son mature understanding and instruction in the biological facts of procreation in the privacy of their home."[48]

## Research Studies

Although parents may argue for the exclusive right to provide sex education to their children, few apparently exercise that right. A 1980 study revealed that only 15 percent of mothers and less than 8 percent of fathers of children up to eleven years old had talked to their children about premarital intercourse, that fewer had discussed venereal disease, and that even fewer had discussed birth control.[49]

Each year, American teenagers bear over half a million children, the vast majority of them reportedly unplanned, and induced abortions terminate a comparable number of adolescent pregnancies.[50] There is general agreement that teenage sexuality can have harmful results: teenage mothers are economically and psychologically unprepared to support the children they bear out of wedlock, and sexual activity increases the transmission of venereal disease. The children of teenage mothers face a higher risk of being stillborn or dying as newborns, and of serious physical handicap.[51] They also perform less well on intelligence measures.[52] The young mothers suffer too. Of a group of one hundred teenage mothers, 60 percent were on welfare, twenty-five of thirty-six who married were divorced in five years, and most dropped out of school. These one hundred teenagers gave birth to 340 babies during the five-year period of study.[53]

Are the sources of information about sex inadequate for adolescents? In 1915, parents were the basic source of sex information for only 4 percent of children.[54] In 1926, 80 percent of boys received their first sex information from other boys.[55] In the 1980s, in a study of a thousand students, peers were still cited as the single most common source of information, and they were the major source for homosexuality, petting, and prostitution. The media were also influential, but schools accounted for only 15 percent.[56]

Within the home, mothers have provided virtually all sex information. Comparing the sexes, females have been more dependent on mothers, males on peers. The areas in which facts have been most distorted are homosexuality, masturbation, and seminal emissions, while the most factually accurate areas are conception and menstruation. Abortion is the third area about which adolescents are most reliably informed, with the media providing most of the information.[57]

Does sex education come too late? Ten thousand males and females aged fourteen to twenty-two were interviewed and reinterviewed about sex education and sexual experiences, thus allowing for the sequencing of these events.[58] For females fourteen or younger at the time of their initial experience of intercourse, only a quarter had taken a sex education course. For females fifteen to seventeen at first intercourse, only half had had a prior course. Males were even less likely to have had a course prior to initial intercourse—12 percent of those fourteen or younger. Even among males whose first intercourse was at eighteen, half had not had a sex education course. Only half of those who began intercourse at fifteen or sixteen had received contraception instruction. Although the initiation of sexual activity at fifteen or sixteen was positively correlated with having had a sex education course, the relationship was weaker than for other variables, such as whether the adolescent was a frequent churchgoer (lower rate), whether parents had more education (lower rate), and whether the adolescent was black (higher rate). In addition, teenagers who had taken a sex education course were somewhat more likely to use effective contraception. Thus, premarital pregnancy rates were not correlated with having taken a course.

Certainly, the state has a compelling interest in reducing unwanted pregnancies and the spread of sexually transmitted diseases. But can it demonstrate that sex education meets these goals? Studies of this assumption offer less than overwhelming support.

National sex education surveys were conducted in 1976 and 1979.[59] Three-quarters of the respondents said they had had a course related to sex education. For seven of twelve categories of

186 · Sex Education

students grouped by age, sex, race, and survey year, those who received sex education were more likely to be sexually active, but in five the reverse was found. "From these results, it would seem that there is no association between sex education (or its absence) and sexual activity."[60]

Black and white teenage females surveyed in 1976 who had had a course containing information about "modern methods such as the pill and the IUD"[61] and women surveyed in 1979 who had been instructed about "different types of contraceptive methods" showed a trend toward lower pregnancy rates. Combining results with various combinations of race and year, "there appears . . . to be fairly strong support for the argument that never-married, sexually active young women who have had sex education experience have fewer pregnancies than those who have not."[62]

Nearly two thousand women, aged fifteen to nineteen, were interviewed in 1986 about sex education and their use of contraception.[63] The study showed that education increased contraceptive use when the measure was whether the teenager *ever* used it (from 70 to 86 percent). But, the association was weaker for current use (about 60 percent). Some 40 percent of teenagers did not receive formal contraceptive instruction before their first intercourse. No consistent relation was found between exposure to contraceptive education and its use in a subsequent first intercourse. Those who received instruction about pregnancy and birth control were more likely to use birth control, but neither pregnancy education nor contraceptive education significantly effected the risk of premarital pregnancy. As with many studies in this area, no data were available on the quantity or quality of the sex education.

One promising report has described a hospital maternal and infant care center that was established in a high school comprehensive health class.[64] Sex education, pelvic exams, contraceptives (provided off campus), and contraceptive follow-up were given. Of the students who began using contraceptives, 86 percent were still using them one year later, and fertility rates declined by 56 percent over three years.

In an ambitious but disappointing major study, one hundred professionals rated the important characteristics of programs believed to facilitate the goals of sex education[65] and then selected sites that offered programs with those characteristics. Thus, the duration and content of the courses were known. There were short programs (one to sixteen sessions) and long courses (at least one quarter, and up to two semesters).

Unhappily for sex education advocates, the programs did not have a "measurable impact on most outcomes . . . most commonly there was very little change between the pre-test mean scores and the post-test . . . mean scores."[66] But many programs did increase knowledge about sexuality, with the shorter courses appearing to be more effective. A greater period of time had evolved from instruction to testing in the longer courses, however, and some increases in knowledge in the short-term disappeared in the second follow-up test.

In the face of generally negative results, the study author was not discouraged to the point of abandoning the cause. "If we abolished all school courses that did not measurably affect behavior outside the classroom, we would probably abolish English, history, all math beyond simple arithmetic, science, [and] foreign languages."[67]

At a commonsense level, providing factual information about methods of contraception and protection against the transmission of venereal disease should reduce unwanted pregnancies and disease. But there are problems in effecting these associations. The information comes too late, a school excusal system may withhold information from vulnerable students, some adolescents may take conscious risks, others may unconsciously deny risks, a sexual partner may exert pressure to ignore risks, and some adolescents may have an emotional need for pregnancy.

The hailstorm of controversy that has met sex education in the public schools has influenced school authorities to provide an excusal system. But there are accompanying risks. Parents whose beliefs are not in the mainstream and may prove a disadvantage to their children can prevent their children from receiving alternative information. And children excused from the classes are marked by peers as "different."

From the perspective of the state, the prevention of disease and unwanted pregnancy is compelling. Therefore, the state's method of meeting the need, if effective, narrowly focused, and minimally intrusive, should prevail. Here is a subject of rich legal potential for sexual science. But if states need to demonstrate program effectiveness, so far they are short of the mark. Research on the effects of sex education has not demonstrated much efficacy due to the factors described above and the difficulties in demonstrating causality in a complex, multidetermined system.

Apologists for the studies with apparently poor outcomes suggest, not without merit, that many academic programs would flunk if subjected to the same standards of effectiveness. But this disclaimer should not dissuade true believers from learning from minimally successful programs, designing better ones, and implementing valid outcome research.

Lost in the tabulated results, with their statistical levels of significance or insignificance, is an in-depth understanding of the experiences of students who participated or were not permitted to participate in sexuality curricula, the sexual decisions they later made, and why they made them.

Additional endpoints for evaluating sex education courses, other than whether the student gets or makes someone pregnant out of wedlock, or transmits or contracts disease, are needed. What of the quality of relating socio-sexually to a partner? What of the quality of parenting? Can these features of a lifelong role in sexual and family life be conveyed? Are they influenced by the courses currently designed to show only effects on the negatives of socio-sexual experience—teenage pregnancy and sexually transmitted disease?

# · 10 ·

# Prostitution

> The truth is that prostitution is one of the most attrac-
> tive of the occupations practically open to women who
> engage in it, and that the prostitute commonly likes her
> work, and will not exchange places with a shop-girl or
> a waitress for anything in the world . . . So long as the
> average prostitute is able to make a good living, she is
> quite content with her lot, and disposed to contrast it
> egotistically with the slavery of her virtuous sisters.
>
> H. L. Mencken, *In Defense of Women*

> The path to prostitution starts with a dysfunctional
> family and usually includes incest, rape, neglectful
> parents, abandonment. That leads to a lack of educa-
> tion and skills, an inability to cope with the pressures
> of a daily job, drug addiction, alcoholism, abusive rela-
> tionships.
>
> "Magdalene: Rehabilitation Project," *Los Angeles Times*

The "oldest profession" was intimately connected with religion as "temple" or "sacred" prostitution. It existed among the ancient Jews and included both male and female prostitutes. "The normal practice was to accept prostitution as a fact of life without any moral condemnation."[1] By 300 B.C., prostitution was highly devel-oped in the Orient.[2] In ancient Cyprus, women were reportedly required to prostitute themselves at least once to a stranger to become eligible for marriage.[3] Greece supported four general classes of prostitutes, ranging from an elite class comparable to contemporary mistresses, to musicians and dancers, to brothel prostitutes, to slaves and women with no social standing.[4] "The only women most Greeks had contact with in a social sense were prostitutes."[5] Among the Romans, "it was probably the main way a woman without inherited wealth or a husband could earn a living."[6]

Although little is known of any lesbian prostitution,[7] male-male prostitution has an ancient heritage. "Homosexual temple prostitutes existed among the Hebrews and in India. Boy harlots plied their trade in the antique civilizations of Egypt, Persia, Greece, Rome, China and Japan."[8]

Moral judgments aside, are there sexual science data that document the effects on the prostitute and the customer of engaging in sex for hire?

## Psychosocial Studies

### Adult Female Prostitutes

Kinsey's classic 1948 work on sexual behavior in males found that 69 percent had experienced sex with a female prostitute. Approximately 4 percent of all sexual outlets by men, single or married, were with female prostitutes.[9]

Several types of prostitute have been studied, among them the "call girl." The apparent benefits of this highest class of prostitution have been described along with the apparent therapeutic potential of client–call girl transactions. In one four-year study, a social worker watched, surreptitiously (to the men) through one-way mirrors and partly open doors, the sexual transactions of sixty-four call girls and twelve hundred male clients.[10] She concluded that "clients turned to the call girls not only for the satisfaction of sexual desires but also for the satisfaction of the emotional needs so often fulfilled by sexual relationships—needs for reassurance, intimacy, relaxation, adventure, self esteem . . . [t]he call girls . . . functioned effectively as paraprofessional therapists."[11] She found similarities between her profession and prostitution (at least as practiced by call girls). "Their work required skills in some ways parallel to those I had tried to develop as a social worker . . . [including] . . . intuitiveness and physical and emotional empathy on a professional basis."[12] Half of the men "put the call girl in the position of meeting a definable therapeutic need for crisis intervention, for ventilation of problems, for the expression of suppressed desires, or for sexual counseling." Others used sessions "to raise self-esteem, to restore their confidence in their own sexuality." Prostitution served as an "underground sexual health service."[13] Thus, she observes "[c]all girls should be trained in mental health principles, licensed and utilized as paraprofessional sexual health personnel: participant therapists."[14]

The women were not seen as exploited: "Someone who makes $50,000 to $100,000 a year [1974 dollars], lives in luxury, and has a work life considerably more interesting than that of a secretary or even many executives, can hardly be called 'exploited.'"[15] Nor were they psychiatrically compromised: "the ones I met were not self-destructive, frigid, nymphomaniacal, or desperate."[16]

Customers appeared to benefit beyond the immediate sexual experience. Some were otherwise lonely and had no other sexual outlet. Those who were married had a dissatisfying sexual relationship and did not want to threaten their marriage with a more serious affair. Some sought the woman's "sympathetic ear," while others used her to enhance their self-image or to answer questions about sexuality and aging.

A different view of brothel prostitution is provided by a French psychoanalyst.[17] "[U]nions in bordellos are consummated only between frigid women and impotent men. Underneath . . . boils an old grudge and pent-up aggression . . . To gain revenge on her father [for his lack of love], the girl seeks to debase his daughter, i.e., herself. To soil the maternal *imago* [for the lack of the mother's love to her son], the boy in his fantasies makes a harlot of his mother and debases her, too." The relations between a female prostitute and the man "are the unbreakable, solid ties between a man-hater and a woman-hater."[18] This researcher also conducted "ethnographic fieldwork." Before her psychoanalytic training, she had spent a month as a chambermaid in a French brothel.

Prostitutes have been classified by two researchers as "voluntary" or "compulsive." The first enters prostitution "more or less" on a rational basis and "mainly" by free choice. The second is psychoneurotically driven or addicted to narcotics. Prostitution offers women positive benefits: enhanced income, adventure, an undisciplined life-style, and an opportunity to be anti-establishment and to meet affluent men. But it can also entail negative features, such as physical and economic victimization, heightened exposure to a drug culture, venereal disease, and a brief professional career span.[19] Observing that "no one knows how to prevent prostitution while preserving fundamental liberties [and that] it has never to anyone's knowledge, and short of absolute tyranny on the one hand or absolute promiscuity on the other, been prevented in any sizable population group," the researchers conclude that "prevention should aim . . . not at prostitution, but at attempting to ensure that no woman who does not wish to be a prostitute should be obliged for any reason at all to become one."[20]

In one of the few studies to compare the psychological status of prostitutes and a nonprostitute control group, researchers interviewed and administered psychological tests to ninety-five prostitutes and ninety-five age- and education-matched women.[21] The prostitutes represented five categories: call girls, in-house workers (employed in brothels, massage parlors, photo studios), streetwalkers, drug addicts, and, interestingly, part-time prostitutes who were also suburban housewives.

Call girls and in-house prostitutes were similar to their matched controls on psychological tests. Although streetwalkers differed somewhat from their controls, the most striking differences were between the addicts and controls and the housewives and controls: these two types of prostitute were the most psychologically pathological. Surprisingly, the biggest difference between groups was between the housewives and controls. Housewives' test scores showed more symptoms of depression, mania, schizophrenia, anxiety, and sociopathy. According to the researchers, they "looked like schizophrenics."

The psychological status of the prostitutes was positive. "The female who engages in prostitution as her major occupation . . . is probably as mature and well adjusted as demographically similar females engaging in other occupations. In fact, if financial success is added to any criteria of successful adjustment, these kinds of prostitutes have a clear 'edge.' "[22]

## Adolescent Female Prostitutes

Of an estimated two million prostitutes in the United States, 600,000 are believed to be under eighteen. The average age of entry into prostitution is reported as fourteen (two years after the first experience with intercourse).[23]

In a recent study, adolescent prostitutes at correctional centers in New York and California were contrasted with two other groups: delinquent nonprostitutes and high school students.[24] On psychological tests, the prostitutes scored in the more pathological direction on most measures. They evidenced more depression and anxiety, more alienation, and a less favorable self-concept. On the "Attitudes toward Men Scale," their view of males was far more negative than that of the other two groups.

A questionnaire, interview, and field observation of adolescent and young adult streetwalkers on the street and in jail focused on early sexual experience.[25] Nearly three-fifths of the streetwalkers reported having been raped, and of these, one-third reported having been raped more than once. Of the adolescents, two-thirds had had a "forced/bad sexual experience," typically before age fifteen. Although half of the 133 prostitutes reported that a male at least ten years older had made sexual advances to them prior to their first intercourse, the authors of the study caution against concluding that "because our sample population of 'deviant' women were disproportionately victims of rape and incest, these sexual abuses were therefore the cause of deviance."[26] Further, some of this study's data are questioned in Chapter 8 on intergenerational sexuality, which reports a study's finding that nonprostitutes of the same social class did not have significantly different histories of sexual abuse.

## Male Prostitutes

According to the authors of an article on male prostitution, "a gay sex market thrives in every big city. It is a profit-oriented street-corner college for the recruiting, training, and selling of boys and men to older, affluent homosexuals."[27] Drawing on interviews with male prostitutes and customers, they describe four types of prostitute: the street hustler, the bar hustler, the call boy, and the kept-boy. Most of the prostitutes did not regard themselves as homosexual but "rationalize[d] [their] behavior" by insisting that the sex was solely for renumeration.[28] Among their motives were the promise of quick, easy money, the need for acceptance, a lack of job training, the unavailability of jobs, broken homes, and parental rejection. The status of the male prostitute was considered poor: "Most prostitutes . . . are self-destructive and their enterprise often ends in either disenchantment, arrest, venereal disease, alcoholism, drug addiction, or social ostracism."[29] Customers were "usually middle-aged and physically unattractive. . . . often they . . . seek bizarre and unusual sex acts which would not meet with acceptance in conventional gay society." "Deep hatred" was observed between the prostitute and customer and "[t]he hatred is mutual."[30]

One study interviewed male prostitutes, aged twelve to twenty-eight, and compared them with boys and men matched for age, educational level, and race.[31] Two-thirds of the prostitutes remembered an early homosexual experience (average age 9.6 years), and three-fifths of these remembered receiving a reward. By contrast, only 15 percent of the control group reported early homosexual behavior (average 9.2 years) and only 13 percent recalled a reward. Nearly three-fourths of the prostitutes were judged to be basically heterosexual. Only 6 percent defined themselves as homosexual.

Another study, also matching male prostitutes with nonprostitutes for age and socioeconomic status, found little support for the broken home hypothesis. But the families of male prostitutes were larger and more dysfunctional as measured by drug abuse and sexual relations between family members. Prostitutes scored higher on a depression symptom checklist. They experienced their initial sexual encounter at a younger age and with a person at least five years older. For two-thirds, the partner was male. In contrast to the previous study, two-thirds of the prostitutes considered themselves homosexual or bisexual.[32]

Although investigators described one hundred male prostitutes, aged fifteen to twenty-three, in seven American cities as "immature, irresponsible, and unstable," they reported that if viewed in another context, "it would be difficult indeed to label the group pathological." The men "drifted into prostitution following the path of least resistance. They were ill equipped educationally, vocationally, and by family conditioning to make their way in our complex competitive society."[33]

When 211 male street prostitutes were tested using a psychological symptom checklist, they showed higher levels of psychopathology than men who were not psychiatric patients but lower levels than psychiatric outpatients. Compared to the nonpatients, they were more suspicious, hopeless, and lonely. For 17 percent, HIV status was positive.[34]

An interview study described male prostitutes according to several categories. "Street hustlers" and "bar hustlers" were usually drifters but occasionally were supporting a wife and child through prostitution.[35] "Call boys" were more "socially presentable" and served as companions for dinner, theater, and so on. "Kept boys" had their school tuition paid, in addition to standard living expenses, and most of them also functioned as houseboys who performed a variety of nonsexual domestic tasks.

Two-thirds of the full-time prostitutes, call boys, and kept boys were runaways. Of those who reported a first sexual experience with a male, over half "were seduced," and two-thirds of these received money or favors. (The two-thirds who reported that their first heterosexual experience was with an older female also said that they were seduced.) More than half of the runaways described their relationship with the older male who introduced them to this work as "warm, affectionate, needed, and desirable. They could identify the father image [in him], the economic security, the acceptance, and the affection, and frequently described [him] as life-saving."[36] The sexual orientation Kinsey score rating of these men was over 3 (on the homosexual segment of the continuum). Call and kept boys were the most homosexually oriented.

The picture of the typical male prostitute was dismissed in this interview study: "As with their female counterparts, male prostitutes proved very different in their personal characteristics as well as in their involvement in prostitution. They were . . . loving, caring individuals and . . . rip off artists."[37] In addition, their backgrounds ran the demographic gamut "from delinquent school dropouts to well-educated, refined, college students; they come from inner-city projects and middle-class suburbs; from completely disintegrated families and from effective loving families."[38] Present involvement and future prospects were also diverse: "Some enjoy the participation, some tolerate it, others hate it . . . they may wind up as derelicts, in prison, or as successful business and professional men."[39]

Among their motives for entering prostitution were "prestige, money, dates," and "pleasurable sexual release." For kept boys, the benefits included "security and to some extent substitute fathers . . . opportunities for schooling, travel, [and] vocational training." One described the benefits as "a very successful blend of needs, my needs for sexual release and money are met, and the customer gets what he wants; everybody is happy."[40]

The sexual orientation of male prostitutes is still in dispute. Two early studies suggested that they were heterosexual. One reported male prostitutes who talked of their relations with girls "to assure themselves that they aren't queer," and only a few who admitted pleasure from homosexual relations.[41] Among adolescents in an institution for delinquent boys, homosexual prostitution was part of a generally delinquent pattern of activity, sanctioned by the gang. Male-male sex for these youths meant being the recipient of fellatio. The boys saw themselves neither as homosexuals nor as prostitutes.[42]

## Legal Aspects

Forty-nine of the fifty United States outlaw prostitution, in contrast to other Western nations such as England, the Netherlands, and Germany.

The American Law Institute's (ALI) proposed Model Penal Code of 1959 did not endorse the decriminalization of prostitution, although it did recommend the legalization of other previously criminal sexual behaviors, including homosexuality. The ALI acknowledged several problems associated with prostitution: that it encourages the spread of venereal disease, that it has become a source of profit for criminal groups who combine prostitution with other criminal activities, that it exerts a corrupting influence on government and law enforcement (with its amenability to bribery and extortion), and the view that it promotes social disorganization and undermines marriage and the home.[43] The ALI then considered these responses: prostitution cannot be eliminated, generally unenforceable laws promote extortion and arbitrary enforcement, legalization would diminish the opportunity for official corruption, the failure to provide prostitution may promote rape, and the spread of venereal disease may be better controlled by registration and health inspections.[44] Yet it still did not endorse decriminalization.

Court cases involving prostitution generally ignore psychological or sociological data describing the prostitute or the customer, focusing instead on whether prior cases that found a right of sexual privacy provide a basis for the protection of commercial sex. The fatal adjective is "commercial." Although a sexual act may be protected (or not, depending on the state), if it occurs for a fee it is relegated to state control. This conclusion follows in the wake of *Paris Adult Theatre I v. Slaton,* the 1973 pornography case in which the Supreme Court found no privacy right for viewing commercially available pornography in a public theater.[45]

A typical unsuccessful argument based on privacy came before the Missouri Court of Appeals in a 1978 sexual massage parlor case.[46] The court refused to apply the compelling state interest standard to protect the massage parlor because it could see no implicated "fundamental right." The state's police power and its concern for protecting the health, morality, and general welfare of the citizenry (a "rational basis") were sufficient. Noting that private sexual massage is not prohibited, but only massage for hire, the court removed the acts from the "sphere of a protectable right of privacy," citing *Paris Adult Theatre I.*

The massage parlor mounted a creative "overbreadth" argument that the statute also prohibited permissible acts. It argued that forbidding "touching, manual or otherwise . . . the anus or genitals of one person by another" for compensation would sweep away the activities of obstetricians, gynecologists, urologists, proctologists, nurses and babysitters."[47] But the court observed that "overbreadth" for conduct is not usually challengeable by those not affected by the law, and "robust common sense" held the posited offensive application to be "frivolous."[48]

Massage parlor operators also lost their sexual privacy argument in the Eighth Circuit, because to the court, the "appellant's right to privacy claim rests on their mistaken premise that the constitutionally protected right to privacy encompasses all sexual acts performed by consenting adults in nonpublic places. We do not agree . . . see [again] *Paris Adult Theatre I v. Slaton.*"[49]

In another case, the city of Detroit's "accosting and soliciting" ordinance was attacked by arguing that the statute prohibited consensual activity.[50] But the court dismissed the assumption that "everyone accosted in a public place will consent to a prostitute's solicitations," and then, in a somewhat disingenuous illustration, stated that in the case before the court, the persons solicited were police officers, who, although they had entered a sexual massage parlor, had not consented to being solicited for prostitution.[51]

The massage parlor argued that since prostitution is not a crime in the city or state, nor is fornication (although adultery is), the First Amendment's free speech provision prohibits criminal prosecution for soliciting someone to perform a noncriminal act. The court rejected this contention with one reasonable argument and another, less relevant one. That the speech is essentially commercial, and thus deserving of less protection, has legal precedent. Calling once again on *Paris Adult Theatre I* to note that "[c]ommercial exploitation of depictions, descriptions, or exhibitions of obscene conduct on commercial premises open to the public falls within a State's broad power to regulate commerce and protect the public environment"[52] is, however, not entirely to the point. Obscenity is by definition illegal, whereas prostitution per se, in the jurisdiction at issue, was not.

The defense in a Massachusetts case argued privacy and discriminatory enforcement against female prostitutes but not against their customers or male prostitutes.[53] The court found no protected right of privacy because the defendants' convictions were not based on acts performed in private (they were arrested for public soliciting). As for not prosecuting customers, the court pointed out that the statute was designed to attack "merely one phase of a problem."[54] Ignoring the customer, to the courts, was similar to not prosecuting a buyer of obscene material along with the seller. Although the statistical data on disparate sex enforcement against prostitutes presented in the appellate brief were not considered by the court because they had not been presented at trial, the court left the door open to future evidence: "[T]he Commonwealth cannot enforce [the statute] against female prostitutes but not against male prostitutes unless it can demonstrate a compelling interest [strict scrutiny]."[55]

An escort service challenged Nevada's strict licensing requirements in federal court.[56] The court noted that "the conduct for which the escort services claim constitutional protection is dating," characterized as a right of "interpersonal association."[57] To the court, however, the relationships protected by the Fourteenth Amendment due process clause are only those that attend the creation and sustenance of a family.[58] But the relationship between escort and client "lasts for a short period and only as long as the client is willing to pay the fee . . . [a]n escort may be involved with a large number of clients . . . [The court does] not believe that a day, an evening, or even a weekend is sufficient time to develop deep attachments or commitments."[59]

The escort service's First Amendment "expressive association" claim of protection fell next: "[T]he escort services make no claim that expression is a significant or necessary component of their activities. The services' advertisements . . . do not tout their employees' skills in conversation, advocacy, teaching, or community service . . . the escort services do not . . . ensure that any expression occurs."[60] The licensing requirements were upheld.

The dissent countered that "the right of two individuals to choose to associate together for reasons short of marriage is . . . deserving of full constitutional protection."[61] Whereas the County's licensing justification was prevention of infectious disease and fraud to patrons, to the dissent there were means less restrictive to meet these compelling state needs. For example, Nevada already had laws to counter disease through required weekly health examinations.

An equal protection argument that the penalties for female prostitutes were greater than for male customers was rejected in Pennsylvania, based on the state's "rational" view that eliminating prostitution and maintaining public health, safety, and morals is served to a greater extent by harsher treatment of prostitutes.[62] A later Pennsylvania case[63] found that, while there is a right to sexual privacy based on Supreme Court decisions, "the proscribed activity is *not* sexual activity but the *business* of engaging in sexual activity for hire . . . [i]t can hardly be maintained that appellant is deprived of a constitutional right to engage in intimate sexual relations merely because she is prohibited from charging a fee for such conduct."[64]

COYOTE (Call Off Your Old Tired Ethics), a national organization whose members are mostly prostitutes promoting sexual privacy, challenged Rhode Island's antiprostitution laws.[65] The privacy portion of the suit charged that not only was private sex for pay outlawed by the statute, but a wide range of consenting adult sexual acts without pay were also barred, including all extramarital sexual intercourse and "unnatural" forms of copulation, whether by the married or unmarried. After trial but before a judgment was made, the state amended its statute so that private consensual sexual activities were no longer criminalized (apparently whether or not for pay), although public solicitation for such acts remained against the law. COYOTE conceded the state's power to regulate or criminalize the public facets of prostitution, but how prostitutes were going to engage in their "protected" sexual activities when all preparatory (soliciting) activity remained illegal was not clear. As for COYOTE's charge of discriminatory enforcement, police had begun to use more female "undercover agents" to arrest male customers.

Massage parlors were handcuffed in federal court in North Carolina by a district court judge who began his discussion with a "light touch": "This case presents a touchy situation in which it will be impossible not to rub one of the parties the wrong way."[66] Administering massages to "private areas" was prohibited by the challenged law (public control of a private area), massage being defined as the "manipulation of body muscle or tissue by rubbing, stroking, kneading or tapping, by hand or mechanical device."[67] The court found no constitutionally based right to privacy, again because *Paris Adult Theatre I* limited this right to the "personal intimacies of the home, the family, marriage, motherhood and child rearing."[68]

A New York family court judge had a sexual privacy field day with a prostitution charge against a fourteen-year-old female. The court declared not only the prostitution law unconstitutional, but also those forbidding private, consensual sexual activity between adults, conventional or "deviate."[69]

The New York prostitution law was held to invade the girl's protected right of privacy and to be in violation of equal protection guarantees to both genders because it was enforced against female prostitutes but not male customers. A statistic introduced in the case showed that, compared to 2,944 female prostitutes arrested, only 60 patrons were charged.

The court then dissected the deviate sexual intercourse statute. (The fourteen-year-old had been charged with offering to perform a "deviate" sexual act for a fee.) "It cannot be said that acts of deviate sexual intercourse are, in and of themselves, intrinsically harmful or unnatural, causing in the participants any deviation from fundamental human nature."[70] Since "deviate" sexual intercourse between married people was no longer a crime, the court found that proscribing it for the unmarried violated their right to equal protection. Behavioral science data were utilized in the analysis. Citing Hunt's *Sexual Behavior in the 1970's*[71] (see Chapter 1 for a discussion of this work in relation to *State v. Saunders*), the court observed that 72 percent of unmarried heterosexuals between eighteen and twenty-four had performed fellatio and 69 percent cunnilingus, and that one person in six under twenty-five who had ever engaged in vaginal intercourse had also engaged in anal intercourse. Kinsey studies on the rates of male and female homosexual behavior were also cited.

The court then considered whether there is evidence that the anti-deviate sex law affects the stability of marriage and the family. "On the contrary, in the 17 states where consensual sodomy has been decriminalized, and the 100 nations that permit consensual sodomy, cooperative social institutions like the family remain."[72] Further, "if the marital contract is breached by promiscuity or the family is undermined by extramarital sexual relations, the burden of responsibility lies with the patron, not the prostitute."[73] The court reasoned that if the consensual sodomy law was really designed to prevent sexual relations between unmarried people, then "normal" sexual relations between the unmarried would also be criminalized.

The various rationales for prostitution laws were the next victims of this judicial tour de force. The court first considered the spread of venereal disease. Data from the American Social Health Organization showed that the amount of venereal disease attributable to prostitution was only 5 percent. Another study showed that less than 1 percent of female prostitutes examined in one large city had syphilis and less than 6 percent had gonorrhea.

The appellate court was not impressed.[74] It reminded the lower court that constitutional questions should not be reached unless there is a need for their determination to resolve the case at hand and the matter is squarely presented. Because the offer of deviate sexual intercourse for remuneration satisfied the definition of prostitution, the validity of the deviate sexual intercourse statute was inappropriately considered. In addition, the state's interest in proscribing the conduct charged to the fourteen-year-old was a legitimate one and within the police power. The unequal protection claim and the consensual sodomy statute, held the court, were not to be treated as affirmative defenses but as motions to dismiss or quash the official action, and so an evidentiary hearing was required (but not held). To the appellate court the discrepancy between the number of prostitutes arrested and the number of customers arrested did not demonstrate unequal application of the law because the two genders had committed "discrete crimes."

Finally, a male prostitute in Oregon arguing for a right to privacy was derailed by the Supreme Court's ruling in *Bowers v. Hardwick,* which permitted a state to criminalize consensual, private, *noncommercial* homosexual conduct.[75]

A sexual utopia integrating state-sponsored prostitution was proposed by a Swedish physician:

> By permitting brothels, one would . . . diminish sexual starvation in society and the number of illegitimate pregnancies . . . Many young people of both sexes would be only too pleased to enter the ranks of this humanitarian profession . . . [t]he most important function . . . would be to alleviate the misery of those who for various reasons cannot provide for themselves sexually . . . there is a great demand for sadistic youths among the homophiles . . . it is obvious that he runs a great risk if he is forced to rely on street prostitutes [this can be alleviated by] the establishment of homosexual brothels . . . [Further] [t]here are sexually active women in their fifties, sixties, and seventies who would like nothing better than the chance of meeting young boys . . . There ought to be mobile brothels to provide for hospitals, mental hospitals, and institutions, paralyzed, housebound patients, and old people . . . [t]he employees of these mobile brothels should be called *erotic Samaritans.*[76]

This humanitarian view of prostitution notwithstanding, sexual science data that have informed researchers about prostitution have not informed the courts. Whether prostitutes benefit from their work (some do, some do not), whether their customers benefit (at least some do), goes unnoticed. Also ignored is the experience from nations otherwise like the United States that regulate prostitution rather than criminalizing it, and the experience of the one state, Nevada, that has followed the European tradition.

The major impediment to removing prostitution from the category of crime is, in the final analysis, a moral one, a vestige of a time (perhaps legendary) when sexual contact only occurred between married male and female partners and with a reproductive goal. Although in contemporary society there is a widely acknowledged erosion of the moral tenet that sex should only occur between partners who are married to each other, or at least between loving unmarried partners, and although many hitherto nonintimate couples date with the implicit understanding that a paid-for dinner will be reciprocated sexually, resistance against the blatant commercialization of sexual exchange remains. Sex-for-hire emphasizes too boldly the passing or undermining of this romantic ideal.

Occasionally, "collateral crimes" provide the rationale for prohibition. But common sense dictates that the crimes often associated with prostitution, such as physical or economic victimization, may be a by-product of the fact that prostitution is outside the law and that neither victimized prostitutes nor customers are inclined to seek police help. At the same time, the amount of rape may increase when prostitution is not available. In Australia, for example, rape or attempted rape increased by 150 percent when legal brothels were closed.[77]

Stopping the spread of sexually transmitted disease is undeniably an important public need. But, at least in the pre-AIDS era, prostitution was reported to account for only a small percentage (about 5 percent) of the spread of venereal disease in the United States.[78] European studies revealed an inverse relation between venereal disease rates and legalized prostitution.[79]

But these arguments, along with any examination of the quality of life of prostitutes and their available alternatives, or the quality of life of their customers with and without access to prostitution, receive no notice in court. Prostitution exemplifies not the misapplication of sexual science to law, as with immigration and homosexuality, but its total circumvention.

# · 11 ·

# Abortion

Embedded within the fifty-seven-page landmark abortion rights decision *Roe v. Wade*[1] are a handful of sentences alluding to the negative psychological significance to the woman of being required to continue an unwanted pregnancy. "Maternity, or additional offspring, may force upon the woman a distressful life and future. Psychological harm may be imminent. Mental and physical health may be taxed by child care. There is also the distress, for all concerned, associated with the unwanted child, and there is the problem of bringing a child into a family already unable, psychologically and otherwise, to care for it. In other cases . . . the additional difficulties and continuing stigma of unwed motherhood may be involved."[2]

There are also concerns about the mental health consequences of terminating a pregnancy. Prior to 1960 most psychiatrists believed that it led to depression, and some wrote that it was a factor leading to severe mental illness.[3] In 1978, however, the World Health Organization concluded: "There is now a substantial body of data reported from many countries after careful and objective follow-up, suggesting frequent psychological benefit and a low incidence of adverse psychological sequelae; moreover, when post-abortion depression does occur, it is often apparently due to stresses other than the abortion."[4] This conclusion is based on a number of studies.

## The Psychological Impact of Permitting
## or Denying Abortion

*The United States*

Psychological reports prior to the 1973 Supreme Court decision were generally positive. A 1958 Kinsey Institute study of four hundred women who underwent primarily illegal abortions found that only 10 percent reported "psychological upset" over the procedure.[5] A 1963 survey of thirty-two California psychiatrists, in practice for an average of twelve years, revealed that only one-quarter had ever seen a moderate or severe psychological reaction to abortion, and this but rarely (the highest figure reported was six cases in fifteen years).[6]

A 1966 assessment of fifty women, three to six months after abortion, one-half of which were performed for psychiatric indications, found only one major negative reaction, and that subsided quickly. Twenty percent experienced some guilt feelings, and one-third mild depression, but these reactions were generally gone at follow-up. Ninety-eight percent of the women said they would choose to have the procedure again under comparable circumstances.[7]

A 1967 description of 116 women who had a therapeutic abortion (90 percent for psychiatric indications) found that two-thirds felt better immediately after the procedure and four-fifths were psychologically improved at 8 months follow-up. Of the 116 women, 110 answered "yes" to the question "Was therapeutic abortion the best answer for you?"[8]

A 1970 report of 147 patients who received abortions under California's liberal abortion law found few serious emotional problems of guilt or remorse. Four women were psychotic or severely depressed after abortion, but they were either depressed or psychotic before the procedure.[9]

In a 1971 study, forty women who requested therapeutic abortion on psychiatric grounds were interviewed and given the Minnesota Multiphasic Personality Inventory (MMPI) psychological test. Thirty were approved for abortion and twenty-two were seen six months later. Five of ten not approved for abortion were also reevaluated; two had received an abortion elsewhere. Of those who aborted, 43 percent were markedly improved and another 20 percent were at least moderately improved. Fourteen percent were more emotionally disturbed, but these women had a previous history of serious psychiatric problems. The MMPI mental disturbance scales for depression, hypochondriasis, hysteria, obsessive anxiety, psychopathic deviation, and paranoia were all reduced from the preabortion scores. By contrast, the few women denied abortion and reevaluated were more emotionally troubled than those who aborted.[10]

A report from sixty-six institutions that performed abortions between July 1970 and June 1971 found only 16 major psychiatric complications from a pool of 73,000.[11]

In a 1975 study of the emotional responses of adult women to abortion, the positive emotions most strongly experienced two to three months later were happiness and relief. Although negative feelings were also present, they were weaker and were internally and socially based (such as guilt or shame). Women who wanted to be pregnant were also more likely to experience loss.[12]

Some studies have shown that women who have repeated abortions may pose a higher psychiatric risk. One-third of a group of 413 women undergoing abortion were repeat abortion patients. On a symptom checklist, distress levels were comparable in both groups before abortion. After abortion, although the repeat abortion women had higher distress scores in anxiety and interpersonal sensitivity (feelings of being easily hurt, of being misunderstood by others, and of being watched or talked about), their depression scores decreased significantly.[13]

Forty percent of the American teenagers who become pregnant each year terminate their pregnancy. Among those younger than sixteen, there are 1.7 abortions for each childbirth. Ninety-six percent of unmarried teenagers who have the child keep it.[14]

A powerful 1989 study of the effects of pregnancy, abortion, and childbirth compared three subgroups of 360 black teenagers who sought pregnancy tests: those who chose abortion, those who carried the pregnancy to term, and those who were not pregnant. Two years later, those who terminated their pregnancy were more likely to have stayed in school or to have graduated from high school and to be better off economically. Those who terminated their pregnancy did not show more psychological problems and were less likely to become pregnant again during the two-year interval.

A positive educational result was found for the teenagers who terminated pregnancy. Although 18 percent had either left school or failed to progress academically, the failure rate was twice as high for those who kept the pregnancy or were not pregnant. (At baseline, more of the teenagers in the abortion group had expected to continue their education beyond high school; thus, their more extended educational goal may have led to their decision to abort.) More of those in the child-bearing group failed to live up to their educational goal than those in the other two groups.[15]

## Other Countries

In England, under the 1967 Abortion Act, abortion became approvable during the first twenty-four weeks of pregnancy to prevent risk of injury to the mother's mental or physical health.

Two hundred English women approved for a first trimester abortion were studied fifteen months to two years later. The proportion of women receiving psychiatric treatment after abortion was less than that receiving treatment before, 19 percent as opposed to 29 percent, and only 10 percent of those who received treatment were in therapy related to the pregnancy termination. Depression scores just before abortion and three months later showed significant improvement at follow-up. Eighteen months later, 7 percent of the women experienced at least moderate guilt, and nine women regretted the abortion. Marital harmony was not affected, and sexual adjustment was improved.[16]

The short-term effects of abortion were assessed in forty-four English women who were interviewed six months after the termination of their pregnancy. Seven regretted the decision and four were depressed, but thirty-nine were improved or unchanged.[17]

In another English study, sixty-four women were interviewed eight weeks after abortion. Although fifteen reported persistent guilt feelings and five thought it had been a mistake, two-thirds had no regrets. Guilt was more common for women whose abortion was performed for a physical rather than an emotional reason.[18]

In a geographic catchment area in England of 1.3 million people, where the estimated number of abortions was 3,550, only one woman was admitted to a psychiatric hospital with a psychosis within three months of the abortion, and she had a history of psychosis following two previous childbirths. By contrast, the estimated rate of psychosis in the same region following childbirth was four times greater.[19]

One study followed 130 English women recommended for termination of pregnancy for from one to three years. Of the 128 who had an abortion, only 2 regretted the decision. Mild feelings of guilt were not unusual, and in 13 percent they lasted longer than three months. Of 120 patients not recommended for abortion, two-thirds gave birth and one-third obtained an abortion elsewhere. Of the 73 women who bore the child, fourteen gave it up for adoption. For the remaining women, about two-thirds of those who were married and kept the baby were satisfied at having done so, whereas one-third felt the burden of the unwanted child and regretted not having terminated the pregnancy. Unmarried women who continued their pregnancy did worse psychologically; four were psychiatrically hospitalized.[20]

In a large study in Scotland, 3,300 women applied for abortion and three-fifths were approved. A follow-up evaluation was conducted at fifteen months. One in nine of the unmarried aborted group was depressed, compared to one in four of those continuing the pregnancy.[21]

Of the nearly five hundred Swedish women who obtained a legal abortion, 2 percent experienced serious self-reproach. This increased to 11 percent two to four years later, although half of these women said they would make the same decision again.[22] Juxtaposed to this report is the Swedish study of 250 women seven years after they were refused an abortion. One-quarter accepted the pregnancy and did well, and one-half showed psychological problems in the intervening two to four years but were doing well at follow-up. Interim problems included incapacity for work, "neurotic reactions against the child," and the need for social placement of the child. A poor adjustment was found in the final quarter more than seven-and-a-half years later. Two-fifths of these poorly adjusted women took sick leave for mental disturbance.[23]

In Denmark, an extensive registry study evaluated the results of 27,000 abortions and 71,000 deliveries by rates of first admission to psychiatric hospitals during the ensuing three months. The risk of admission was the same for either abortion or delivery—12 per 10,000 (compared to 7 per 10,000 for all women of reproductive age). Among women who were separated, divorced, or widowed, those who terminated pregnancies had four times the rate of admission compared to those separated, divorced, or widowed who carried to term (64 compared to 17 per 10,000).[24] The authors suggest that the separated, divorced, or widowed women who had abortions may have been especially vulnerable due to disturbed partner relationships and/or may have terminated a pregnancy that the partners had wanted when they were together. Another interpretation of the finding is that physicians are less likely to hospitalize a recent mother.[25]

A 1990 summary report of the psychological effects of abortion is consistent with the World Health Organization conclusion of 1978: "Women who report little difficulty in making their decision, who are more satisfied with their choice, and who are terminating pregnancies that were unintended and had little personal meaning for them show more positive responses after abortion. Women with negative attitudes toward abortion, and who perceive little support for their decision have more difficulty deciding about abortion."[26]

In the abortion debate, the male partners of women contemplating abortion are rarely considered. The 1958 Kinsey Institute study found that about 4 percent of the male partners of women undergoing abortion experienced psychiatric consequences.[27] A more recent German study looked at the relationship between the man and the woman after an induced abortion. Researchers interviewed ninety-two women and administered psychological tests before and one year after the abortion and compared this group with a group of nonpregnant women and their partners, who were using contraceptives. The groups were matched for the number of previous children. Prior to the abortion, the partnerships in the abortion group showed more conflict. One year later, there were no significant differences between the two groups for those couples still together. The percentage of both groups that separated was comparable. When separation occurred, it was more often initiated by the women in the abortion group.[28]

## Unwanted Children

The status of children born of unwanted pregnancies after abortion was denied reflects another aspect of the pregnancy termination versus childbirth decision. A review of the world literature on infanticide found that 83 percent of newborns and 11 percent of infants killed by their mothers were born of an unwanted pregnancy.[29]

A landmark Swedish study reported a twenty-one-year follow-up on sixty-eight children whose mothers were refused an abortion requested on psychiatric grounds. These children were compared with a control group obtained by selecting the next child of the same sex from birth registers. One index of psychological adjustment was whether the child had been seen in a child guidance clinic or psychiatric center. Researchers also studied central penal registers of criminal records, social agency reports, and school records to determine the children's status.

The findings revealed negative consequences for the unwanted children. Twenty-seven percent of them were born out of wedlock compared to 7 percent of the controls. Five times as many were placed in foster homes (19 percent as compared to 4 percent). Parents of unwanted children divorced twice as frequently. Nearly twice as many unwanted children had attended a psychiatric clinic (28 percent as compared to 15 percent). Eighteen percent were registered with child welfare boards for complaints of delinquency compared to 8 percent of the controls. Eight percent of the unwanted children compared to 2 percent of controls had records in the penal register. Fourteen percent of the unwanted children compared to 2 percent of controls received public assistance. Advanced education beyond that required by law was obtained by 14 percent of the unwanted children, but by over twice that number (33 percent) of the controls.[30] A follow-up at age thirty-five found that the unwanted children remained more likely to be on a registry indicating psychiatric care, crime, or public assistance.[31]

These differences may be modest compared to what could have been found had no abortions been available, since the mothers who were denied abortion were relatively healthier than those whose therapeutic abortions were approved, and those pregnant women who were refused abortion but obtained one elsewhere were the most negatively disposed to childbearing.

The findings of a Czechoslovakian study also revealed the negative impact of unwanted childbirth. The study assessed 220 children born to women denied legal abortion and 220 controls whose mothers did not apply for abortion, when they were nine years old.

The "unwanted" children were more often described as "bad-tempered" in preschool. They were rated by mothers and teachers as more excitable and less able to concentrate. The mothers of unwanted children were rated by teachers and social workers as more detached and less informed about their child. The school grades of unwanted children were somewhat poorer, significantly so in the use of language. The children's playmates ascribed less socially desirable characteristics to them, and they were less often the "best friend" and more often those who "fight a lot." Unwanted boys showed more chronic disease. Parents reported less marital harmony.

The higher incidence of illness and hospitalization among the unwanted children contrasts with the absence of medical differences between the groups of children at birth, and their slightly poorer school grades with the absence of any differences in measures of intelligence.[32]

At ages fourteen to sixteen, the school performance of the unwanted children continued to deteriorate.[33] In their early twenties, more social problems were in evidence. They showed more criminality, and there was a trend toward more problems with drugs and alcohol.[34]

Not every study shows a significantly negative effect on unwanted children, however. Another Swedish study looked at two hundred children age 7 to 11.5.[35] Thirty mothers gave their newborn child up for adoption or to a foster home. Of the children raised by the biological mother, the school health records of 22 percent made some mention of mental disturbance or indicated that the child was referred to a psychiatrist during the first three or four years of school. This was not substantially different from a comparison of Stockholm children of whom 20 percent had such a referral up to the seventh or eighth grade.

## Legal Rights of the Pregnant Woman's Partner

Although these reports generally ignore the issue of specific effects on the male partner of the woman who undergoes an abortion or continues the pregnancy, the role of the father has not gone unnoticed by the United States Supreme Court. In 1976 Missouri granted the father veto power (his written consent required) over the woman's decision to have an abortion during the first twelve weeks of pregnancy. The rationale was the "perception of marriage as an institution" and that "any major change in family status is a decision to be made jointly by the marriage partners. The consent of both parties is generally necessary . . . to begin a family . . . a change in the family structure set in motion by mutual consent should be terminated only by mutual consent."[36]

Although the Supreme Court acknowledged the importance of the father in the abortion decision, it did not give him priority over the power of the state.

[The court is] not unaware of the deep and proper concern and interest that a devoted and protective husband has in his wife's pregnancy and in the growth and development of the fetus she is carrying . . . Moreover, we recognize that the decision whether to undergo or to forego an abortion may have profound effects on the future of any marriage . . . Notwithstanding these factors, we cannot hold that the State has the constitutional authority to give the spouse unilaterally the ability to prohibit the wife from terminating her pregnancy, when the State itself lacks that right.[37]

Nor did the Court see the father's interest as symmetrical with that of the mother:

It seems manifest that, ideally, the decision to terminate a pregnancy should be one concurred in by both the wife and her husband . . . But it is difficult to believe that the goal of fostering mutuality and trust in a marriage, and of strengthening the marital relationship and the marriage institution, will be achieved by giving the husband a veto power exercisable for any reason whatsoever or for no reason at all . . . Inasmuch as it is the woman who physically bears the child and who is the more directly and immediately affected by the pregnancy, as between the two, the balance weighs in her favor.[38]

The dissenting justices, however, would not penalize the father for his inability to conceive: "A father's interest in having a child—perhaps his only child—may be unmatched by any other interest in his life."[39]

## Other Legal Cases and the Psychological Effects of Abortion

The allegedly negative psychological consequences of abortion provided the rationale for one man's attempt to disrupt the office practice of an Arkansas gynecologist. His defense was "choice of evils," that he broke the law to serve a higher goal. A mental health counselor, he claimed that "from his experience in counseling young women who had undergone abortions, he had formed a belief that serious psychological consequences could result and that those contemplating abortion should be advised by him of the possible results."[40] His argument was rejected by the court.

The psychological consequences of termination of pregnancy also constituted part of the "informed consent" document that was required reading for women under a 1983 Akron, Ohio, law. Abortion applicants were warned, among other things, that the procedure "may leave essentially unaffected or may worsen any existing psychological problems [they] may have, and can result in severe emotional disturbances."[41] The Supreme Court characterized the document as a "parade of horribles" and held that "Akron has gone far beyond merely describing the general subject matter relevant to informed consent [by] insisting upon recitation of a lengthy and inflexible list of information."[42]

The question of "when life begins" is not within the scope of this chapter. That debate, coopted from medical science by philosophers and theologians, is not sexual science. Legislators can decide that life begins with conception, tort law acknowledges that the unborn fetus has some rights, and nonsexual medical science attempts to identify "viability": when a fetus can survive in an extrauterine environment. But this last criterion is also lacking in precision as new technology permits the smaller and less mature to "survive," although often not without handicap. Technological innovations are not without legal import, however. The key variables in the quixotic formula for balancing maternal and unborn rights created in *Roe v. Wade* were viability and the medical risk of abortion compared to childbirth. But the progression to earlier gestational times of viability (on the one end) and the increased safety of abortion (on the other) were described graphically by Supreme Court Justice Sandra Day O'Connor as being "clearly on a collision course."[43]

In 1989, when Surgeon General C. Everett Koop stated that there was insufficient evidence to conclude that abortion was psychologically harmful to women, and that the development of significant psychological problems from abortion was "miniscule from a public health perspective,"[44] he surprised and displeased his president and the "prolife" movement. In 1991 a review of 225 science papers on the psychological impact of abortion also concluded that there were few negative sequelae.[45] Although distress is common in the immediate postabortion period, "these symptoms seem to be continuations of symptoms present before the abortion and are more a result of the circumstances leading to the abortion than a result of the procedure itself." Long-term results are generally positive: "only a small minority express any degree of regret."[46] When abortion is denied, up to 40 percent have abortions elsewhere. Of those who give birth, most do not put the child up for adoption. And, "[a] significant minority—about 30 percent . . . continue to report negative feelings toward their child and difficulty adjusting." The status of the children born after abortion is denied is "the most disturbing part of the whole issue." The effects are "long-lasting, broadly based, and negative."[47]

The research results are consistent and clear, notwithstanding the methodological problems inherent in researching a complex area involving multiple psychological and social influences and their impact on romantic relationships, procreative drive, and moral and religious values. For those who believe that abortion is murder, however, their conviction trumps the results of the sexual science studies demonstrating the positive effects on the woman that result from permitting abortion or the negative effects on the unwanted child.

Although researchers have generally ignored the role of the father in this pregnancy complex and courts have relegated his rights to second or third tier status, the increasing vigor of men's groups may result in a reappraisal of the father's right to have or raise a child (a fundamental right) if it is not desired by the mother. Because only women can experience pregnancy, the Supreme Court has concluded that their needs must receive priority. However, this argument is regarded by some as proving too much. Because men cannot experience pregnancy, their needs, according to the men's rights position, must not be relegated to lesser protection. If the Court overturns *Roe v. Wade,* then *Planned Parenthood v. Danforth,* which refuses to grant fathers the veto power over the mother that is denied to the state, would be without that source of vitality.

When the Supreme Court wove its way through the Constitution and found that a woman's liberty interest under the Fourteenth Amendment was violated when abortion was categorically denied, it paused only momentarily to consider the psychological impact of an unwanted pregnancy. But now that the Rorschach inkblot of that amendment is not likely to be seen by new Court members as providing a textual basis for protecting the woman's decision, the psychological dimension of abortion or its denial should command greater attention. That attention may be evidenced in state legislatures and courts if the "choice" is once again theirs.

# · 12 ·

# Surgical or Chemical Castration
# of Sex Offenders

The theory behind the anti-androgen (anti-male hormone) treatment of sex offenders is simple. Critics have argued that it is too simple. The hormone testosterone and its metabolites constitute the primary source of sexual interest and sexual functioning in the adult male. Although correlations between blood testosterone levels and male sexual behavior within the normal range of hormone are not precise, markedly deficient levels are usually associated with a reduction in male sexuality.[1] Thus, a drug that blocks the effects of male hormone should block sexual behavior. The phenomenon is more complex, however.

Prepubertal males, who have minimal levels of testosterone, experience erections frequently, although systematic reports of sexual interest during this period are lacking. In addition, sexual aggression is complex behavior. By its term, it is not purely sexual. As one researcher notes, rape is "concerned much more with status, hostility, control, and dominance than with sexual pleasure or sexual satisfaction."[2] Rapists are not merely sexually frustrated. "The commonest variety," as the authors of a study of sex offenders point out, "are men whose behavior includes unnecessary violence; it seems that sexual activity alone is insufficient and that in order for it to be maximally gratifying it must be accompanied by physical violence or serious threat."[3] Because research attempting to link aggression and testoterone levels finds poor correlations,[4] the extent to which sexual assault is aggressive, as opposed to sexual, becomes problematic when treatment is directed at testosterone reduction. Nevertheless, the poor results of psychiatric treatment of sex offenders with insight therapy and the less than satisfactory results with behavior modification (conditioning) therapy have prompted intervention based on hormonal control.

# Treatment

## Surgical Castration

A 1979 review of European research on the castration of sex offenders focused on recidivism rates—how many offenders committed another sex offense—and on sexual function.[5] Over a thousand sex offenders, castrated in Germany by court order and then released from prison between 1934 and 1944, were compared to 685 sex offenders who were released uncastrated. Of the castrated males, 2.3 percent were recividists and repeated their offenses (before castration their recidivism rate was 84 percent), while for the noncastrated men the recidivism rate was 39 percent.[6] Sexual functioning after castration varied among the 58 men who were interviewed. Two-thirds reported the extinction of sex drive and potency soon after castration, and 17 percent reported a gradual fading. Eighteen percent, however, stated that they were able to engage in sexual intercourse *more than twenty years later.* The study does not mention whether these were the repeat offenders. The lower the adult age at castration, the more enduring was sexual function.

One hundred and twenty-seven Swiss offenders assessed at least five years after castration were compared to fifty offenders who had refused castration and so remained in prison longer.[7] The recidivism rate among castrates was 7 percent, compared with 77 percent before surgery. Repeat offenses occurred within five years, and younger castrates had a higher rate. In the noncastrated group, 52 percent committed sexual crimes again within ten years. The prior recidivism rate of this group had been 66 percent. Of interest is that the number of repeat prison sentences decreased from 130 to 56 after castration had been *proposed* to, but *rejected* by, the second group. Of the sixty-eight castrates who were interviewed, two-thirds stated that their sexual interest and drive had been extinguished shortly after surgery, and one-quarter reported a gradual fading, but 10 percent reported having intercourse eight to twenty years after surgery.

A Norwegian study that assessed 102 castrated sex offenders, observing 41 of them for five to ten years, found a recidivism rate after castration of 7 percent. Before castration it had been 58 percent. For two-fifths, sexual interest disappeared shortly after surgery, and for one-fifth, it diminished gradually. For one-quarter of the men, however, sexual interest persisted for at least a year. Five percent of the men were sexually inactive before and after castration; for 10 percent there were no data.[8]

A large Danish study of 3,185 men looked at relapse rates and long-term follow-up (at twelve to twenty-four years) for noncastrated offenders.[9] Relapse rates were higher among those who had committed more than one previous offense. Thus, while 17 percent of first offenders relapsed, more than half of the five-time offenders were rearrested. The total relapse rate was about 10 percent.

These data on noncastrated sex offenders may be compared with those from nine hundred Danes castrated between 1929 and 1959. When castrated, 44 percent were in institutions for mental defectives, 30 percent were incarcerated, 8 percent were in mental hospitals, and 18 percent were not institutionalized. Forty percent had been convicted once, 18 percent a second time, and 24 percent several times. Another 18 percent had no convictions.

Two-thirds of the men were followed for at least six years, two-fifths for more than 10 years, and the remainder for at least fifteen years. "Desexualization," the loss of potency and sex interest, was attained in 90 percent. In the six months following castration, "desexualization" occurred among one-half, and the rate rose to 87 percent at one year. In 3 percent, it did not occur for at least six years. No rapist raped again. The recidivism rate for all sex crimes was 1.1 percent.[10]

A study of thirty-nine sex offenders in the Federal Republic of Germany who underwent "voluntary" surgical castration reported mixed results. The frequency of masturbation, intercourse, and sexual fantasy was markedly reduced, but sexual capacity was not eliminated. In fact, eleven of the thirty-five men stated that they were capable of sexual intercourse at an average of 4.8 years after castration (the range was from 1.3 to 9.5 years).[11]

The basis for continuing sexual function in men years after surgical castration may be androgens (male hormones) originating in the adrenal gland. In the treatment of prostatic cancer, an androgen-dependent tumor, attempts have been made to block the effects of these hormones by the use of "pure anti-androgens," drugs that block all androgens at their tissue receptor sites, rather than drugs that only interfere with the release of testicular androgens.[12] This approach suggests possible applications in the treatment of sex offenders.

## Hormonal "Castration"

Anti-androgen treatment for sex offenders in the United States has employed the drug medroxyprogesterone acetate (MPA), originally manufactured by Upjohn as Depo-Provera. As the name implies, it is a progesteronelike ("female" hormone) compound. In countries other than the United States it has been used for birth control, and in the United States in the treatment of uterine and kidney cancer.

The first U.S. reports on treatment of sex offenders with MPA were published in 1968 by the medical psychologist John Money.[13] He described ten men on MPA, all of whom reported diminished erotic imagery and decreased erections and ejaculations. Reports of two larger studies appeared in 1981, one from the United States, the other from Canada. The U.S. study presented follow-up data on twenty men, some of whom had been studied previously by Money. In the follow-up, three of the twenty demonstrated a recurrence of the offending behavior while on the drug. Eleven discontinued drug treatment against medical advice, and ten of the eleven relapsed. The two who discontinued drug treatment with medical approval had not relapsed. The study report concluded: "In general these men appear to do well in response to anti-androgen medication as long as they continue taking it and as long as their problems are rather clearly confined to unconventional sexual cravings."[14] The Canadian study reported on forty-eight patients who were treated with MPA. Testosterone levels in these patients were markedly lowered, and forty reported diminished erotic interest and responsivity.[15]

A review of MPA studies in 1986 looked at ten reports covering a total of ninety sex offenders. The categories of offenders were exhibitionists, 25 percent; homosexual pedophiles, 27 percent;

bisexual pedophiles, 14 percent; rapists, 3 percent; and perpetrators of incest, 4 percent. Although it is generally agreed that this drug reduces sexual interest and sexual functioning with minimal side effects, the author of the review notes that "the outcome of therapy was assessed mainly using self-report questionnaires. These were of uneven quality and unproven validity."[16]

In European and in some Canadian studies, cyproterone acetate (CPA) has served as the primary anti-androgenic drug.[17] This drug, which is manufactured by Schering in Berlin, is more specifically anti-androgenic than MPA and appears to act on peripheral (non-brain) androgen tissue receptors as well as on the central neuroendocrine system production of male hormone.[18]

CPA treatment results were tabulated in one review of seven studies, which followed a total of one hundred patients for from three months to 4.5 years. Prior to CPA treatment, relapse rates approached 100 percent. After treatment, there was no recidivism in five studies, no data available for one, and a recidivism rate of 17 percent in another.[19]

Another review of ten CPA studies covered two hundred patients. Two studies used placebo, or inert substance, controls. In one, CPA or estrogen was superior to the placebo on verbally reported measures of sexual function but not when penile responsivity to erotic photos was assessed. In the other, CPA was superior to the placebo on self-report and masturbatory function; no penile responsivity measures were made.[20] In a study of pedophiles, in which neither the physician nor the patient knew whether an active drug or a placebo was being taken, the changes included decreases (on a scale of most to least) in testosterone level, reported sexual activity, reported arousal to erotic slides and fantasy, and measured penile response to erotic slides and fantasy.[21]

Evaluating early CPA and MPA treatment reports is difficult. Control subjects were generally absent. Physiologic measures of sexual arousal were not utilized, and the patients' subjective reports of sexual interest or arousal may not be valid. In addition, self-serving or placebo effect reports may suggest drug efficacy where no valid change was effected.

The most meaningful indicator of male sexual responsivity is the measurement of change in penis size (penile plethysmography) accompanying sexual fantasies or erotic photographs. Although some voluntary control over erection is possible, the potential for falsification of such physical changes is less than with verbal reports. But few early studies used penile change as well as the subjects' self-report to evaluate drug efficacy. The early MPA study in which penile measurements were assessed found only minimal changes while the more recent CPA study with pedophiles found penile responsivity to be the weakest result of treatment.

Nocturnal penile tumescence (NPT), the reflex erections that occur with dreaming or rapid eye movement (REM) sleep, provide another physiological measure of arousability. Although these erections are not in response to external erotic stimuli, they demonstrate the man's capacity for erection and are even less amenable to conscious distortion.

Three pedophiles, who received MPA, were monitored for NPT and penile circumference changes over a three-month period. Sexually arousing slides (of nude children) were used as erotic stimuli. The men showed minimally reduced penile responsivity with MPA compared to the placebo. Only one man showed a decrease in his average maximum erection response to the stimuli; the other two showed no changes. By contrast, all three reported diminished subjective arousal to erotic fantasies. For the two men who had NPT assessments, both showed a decrease in the average change in penile circumference. Erection decreases were associated with markedly lower levels of testosterone.[22]

Criminal paraphilias, or sexual aberrations, may coexist in an individual along with noncriminal sexual behaviors. Thus, the ideal treatment for those with both patterns would specifically reduce or eliminate the paraphilia while leaving normal sexuality intact. Results in the direction of such specificity of treatment have been reported with the use of CPA.[23] In the treatment of a male with conventional and criminal sexual interests, there was more reduction in sexual arousal in response to depictions of illegal conduct, so that the relative strength of the two sexual patterns was changed.

A general overview of anti-androgen administration identifies several effects. Testosterone levels are lowered, at least during the initial months of administration. Subjective reports of erotic interest and arousal are diminished concurrent with anti-androgen, usually to a greater degree than with a placebo. Penile responsivity generally shows less change. And over time, during continued anti-androgen administration, testosterone levels may increase and even approach predrug levels. However, subjective reports of erotic interest and frequency of erotic arousal usually remain diminished.

## Court Cases

Using anti-androgens in the treatment of sex offenders has touched off a major controversy. The popular term for such treatment, "chemical castration," invokes the specter of surgical castration, usually performed on unwilling prisoners. At more subtle levels, medical ethicists have argued over whether a person can give meaningful consent to participation in a research/treatment protocol with anti-androgen while incarcerated or as a condition of probation or parole outside of prison.[24] Published legal cases highlight the issues.

A man charged with sexually abusing his two stepchildren was convicted and sentenced to five years probation on condition that he be treated with Depo-Provera (MPA). He appealed this condition of probation. Ironically, he is an heir to the Upjohn Company, which manufactures the drug.[25] The trial court was compassionate toward the defendant: "On your behalf, there are many things that you are not. You are not a violent rapist who drags women and girls off the street and into the bushes or into your car from a parking lot; you are not a child chaser, one whose obsession with sex causes him to seek neighborhood children or children in parks or in playgrounds . . . you are a man who has warm personal feelings for your stepchildren, but you let them get out of hand." Using this reasoning, the trial court ruled that "within 30 days [you] submit yourself to castration by chemical means patterned after the research and treatment of the Johns Hopkins Hospital in Baltimore, Maryland, and continue same for five years of your probation under the supervision of this Court."[26] The ruling added that, if it were not possible to carry out the Depo-Provera treatment, the probationary part of the sentence would be set aside and the defendant would be resentenced.

The appellate court observed that the drug was not approved by the FDA for suppressing sex drive in the male, even though its experimental use for that purpose was allowed. And, although the trial judge "crudely referred to Depo-Provera treatment as 'castration by chemical means,'" the appellate court noted that the therapy "is neither castration nor sterilization." To the court, Depo-Provera treatments should not be considered "within the gambit of numerous cases which discuss sterilization (or sometimes castration) of sex offenders because, in all cases where sterilization is allowed, the sanction is specifically authorized by statute."[27] Furthermore, studies of the efficacy of MPA had involved voluntary patients. The appellate court held that the condition of probation was "unlawful": "The Depo-Provera treatment prescribed by the trial judge fails as a lawful condition of probation because it has not gained acceptance in the medical community as a safe and reliable medical procedure."[28]

In another case with a different twist, a pedophile on probation who had committed another sex offense appealed his reconviction because he received psychodynamic-oriented therapy rather than behavior modification or anti-androgen therapy.[29] As a condition of probation, the trial court had imposed two years in jail and psychiatric therapy. A presentence report had recommended that the man be treated with behavior modification techniques rather than insight therapy, and that "chemical castration" could also be used. But the treating doctor used insight therapy, and the offender again molested children.

The appeal of this new sentence argued that "being placed on probation constitutionally entitled him to be effectively treated and rehabilitated." The appellate court rejected the argument that his Eighth Amendment (cruel and unusual punishment) or Fourteenth Amendment (due process) rights were violated. The trial judge "is not constitutionally required to give the most weight to the goal of rehabilitation." To the court, neither the due process clause nor the cruel and unusual punishment clause "require[s] a state to provide incarcerated prisoners with a rehabilitation program" because "probation itself is a matter of grace and not of right."[30]

Another prisoner, serving *eighteen consecutive life sentences* for rape in a maximum security prison was found to have a testosterone level twice normal. He sued to obtain Depo-Provera treatment. The court ordered anti-androgen treatment and psychotherapy. After treatment was commenced, the prisoner applied for a transfer to a minimum security facility and for a parole hearing. The prison commissioner's refusal of both demands was upheld by the court, which reasoned that the defendant might escape from the minimum security facility and that without continued drug treatment he would be dangerous. Parole could be refused because of the absence of assurance that he would remain on medication.[31]

In another case, a prisoner, who was scheduled to be released within a few years, was denied permission by the Connecticut Department of Corrections to commence MPA treatment while in prison. The prisoner took his argument to court, where the penal system capitulated and agreed to begin treatment.[32]

The second child sex offender case above suggests that prisoners may not have a right to rehabilitation and that convicted persons on probation may not have a right to the most effective treatment. On the other hand, courts have also upheld prisoners' right to treatment, both medical[33] and psychological.[34] In a 1977 case, a federal court saw "no underlying distinction between the right to medical care for physical ills and its psychological or psychiatric counterpart." It observed that "[m]odern science has rejected the notion that mental or emotional disturbances are the products of afflicted souls, hence beyond the purview of counseling, medication, and therapy." The court held that a prison inmate is entitled to psychological or psychiatric treatment if the "prisoner's symptoms evidence a serious disease," if the disease "is curable or may be substantially alleviated," and if there is "the [substantial] potential for harm to the prisoner by reason of delay or denial."[35]

*Involuntary* anti-androgen treatment of incarcerated offenders, and not only those on probation, may not withstand a court challenge. In a 1974 case, the Ninth Circuit Court of Appeals held that a prisoner had a cause of action for a hemorrhoid operation performed over his objection.[36] In the short run, that surgery, a well-established procedure, would appear to be of greater benefit to the prisoner than the experimental anti-androgen, unless perhaps anti-androgen was linked with early release.

Cruel and unusual punishment, prohibited by the Eighth Amendment, continues to defy precise constitutional formulation. One principle, advanced by Justice William Brennan in a death penalty case, asserts: "If there is significantly less severe punishment adequate to achieve the purpose for which the punishment is inflicted, the punishment inflicted is unnecessary and therefore excessive."[37] Anti-androgen is less severe than surgical castration and has a more positive outcome than nonhormone treatment. Verbal insight therapies have had poor results, and although behavior modification treatments may be more effective than insight therapy, they pose constitutional issues similar to those surrounding anti-androgen treatment when they employ temporarily paralyzing drugs, nausea-inducing chemicals, and electric shocks.

Should chemical "castration" be considered treatment or punishment? Although anti-androgen may inhibit unlawful sexual interests that are acted out, it usually inhibits normal sexual expression as well for persons capable of both. Procreative ability is also severely curtailed (albeit probably reversibly) due to the loss of erectile capacity and reduced sperm production. Thus, legal issues related to sterilization provide additional perspectives on the use of anti-androgen.

In the early part of the twentieth century, vasectomy, a method of sterilization, was considered by state courts to be comparable to castration. In 1912, a Washington state court upheld mandatory vasectomy for a person found guilty of statutory rape.[38] In 1914, on the other hand, an Iowa court held that when performed on "sexual perverts" it was unconstitutional.[39]

Sterilization per se has a mixed record in the United States Supreme Court. In 1927 it was held to be constitutional when imposed on inmates in a state institution who were believed to have hereditary forms of insanity or retardation.[40] Later, however, it was ruled unconstitutional.[41] There, the basis for the ruling was not cruel and unusual punishment, but rather a violation of equal protection. Sterilization had been arbitrarily designated for the punishment of some crimes but not for comparable offenses. The earlier case was distinguished by the court because there, sterilization would make some prisoners eligible for release, thus freeing up prison space. This case may therefore be more analogous to treatment with anti-androgens.

An array of issues relating to sexual science and the law as they apply to sex offenders remain unresolved. Not only does a typology of sex offenders that permits the prediction of their response to anti-androgen treatment need to be developed, but the most effective concurrent nonpharmacological treatment for specific offenders also needs to be clarified. At the most fundamental level, sexual science does not know what leads some individuals to commit sexual offenses. Undoubtedly, the categories of offenders include many subtypes. Found among offenders are admixtures of aggression and sexuality that result in offenses ranging from unwanted touching, to the threat of force, to brutalization, to lust murder.

The specific role of reduced testosterone in treatment is still unclear. Reduced subjective arousal to sexual stimuli can persist after cessation of the drug, or after long-term administration of the drug, without continued suppression of testosterone. Perhaps the disconnection of erotic stimuli and penile arousal interrupts a conditioned reflex, and that dissociation persists without pharmacologic intervention. Or perhaps the drug effects the tissue receptors so that the available testosterone is less effective.

Informed consent for those faced with imprisonment and/or drug treatment may constitute a two-edged sword. While coercion is clear when a person is given a choice between treatment or incarceration, to deny the choice because it violates the ethic of informed consent results in a loss of freedom. Permitting a prisoner to participate in treatment when consent does not influence the duration of incarceration may reduce coercion, but it may also prolong prison time for the person who responds favorably.

Anti-androgen treatment is not the only intrusive means of controlling prisoners on probation or parole. A variety of other procedures that compromise the probationer's or parolee's liberty have been developed. Some felons wear radio transmitters that track their movements. Some are confined to prescribed areas outside of prison. Many are not permitted to participate in certain activities or to associate with particular people. Pharmacologic treatments have also been mandated. Thus, repeat alcoholic offenders have been required to take Antabuse (a drug that induces a severe reaction when the person ingests alcohol) as a condition of probation. Heroin addicts may be required to take methadone. In England, women who have had murder charges reduced after successfully pleading the "raging hormone" defense of premenstrual syndrome (PMS) (in contrast to the "testosterone poisoning" of sex offenders), have been required to take the hormone progesterone as a condition of probation (see Chapter 13). The duration of treatment is also problematic. When a prison sentence is of a fixed duration and has been fully served, governmental authority to mandate treatment is not likely to survive release from prison. However,

Washington State has enacted a "sexual predator" law, which allows the state to detain an offender, due to be released, as long as the person "suffers from a mental abnormality or personality disorder that makes the person likely to engage in predatory acts of violence."[42] A sexual science problem here is the poor record of psychiatrists and psychologists in predicting violence. "The large body of research in this area indicates that, even under the best of conditions, psychiatric predictions of long-term future dangerousness are wrong in at least two out of every three cases."[43] The law is being challenged by the state's Civil Liberties Union.

Striking a balance between the protection of the public and renewed freedom for sex offenders who have been judged to be reasonably safe must take several science, legal, and public opinion variables into consideration. Statistics document moderate to high rates of recidivism. Even if a small minority become repeat offenders, public tolerance of recidivism is zero. Any humane interventions that reduce recidivism should be encouraged. First, however, it is necessary to identify the baseline for the recurrence of a particular offense for a given type of offender.[44] Then the group prediction must be tailored to the individual offender.

Some states require the registration of sex offenders, the rationale being that when a sex offense occurs, those with a history of similar crimes provide an initial lead in apprehending the perpetrator. But this rationale is reminiscent of the end of the film *Casablanca,* when the police inspector issues the order to "round up the usual suspects." Perhaps registration serves as a deterrent to recidivism. Recidivism and offender apprehension rates should be studied in states with and without mandatory registration.

A final point concerns offenders who have not yet come to the attention of the criminal justice system. All states mandate the reporting of suspected cases of sexual abuse of children, and this may lead to the prosecution of sex offenders. But laws mandating the reporting of sexual abuse may be counterproductive. As I noted in Chapter 8, in Maryland such reporting was not mandated when the offender voluntarily sought treatment. Because of this, "several persons [came] to Johns Hopkins Hospital [in Maryland] from adjacent states in order to receive treatment without having to self-incriminate. All came seeking help, including the use of Depo-

Provera. Each made it clear that he would probably not have, had he not first been reassured that [he was] not running the risk of self-incrimination."[45] In 1990, however, when the state enacted legislation mandating the reporting of suspected abuse, self-referrals stopped.[46]

Sexual science must collaborate with the law to strike the thus far elusive balance between protecting the public against unwanted sexual contact and providing help for those whose psychosexual development has evolved along an antisocial spectrum. These goals will be unattainable until we better understand the roles of aggression and sexuality in sexual assault. They will be unattainable until we better understand the individualized motivators that contribute to a sexual offense. Then, compassion in the courts must integrate these data from sexual science.

# Sex-Linked Defenses
# to Criminal Behavior

Goals of the criminal law include retribution, prevention, restraint, deterrence, education, and rehabilitation.[1] Exceptions to punishment are allowed when the mental state of the offender renders such goals meaningless.

## Tests of Insanity

Although in thirteenth-century England, "a man who has killed another by misadventure, though he may deserve a pardon, is guilty of a crime; and the same rule applies to a lunatic,"[2] by the fourteenth century, insanity or "madness" had emerged as a defense for crime. It allowed the accused to avoid the otherwise mandated death penalty.[3] In the seventeenth century, those considered mentally ill included "congenital idiots," the mad, with neither memory nor understanding, and the person who "hath not understanding" but was not always so.[4] By the eighteenth century an English defendant was accountable in court "unless totally without reason and memory, like an infant, brute, or wild beast."[5]

In the nineteenth century, the major contemporary test of insanity crystallized when a man named M'Naghten, who had failed to kill the prime minister but succeeded in killing his secretary, was aquitted as insane. Several questions regarding M'Naghten's defense were addressed to the Lord Justices, and the answers became the "right-wrong" test: "To establish a defense on the grounds of insanity, it must be clearly proved that, at the time of the committing of the act, the party accused was labouring under such a defect of reason, from disease of the mind, as not to know the nature and quality of the act he was doing; or, if he did know it, that he did not know he was doing what was wrong."[6]

Other tests of sanity are not as cognitively based. Under the "irresistible impulse" test, the defendant is not criminally responsible if, by reason of mental illness, he or she was unable to exert control over an offending act, even if he or she knew that the act was wrong.[7] Here, the dilemma for psychiatry is distinguishing between an act that is *uncontrolled* and an act that is *uncontrollable*. Under the Durham or "product" test, the defendant is excused if the offending act was the product of a mental disease or defect.[8] The Model Penal Code of the American Law Institute is a hybrid of the cognitive and irresistible impulse tests. Thus, the person is not responsible if a mental disease or defect resulted in the lack of a "substantial capacity" to appreciate the wrongfulness of the act or to conform behavior to the requirements of law.[9]

The "diminished capacity" test supplements the insanity defense by permitting evidence that the defendant did not have the requisite capacity to formulate one of the specific mental elements of the crime because of a mental disease or defect.[10] A person under the influence of a drug might argue, for example, that he or she was unable to formulate an *intent* to murder, allowing conviction for a lesser offense. Finally, with a guilty but mentally ill plea, the defendant is judged guilty but the sentence may include treatment in a mental hospital.[11]

## Sex-Linked Defenses

### XYY Chromosomes

The "supermale" syndrome of XYY (an extra Y male chromosome) was popularized in 1968 when two men, one in France,[12] the other in Australia,[13] who were charged with murder, used it in their defense. The Frenchman was found guilty but received a reduced sentence. The Australian was acquitted as insane, although the verdict may have been the result of factors other than his XYY status: "It is, in fact, quite possible that the jury would have returned the same verdict on the basis of his mental deficiency alone, his abnormal electro-encephalograph and his epilepsy alone, or both."[14] When it was (incorrectly) reported that Richard Speck, the American murderer of eight nurses, was also XYY, the result was a widespread belief that men with a double dose of the male sex chromosome were violent and that "their chromosomes made them do it."

The first report of the XYY pattern occurred in 1961 in the chromosome study of a man who had fathered a child with Down syndrome.[15] Excitement about the relevance of the extra Y increased in 1965 when the additional chromosome was found in 3 percent of men studied in a maximum security prison in Scotland.[16]

A 1969 account of XYY males in institutions (most of whom were characterized as "antisocial") identified 50 out of 926, or 4.3 percent. Since the estimate for the general population is one in a thousand, this institutional rate was forty-three times higher than expected. When minimum height restrictions were imposed on the subjects tested, the figure rose: if the minimum was six feet, the rate was over a hundred times higher.[17] Further surveys of penal institutions were carried out, and a 1973 summary of results from sixteen facilities found 26 XYY males among 5,805 *height-unselected* males (1 in 225), or about four times the expected frequency.[18] Indeed, the population estimate of one in a thousand may be high, rendering the institutional rate even more impressive. In samplings of a total of 6,500 infants, 12 XYY males were found (1 in 550).[19]

Because of the posited association between the extra male chromosome and violence, early studies of prisoners focused on those confined to maximum security facilities. The fact that XYY males are taller than most prisoners, however, was a study confound. Possibly, taller prisoners are found more frequently in maximum security areas because they *appear* to pose a more formidable threat. In addition, an extra Y chromosome may contribute to lower intelligence. Less intelligent criminals may be more easily apprehended, again skewing the samples studied. By the late 1960s the only non-institutionalized sample of tall men surveyed for the extra Y consisted of thirty-six basketball players. They tested normal.[20]

The least biased study of XYY men was conducted in Denmark, where males born between 1944 and 1947 and in the top 16 percent for height were studied.[21] To increase the chances of locating XYY men, the study tested taller Danish males only. Since XXY men—

who have an extra X (female) chromosome—are also tall, these men were also studied. Of 4,591 men six feet or taller, 12 XYY and 16 XXY men were identified.

Penal registers provided data on convictions for criminal offenses, and rough intellectual levels were obtained from a military draft board test and from the men's achieved educational level. Of the XYY men, 42 percent (5 of 12), and of the XXY men, 19 percent (3 of 16) had been convicted of one or more offenses, compared to 9 percent of the normal XY male controls. The difference between the XYY men and the XY men is statistically significant. The difference between the XXY and XYY men and that between the XXY and XY men is not.

Only one of the XYY men's offenses constituted an aggressive act against a person. One XYY man with an extensive criminal record was mentally retarded, and the remaining four were below average in intelligence. Of the three XXY men with a criminal history, one was convicted of a brutal attack. All three had below average intelligence scores. In all three groups of men lower intelligence scores were related to convictions. When researchers controlled for intelligence, educational level, and socioeconomic status for the groups, an elevation in the crime rate remained for the XYY men but not for the XXY men, but their offenses were against property, not persons.[22]

The hormone levels of the XYY men were also measured. Testosterone, the male hormone driving sexuality (see Chapter 12), was higher. XXY men, by contrast, had lower levels of testosterone. A study of the sexuality of the XYY men found that they masturbated more frequently in boyhood, experienced their first intercourse earlier, reported more sexual desire, and were more sexually active. The XXY men, however, had more "problems with masculine role" and were more "submissive."[23] Although the XYY men had elevated testosterone levels compared to the controls, they were within the normal range. But for *all* subjects a relationship was found between testosterone levels and criminal convictions, especially among those convicted of violent crimes.[24] No relationship was found, however, between testosterone and *psychological test* measures of aggression, and the mean testosterone concentrations did not differ for XYY men who had criminal convictions and those who did not.[25]

Each sex chromosome atypical male was compared with two XY normal males, one matched for socioeconomic status, height, and age, and the other for these variables plus intelligence. When compared with controls for delinquent and aggressive behavior, the XYY men were higher in one item, "aggression toward wife." They also reported more impulsivity in their delinquent acts.[26]

Other studies of XYY males also suggest a problem with impulsivity control.[27] In a psychological assessment of XYY and XY males, eight of fourteen XYY men showed more need for immediate gratification and more impulsivity. "Fits of temper" were also more common.

The relevance of these findings for a criminal defense is related to the operant legal definitions of "excuse" or "mitigation" as well as the extent to which sexual science data are accepted by the court. Under the widely used M'Naghten "right-wrong" test, defendants pleading the XYY defense face a major hurdle because of the current state of knowledge about the anomaly. Data do not show that the extra Y radically impairs a person's ability to appreciate the nature of his acts or to understand that they are wrong. Impulsivity of action is not enough. By contrast, under the "irresistible impulse" test, XYY men might fare better. Although their cognitive capacity to appreciate wrongfulness is not lacking, their impulse control, a feature commonly reported as a problem for some XYY men, might be impaired. With the Durham or "product" test, the XYY defendant also has a chance. Here he must demonstrate that the criminal act was the product of a mental defect. Unfortunately for the defense, this test is almost extinct. With the ALI Model Penal Code, which combines the cognitive and product tests, the defendant may have a relevant argument if the court accepts the notion that the extra Y leads to a mental defect and that the defect is manifested as a *substantial* incapacity to conform to lawful conduct. Under a "diminished capacity" defense the defendant could argue for less than full culpability because of the lack of full requisite intent to commit the crime.

The admissibility of sexual science data generally depends on the "Frye" test or rule.[28] As the *Frye* court wrote,

Just when a scientific principle or discovery crosses the line between the experimental and demonstrable stages is difficult to define. Somewhere in this twilight zone the evidential force of the principle must be recognized, and while the courts will go a long way in admitting expert testimony deduced from a well-recognized scientific principle or discovery, *the thing from which the deduction is made must be sufficiently established to have gained general acceptance in the particular field to which it belongs.*[29]

In some courts, the applicable test of admissibility is relevancy. Does the evidence have sufficient probative value (as an aid in proof)? The question of scientific reliability goes to the *weight* of the evidence.[30]

Compared to the French and Australian defendants who first popularized the notion of the "supermale" syndrome, Americans pleading excuse or mitigation on the basis of an extra Y chromosome have not fared well. In a 1970 Maryland case, *Millard v. State,* a defense witness could not connect the chromosome in any legally recognized way with a mental defect that would contribute to robbery with a deadly weapon. The court followed the ALI Model Penal Code test. The defendant's medical witness, a geneticist, described the published reports of XYY and opined that the defendant had a mental defect. Because the expert was not a psychiatrist, however, he could not testify as to whether the defect met the standard for insanity. The psychiatrist who testified for the state declared that the chromosomal anomaly did not constitute a mental defect and that the defendant was not insane. The defense of insanity was not submitted to the jury.

The conviction was upheld on appeal. The court noted the geneticist's inability to "meaningfully relate the effect of such 'mental defect' to which he had testified to the 'substantial capacity' requirement," but it also indicated that "in so concluding, we do not intend to hold, as a matter of law, that a defense of insanity based upon the so-called XYY genetic defect is beyond the pale of proof."[31]

A California appellate court dealt with the XYY syndrome in another 1970 case, *People v. Tanner.*[32] The defendant, who was accused of attempted murder, was discovered to have an extra Y while committed to a state hospital. At trial "medical testimony introduced by [the] appellant was that of two geneticists . . . [who] described the physiological manifestations of this chromosomal abnormality" and testified to some of the behaviors attributed to it. "These studies suggest that such individuals exhibit aggressive behavior as a causal result of this chromosomal abnormality."[33]

The court was not impressed.

> Studies of the 47 XYY individuals undertaken to this time are few, they are rudimentary in scope, and their results are at best inconclusive . . . The testimony of appellant's expert witnesses suggests only that aggressive behavior may be one manifestation of the XYY Syndrome. The evidence collected by these experts does not suggest that all XYY individuals are by nature involuntarily aggressive . . . [Furthermore] the experts could not determine whether appellant's aggressive behavior, namely, the commission of an assault with intent to commit murder, resulted from his chromosomal abnormality . . . none of the expert witnesses on genetics testified that possession of this extra Y chromosome results in mental disease which constitutes legal insanity under the California version of the M'Naghten Rule.[34]

Five years later, a New York defendant fared no better.[35] As part of an insanity defense, his attorney sought the appointment of a cytogeneticist to conduct chromosomal testing. But in its analysis, the court considered the scientific status of the extra Y as a criminal defense: "Early studies of chromosome imbalance focused almost exclusively on prison populations . . . the sampling, thus far, has been inadequate and inconclusive . . . Scientists and legal commentators appear to be in agreement that further study is required to confirm the initial findings and to concretely establish a causal connection between one's genetic complement and a predisposition toward violent criminal conduct."[36] Noting that in another New York case the XYY statute was admitted into evidence, the court commented, "Judge Farrell has taken a different approach and permitted, in *People v. Farley*[37] evidence of an XYY condition to go to the jury . . . The jury rejected the insanity defense . . . [Later] Judge Farrell, writing for [a law review], indicated that 'Its [the XYY syndrome's] relevance as part of an insanity defense should not be opened to serious dispute.'"[38]

The appellate court was not persuaded: "Notwithstanding the comments of and the practices followed by Judge Farrell in the trial over which he presided and the acceptance by some foreign courts of the XYY syndrome, it appears on the whole that the genetic imbalance theory of crime causation has not been satisfactorily established and accepted in either the scientific or legal communities to warrant its admission in criminal trials."[39] The defendant's motion for the appointment of a cytogeneticist was denied.

The skeptical analyses of XYY research by American courts is generally warranted. Yet there is evidence of reduced impulse control in association with this genetic anomaly, at least for some individuals. Rejecting such evidence as inconsistent with a psychiatric disorder because it is based on a chromosomal anomaly invokes a false mind-body dichotomy in human behavior. It is analogous to contending that the intellectual retardation of those with Down syndrome (once popularly called "mongolism") is not a mental problem because it is due to a chromosomal abnormality.

The extra Y chromosome need not affect all males uniformly. It may interact with other genetic and environmental contributors to find expression in behavior. All persons with Down syndrome are not mentally retarded to the same degree—some are employable, while others require custodial care. In legal jurisdictions that do not require the exacting M'Naghten standard for excuse or mitigation of criminal conduct, consideration should be given to the individualized experiential factors brought to each case.

If the XYY defense is successful, has the defendant painted himself into a corner? A successful insanity plea based on a fundamental genetic defect could result in a life commitment to prison or a hospital. What this view ignores, however, is the potentially beneficial effect of psychopharmacology on mental states that may have some physiological basis, including schizophrenic and manic-depressive illness. And, although a follow-up study using the anti-androgen medroxyprogesterone acetate (MPA) (Chapter 12), on a dozen XYY men who had committed sex offenses found no benefit,[40] treatment with major tranquilizers might be beneficial.

## Premenstrual Syndrome

According to one sixth-century B.C. commentator, "One day she smiles and is happy. A stranger who sees her in the house will praise her, and say 'There is no woman better than this among all mankind' . . . But on another day she is unbearable to look at or come near to; then she raves so that you can't approach her."[41] These words are evocative of "premenstrual tension," which was characterized over sixty years ago as a feeling of "indescribable tension and a desire to find relief by foolish actions difficult to restrain."[42] In 1953, Katharina Dalton described premenstrual behaviors that included aggressive and suicidal tendencies, and with Raymond Greene coined the term "premenstrual syndrome" (PMS).[43] Eventually, the list of reported symptoms totaled over 150.[44]

Several criminal and psychiatric behaviors reportedly occur more frequently premenstrually. An early study found that 62 percent of violent crimes by females were committed then.[45] Another study found that half of all emergency room admissions of women due to accidents occurred then.[46] More women reportedly commit suicide during that time.[47] And half of women convicted of committing a crime did so during the four days before or after the onset of menses. This was true for two-thirds of those women who reported a history of PMS.[48]

In England, PMS has had a successful run in the courts as a mitigating or excusing factor. In a 1981 case, Sandie Craddock, a London barmaid with a history of forty-five convictions and twenty-five suicide attempts, had stabbed another barmaid through the heart three times.[49] The barmaid's actions came "as a surprise," in that she reportedly spent a "happy evening with the [other] barmaid she later murdered [and] had even defended her in a quarrel with another couple only minutes before the stabbing."[50] Katharina Dalton used Craddock's diaries and other records to demonstrate the periodicity of her acts of violence. Both her crimes and her suicide attempts occurred at intervals of about twenty-nine days. Dalton diagnosed PMS and treated Craddock with large doses of the female hormone progesterone, which reportedly calmed and smoothed out her behavior. She became a "model prisoner, busy writing poetry and reading one book a day."[51] Her criminal charge was reduced to "man"slaughter on the basis of PMS-induced diminished responsibility. She was then given probation so that she could receive hormone therapy.

A year later, Craddock, now named Smith, missed four progesterone treatments within a span of four days.[52] She subsequently threw a rock through a window and then reported herself to police. She was permitted to remain on probation with continued hormone treatment. But over the next eight months, Dalton reduced her progesterone dosage, and Smith then slashed her wrists and threatened the life of a policeman. She was convicted but again placed on probation.

Christine English had no record of periodic (or otherwise) violent acts. But she had experienced severe postpartum depression after the birth of a son and had attempted suicide. Following a verbal dispute with her lover, she fatally pinned him against a utility pole with her car. The next morning she began to menstruate.[53]

Both Craddock and English were convicted of manslaughter due to PMS-caused diminished responsibility. Craddock received a probationary sentence. English lost her driver's license!

Dalton reports a case in which a woman was charged with shoplifting. In court, her husband gave evidence that one day a month she would bring home a bizarre item, such as dog food for a dogless home or baby clothes for adult children, but would have no memory of obtaining them. With the help of the husband's diary, the charges were dismissed.[54]

Dalton also reports other cases with spectacular treatment results. One is of a young woman whose first suicide attempt occurred eighteen months after her first menstrual period. By her midteens she had begun to exhibit bizarre behavior, including swallowing weed killers, shaving her eyebrows, and setting fire to her home. While in prison for arson, during the following three premenstrual cycle phases she attempted arson, cut her wrists, and attempted self-strangulation. After the administration of progesterone her behavior normalized and she was released on probation. At a two-year follow-up she was married and employed in a managerial position with no further episodes of troubled behavior.[55]

Another woman exhibited criminal behavior at monthly intervals that included making false police emergency calls, assaulting the police, attempting to hang herself, and arson. Daily injections of progesterone were associated with the cessation of her bizarre behavior, and she was released from prison. Then, in error, she received no injections for a week. The woman reoffended. While in custody three weeks later she told personnel that she felt violent, and before an injection was available she threw a knife at a man, escaped, and assaulted three policewomen. That evening she began to menstruate. She received a two-year prison sentence, but the periodic violence continued. Five months later she received progesterone and remained in control over the next four months, up to the time of Dalton's report.[56]

English law is more sympathetic to the type of defense available for PMS defendants. "Diminished responsibility" grants the court discretion in sentencing a defendant charged with murder and affected by an abnormality of the mind arising from arrested development, inherent causes, or a disease or injury that results in substantial impairment of mental responsibility.[57]

The female hormone progesterone was initially used in treating PMS in 1934.[58] Dalton and Greene were the first to suggest a rationale for its use and described its success (absent a placebo) in seventy-two of seventy-eight cases.[59] Treatment studies with PMS are inconclusive, however. The placebo response is high (60 to 80 percent); thus, one study found that although progesterone was an effective treatment for some symptoms, a placebo was equally effective.[60] Nevertheless, by 1982 Dalton had treated 1,095 women with PMS using progesterone and claimed that PMS is "progesterone responsive."[61] The fact that progesterone *deficiency* has not been proven as the *cause* of PMS does not discourage Dalton's co-author Greene, who asserts that the efficacy of progesterone treatment is not tethered to progesterone deficiency: "This no more proves that progesterone deficiency is the cause of the trouble than that aspirin deficiency is the cause of headaches."[62] And Dalton is not overly sympathetic to the call for double-blind placebo controlled research in which neither patient nor physician know whether the patient is receiving progesterone or placebo: "Had the obsession with [such scientific methods] existed when insulin was first discovered, on whose conscience would lie the death of the placebo-receiving diabetic?"[63]

For all Dalton's effort, one critic characterizes her career as one in which she "has treated thousands of women with progesterone during the past 30 years—undoubtedly encompassing the largest uncontrolled trial in history of a single medication by one physician for one disorder!"[64]

Distinguishing "genuine" PMS has also been a problem, especially for legal purposes. According to Dalton, the "only positive method of diagnosis is by the menstrual chart, on which the patient records co-instantaneously the presence of symptoms in relation to her menstrual cycle."[65] The patient's personal diary, where women often keep records of menstruation, may also be used. "Such evidence can be used when combined with other retrospective sources such as police files, hospital admission records for previous suicide attempts or self-mutilation, and employer's records of absences or lateness for work."[66]

PMS women whose criminal behavior can be modified by hormonal intervention should show "[t]he recurrence of monthly symptoms in the premenstruum or early menstruation with a complete absence of symptoms after menstruation."[67] For Dalton, there must be recurrence "in every cycle, which, for practical purposes, may be taken as recurrence in at least the last three consecutive menstrual cycles."[68]

United States courts have been far more conservative in their acceptance of the PMS defense. In one case, a bankruptcy proceeding concerning two female romantic partners,[69] one woman filed for bankruptcy to discharge, among other debts, a judgment from the other woman for multiple stabbing injuries. The issue facing the bankruptcy court was whether the debt was nondischargeable because it was the product of a "willful and malicious" action or whether the PMS defense negated the willfullness of the act. Unfortunately for the PMS defense, previous roommates of the alleged "sufferer" claimed that she had threatened suicide and murder several times a week. Another roommate claimed to have been threatened at knife point over a hundred times and to have had a shotgun held to her head for two hours, again with no periodicity to the assaults. Thus the defendant's statement that she began menstruating on the day she attacked the present roommate did not impress the court. There was "no competent evidence to establish that her conduct on the occasion was proximately caused by this disorder." In addition, the woman had not asserted PMS as a defense in the earlier criminal proceeding for the stabbing.

Another PMS defendant was found incapable of forming the requisite intent to commit larceny (the object of the theft was a $3 piece of meat).[70] Another argued (unsuccessfully) that she should be able to withdraw a guilty plea because of its involuntariness due to PMS.[71] Still another, an employee with PMS, quit her job in a huff and shortly thereafter attempted unsuccessfully to revoke her quitting. When she was denied unemployment benefits, she sued and won, in part because of her irrational behavior, allegedly due to PMS, but in part also because her employer was irrational.[72]

The criminal case that came closest to testing the PMS defense in the United States involved felony child beating, but prior to trial, the woman dropped that defense and pled guilty to a misdemeanor.[73]

The fact that PMS symptoms are not uniform across cultures provides ammunition to critics of its legitimacy as a biological aberration.

> The difference in the cyclic timing of emotional changes between Western and non-Western women, as well as the absence of emotional shifts among some non-Westerners, has implications for the interpretation of menstrual cycle mood changes . . . the notion that PMS is a biologically-induced condition must be examined carefully. The biology of the menstrual cycle is the same for women regardless of culture, so that the absence of important premenstrual mood shifts among women in Third World nations must be accounted for by something other than biology."[74]

Although there is disagreement over the uniformity of PMS symptoms across cultures, the constellation of behaviors that may constitute PMS, and its prevalence (not to mention its etiology and treatment), many women do report extensive mood and behavioral changes in the premenstrual phase of the cycle. Yet the American Psychiatric Association Diagnostic manual, DSM IIIR, does not include PMS as a distinct entity. It does, however, include its more severe manifestations—where there is "marked impairment in social or occupational functioning"—under the term "late luteal phase dysphoric disorder" in an appendix of proposed diagnoses "needing further study."[75] In a preliminary 1991 version of its successor, DSM IV, the inclusion of PMS remained undecided.[76] The politics surrounding the controversy make the ultimate entry or exclusion of premenstrual syndrome less than a purely scientific decision. Some feminists argue, for example, that legal recognition of a periodically compromised emotional state in women would impede their pursuit of equality in the workplace and call into question their eligibility for important leadership roles.

As is posited for XYY men, individual women may experience a substantial impact from their underlying physiological state. When well documented, PMS should be admitted as a defense grounded in psychiatry, consistent with the legal requirements in the defendant's jurisdiction.

## Postpartum Psychosis

"The problem of post-partum mental disorders is almost as old as medicine itself. Hippocrates, Celsus and Galen . . . all observed postpartum psychosis."[77] For Hippocrates, "the bleeding of a nipple of a woman recently delivered of a baby was an ominous sign . . . [T]his view had established itself as such a strong tradition that twenty-three centuries later we found Esquirol earnestly presenting the clinical evidence for and against it."[78] The theory behind this notion was that when milk stopped being secreted from the breast it went directly to the brain.[79]

In 1847 in a suburb of Boston, a few days after a woman gave birth, her troubled behavior caused neighbors to call her physician. He diagnosed postpartum psychosis and prescribed the separation of mother and baby. But a few days later, she obtained access to the baby and killed it. The woman was tried and found not guilty by reason of insanity.[80]

Postpartum mood disorders range from "baby blues" to postpartum clinical depression to postpartum psychosis. *"Baby blues"* are characterized by crying, anxiety, or fatigue, and may occur after childbirth in half of women. The condition commences within the first week and is gone within a couple of weeks. Postpartum *depression* displays the same symptoms but with greater severity, and includes difficulty in caring for the baby and concern by the mother about her ability to be an effective parent. It may occur after 15 percent of births. The time of onset is variable, and it can persist from a few weeks to months. Postpartum *psychosis* includes, in addition to these symptoms, delusions (false ideas) and auditory hallucinations (internally induced or "imaginary" voices). A common delusion is the belief that the infant is defective or dead. Hallucinations may involve voices that order the mother to kill her baby. Postpartum psychosis starts within a few weeks of childbirth and affects one or two women in a thousand. Over 90 percent recover with antidepressants or electroconvulsive (shock) therapy within a few months,[81] but about 3 percent of mothers with postpartum psychosis kill their infants.[82]

In an early California case,[83] a mother drowned her nine-month-old in a bathtub. She claimed that God told her the boy was the Devil. With a previous childbirth she had suffered a severe postpartum illness. Originally charged with murder, she was tried for manslaughter and found not guilty by reason of insanity due to postpartum psychosis (PPP). She spent several months in a psychiatric hospital.[84]

In a 1988 California case, a mother who was experiencing auditory hallucinations was convicted of second degree murder after strangling her eighteen-month-old son and sentenced to fifteen years to life in a state mental health facility. On appeal, the conviction was reversed because the trial court had disallowed jury instructions on the lesser included offenses of voluntary and involuntary manslaughter and the jury should have been allowed to consider whether she formed the required mental state for the higher level crime.[85] Subsequently, the California supreme court criticized the appellate court decision because it failed to consider a recent law affecting the mental state required for conviction.[86]

A 1989 California case focused public attention on postpartum psychosis with conflicting views of medical experts and conflicting conclusions of judge and jury. In *People v. Massip*[87] the court described in detail the events leading to the arrest and trial of Mrs. Massip.

On March 17, 1987, Massip gave birth to a son, Michael. Although she was a caring, loving mother, Michael cried 15 to 18 hours a day . . . He was in a great deal of pain and nothing Massip did helped to alleviate it. She tried feeding him different formulas but he just vomited . . . she began feeling confused and worthless; and during the next six weeks she could neither sleep nor eat. She began having suicidal thoughts . . . [A few days later] when Michael began crying again, Massip took him for a walk. During the walk, she heard voices telling her the baby was in pain and to put him out of his misery . . . She was watching her own actions from outside of herself . . . At one point during the walk, she saw herself throw the baby in front of a car. The driver did not recognize the bundle as a baby, but was able to swerve and missed it. Massip later that day placed Michael under the tire of her car and drove over him. She then picked him up and walked with him, but did not remember what he looked like. At that time, she saw him as a doll or an object . . . afterward [she] plac[ed] him in a trash can, where he was later discovered. She told her husband the baby had been kidnapped and gave a description of the kidnapper. Later, when they were at the police station, she admitted to her husband she had killed Michael.[88]

The jury found Massip sane, but the judge set the verdict aside and ruled Massip insane. The trial court then reduced the offense from second degree murder to voluntary manslaughter. In explaining his decision, the judge noted:

The court is required to independently weigh the evidence. . . . In doing so, I have determined from the evidence that on the day of the killing the defendant's mental condition was disrupted and delusional from a postpartum depression and at times a postpartum psychosis. I do not believe the People's evidence has established beyond a reasonable doubt that the defendant possessed the requisite mental state of malice aforethought at the time of the killing. Therefore, the court, having the power and responsibility to effect justice, does set aside this jury verdict . . . this defendant is guilty of voluntary manslaughter and not guilty of second degree murder.[89]

The state appealed. The appellate court dealt with the court's finding of insanity first: ". . . the court clearly had the power to set aside the jury's finding of sanity when it found 'as a matter of law' Massip's insanity had been established. But we have no trouble finding it exceeded its power, as expressly defined by the Legislature, in entering a new finding of insanity." (The court had only the power to grant a new trial on the sanity phase.)

For the appellate court, "the real thrust of the People's argument is that the evidence established Massip intended to kill and malice was thus necessarily present . . . The People point to conflicts in the evidence which indicate Massip was behaving in a rational manner."

Experts for Massip provided enough evidence for the appellate court. Three mental health professionals testified that she was psychotic and "operating under hallucinations and delusions resulting from severe mental illness, causing her to lose touch with reality."[90] However, on appeal, the California supreme court vacated the appellate court decision for reconsideration in light of *People v.*

*Saille*. There, the court held that California does not permit reduction of what would otherwise be murder to nonstatutory voluntary manslaughter due to mental disorder.[91]

A woman in Michigan who dropped her child into a river and reported him kidnapped was found not guilty by reason of insanity due to PPP and was psychiatrically hospitalized for two months.[92] Another California woman who killed her infant pled guilty to voluntary manslaughter and was sentenced to four years in the psychiatric ward of a state prison.[93] A pediatric nurse in New York was charged with murdering her daughter in 1980, her son in 1982, and with attempting to murder another son in 1985. Before her arrest, she underwent voluntary sterilization. She pled insanity based on PPP. She was acquitted and ordered to undergo outpatient psychiatric treatment.[94]

A Pennsylvania mother who killed her infant was found guilty of third degree murder but mentally ill, and received the same sentence she would have received if she had not been mentally ill (eight to twenty years), although she had undergone sterilization.[95] The woman had experienced postpartum depression with her one prior childbirth. She dropped her second infant into a stream in January, where it either drowned or died of exposure to cold, and reported the child kidnapped. She pled guilty but mentally ill, and on appeal argued excuse for the killing. The appellate court observed that "the sentencing court found that appellant was aware at that time that her conduct would cause serious harm." As for the sentence, "the court's focus in rejecting probation was not appellant's mental condition at the time of the murder, but rather the future undue risk the court believed appellant represented as a result of her current mental illness . . . the sentencing court was well aware of the fact that appellant could no longer have children."[96]

Postpartum psychosis was not included in the American Psychiatric Association DSM IIIR list of mental disorders. But category 298.90 does include "Psychiatric Disorder not otherwise specified. (Atypical Psychosis) Disorders in which there are psychotic symptoms that do not meet the criteria for any other nonorganic psychotic disorder. Examples [include] . . . postpartum psychoses."[97] In the preliminary version of DSM IV, there is a proposed diagnosis of "postpartum mood disturbance" if the onset of symptoms is within four weeks of childbirth.[98]

Postpartum psychosis is an easier defense in England, "where a woman by any wilful act or omission causes the death of her child . . . under the age of twelve months . . . [if] at the time . . . the balance of her mind was disturbed by reason of her not having fully recovered from the effect of giving birth . . . or by reason of the effect of lactation . . . she shall be guilty of . . . infanticide." Infanticide is punishable as manslaughter, not murder. Alternatively the jury can return a verdict of "guilty but insane."[99]

Postpartum psychosis is a long-recognized entity. Emphasis on "psychosis," whether or not it is caused by recent childbirth, should constitute a sufficient basis for arguing legal excuse or mitigation based on precedents from other psychotic states. In contrast to the PMS defense, there may be no psychiatric history supporting a diagnosis of postpartum psychosis. Thus, a challenge for psychiatry and law is that of distinguishing overburdened new mothers from the actively delusional.

## Homosexual Panic

"Acute homosexual panic" was first described in 1920.[100] Early reports profiled seventeen case histories (including those of two females). Precise diagnosis however, has hardly been a strong feature: "It is doubtful if many terms in the lexicon of psychiatry and psychoanalysis have been subject to more variegated usage than that of homosexual panic."[101] A major problem in diagnosing acute homosexual panic is that "it is as much an interpretation as it is a diagnosis."[102]

The psychological dynamics of homosexual panic have been characterized in varied ways. One researcher states, "the unconscious, infantile wish in all cases of homosexual panic in males is to submit, or offer oneself, sexually to the father."[103] Others claim that "the unassertive male's conviction of inadequacy is so strong that he concedes defeat in advance. The result is a chronic pseudohomosexual anxiety that flares up acutely in self-assertive crises as a paranoid expectation of homosexual assault, often symbolized in the form of anal rape[104] . . . In a particular patient the perceived threat of homosexual assault may specifically cause rage and fear . . . For some patients the fear of homosexual assault in a power struggle may lead to violent acts to ward off the humiliation of mas-

culine pride . . . The pseudo-homosexual equation is . . . I dominate, control, annihilate, therefore I am not castrated, I am not a
woman, I am not a homosexual."[105]

Although homosexual panic was legitimized in an earlier version
of the American Psychiatric Association Diagnostic Manual, DSM
I (1952) (diagnosis 082),[106] it is not listed in DSM IIIR, the current
manual.

The courts have not been terribly sympathetic to this defense. A
California court rejected it in *People v. Huie*.[107] Huie was convicted
of murdering a homosexual man during a robbery. At his trial he
alleged that the victim had made a sexual advance to him and
sought to admit evidence that the alleged advance triggered a violent "pseudohomosexual panic." The court held the defense inadmissible. On appeal, Huie argued that his experts were not going to
testify "that the defendant at the time of this alleged incident was
suffering from any mental disease or disorder, defect or illness."[108]
Rather, they were going to address events in his childhood that constituted a "compelling trauma" ostensibly relevant to the formation
of the necessary criminal intent.[109] Huie contended that his conviction must be reversed, since expert testimony would show that he
"actually lacked the mental state necessary to support the charged
offense of murder"[110] as a result of childhood events that bore
"directly upon his state of mind at the time of the incident."[111] But
because the California Penal Code excludes evidence of mental
condition except where it reveals a mental disease, defect, or disorder, the exclusion of this defense by the trial court was upheld.

Two other courts have also ruled against the homosexual panic
defense. The Massachusetts Supreme Court found that an appeal
based on the ineffective assistance of counsel was not established
by the fact that the defense did not raise a homosexual panic insanity defense.[112] The defendant claimed that he killed his victim by
repeated stabbing in reaction to an attempted homosexual attack.
A doctor's report in the jail infirmary characterized the defendant's
actions as homosexual panic, but this defense was not pursued at
trial and its omission was held not to be ineffective assistance of
counsel: "[T]he defendant fails to demonstrate how the phrase
'homosexual panic' used in an infirmary report compels the inter-
position of an insanity defense. The term, as we see it, merely
described the defendant's version of the events which occurred in

the motel room. The defendant points to no express mental disorder which may have been the source of the panic . . . Therefore we conclude that the defendant was not deprived of a valid insanity defense."[113]

A protracted, procedurally convoluted case involving homosexual panic as a defense began in the Illinois courts in 1969 and was finally concluded in the federal courts in 1983. Parisie, the defendant, was convicted of murder after being unable to introduce the testimony of three prisoners about the victim's sexuality purporting to show that the deceased was homosexual. Parisie's conviction was upheld by the Illinois courts.[114] When the case entered the federal system, Parisie lost again in a summary judgment at the district court level, but then found two pairs of sympathetic ears in a three-judge panel of the Seventh Circuit. In *Parisie v. Greer*,[115] the federal appeals court described the circumstances of the killing and their rationale for ordering a new trial.

Parisie had argued that the deceased, a married man with three children, had put his hand on the defendant's crotch and said, "John, I'd like to blow you." Parisie's counsel had made an offer of proof to the trial court consisting of his statement "that a witness would testify to having participated in three homosexual acts with the decedent and that the decedent was reputed in the community to be a homosexual."[116] Another affidavit stated that "two witnesses had seen the decedent in known male homosexual locations making homosexual manifestations." But the Illinois appellate court held that "the 'offer of proof' regarding the three witnesses [was] patently inadequate [and] amount[ed] to nothing more than conclusionary, broad-sweeping statements of defense counsel and offer[ed] no acceptable foundation for admission as reputation evidence."[117]

The federal appellate panel disagreed. "The proffered testimony of the three witnesses involved a great deal more than mere reputation evidence. The testimony involved actual homosexual acts and manifestations on the part of the decedent."[118] Parisie's defense, as interpreted by the federal panel, was that "he did not have the requisite intent or mental capacity at the time of the incident because he was undergoing a 'homosexual panic,' a state of mind in which an individual acts instinctively."[119]

A court-appointed psychologist had found the defendant to be "a highly latent homosexual with strong feelings of inferiority and testified that a severe stress of any type could result in an acute schizo-phrenic reaction with accompanying amnesia." Further, "a court-appointed psychiatrist defined homosexual panic as a fear reaction precipitated by a psychological trauma such as a homosexual advance. In such circumstances, the person . . . loses control and acts purely instinctively, 'almost like an animal,' causing the person to be unable to control the nature of his acts . . . Homosexual panic, the psychiatrist stated, is a mental defect and symptomatic of a mental disease."[120]

The problem for Parisie, as stated by the federal panel, was that, "while these defense expert witnesses supplied opinion evidence as to the existence of Parisie's latent homosexuality, the trial court's exclusionary ruling left the jury with the testimony of Parisie, an admitted latent homosexual, as the only evidence of homosexuality on the part of the deceased, a well known and respected citizen of the community."[121] Parisie's conviction was overturned and a new trial ordered.

The state, however, was granted a new hearing before the Seventh Circuit Court of Appeals sitting with nine judges "en banc."[122] The en banc decision is a wonder to behold. No single opinion commanded a majority of the court's members. Only five of the nine were of the view that the court even had jurisdiction, the authority to rule on Parisie's appeal from the state court, and they could not agree on its basis. Furthermore, five judges believed that if they did have jurisdiction, the court could decide the merits of the appeal even though the petition for rehearing was limited to the question of jurisdiction.

The court was divided equally on whether to affirm the district court or reverse and return the case for further consideration. Therefore, because of the tie, the district court decision was affirmed. A similar result of affirming the lower court was reached when four members believed that the appellate court should not hear the case, and a fifth believed that there was jurisdiction but that the district court's decision should be upheld, yielding five votes, out of nine, that the judgment of the lower court should not be disturbed. Six of the court members then voted, for different reasons, that the three-judge panel's decision should be vacated.

What appears to emerge from this byzantine ruling was that the "offer of proof" by the defendant failed to meet the standards of Illinois law. Prior homosexual actions may not be admitted to prove reputation, which was how the evidence was put forward. As stated by Judge Posner in a separate opinion, "It is no business of mine whether the State of Illinois chooses to recognize a defense of 'homosexual panic' as a subcategory of the insanity defense, but I cannot believe that the Constitution of the United States requires a state to allow defense counsel in a murder case to defame the murderer's victim as a homosexual without satisfying the normal prerequisite to admitting evidence of reputation—that the evidence 'be based upon contact with the subject's neighbors and associates rather than upon the personal opinion of the witness.' "[123]

The three judges who disagreed would have upheld the appellate panel, reasoning that Parisie was only permitted half a defense. He had been able to "submit psychiatric evidence that certain circumstances were likely to trigger [homosexual panic] in him. [But] [h]is attempts to bolster his assertion that the triggering event—the homosexual advance—had occurred, were frustrated by the trial court's exclusion . . . [which] . . . was particularly damaging to Parisie's defense because during closing argument the prosecutor stated that '[n]o evidence [had been presented] that this man [the deceased] is or was a homosexual.' "[124]

A more bizarre case that is tangentially related to "homosexual panic" involved the killing of a man who at the hospital was found to be wearing an artificial penis.[125] The defendant wanted to argue that because the decedent was carrying a dildo, he was an aggressive homosexual, and that the defendant had been the victim of a homosexual attack. The state argued that "the admission of the penis would arouse 'prejudicial emotion' among the jurors."[126] The appellate court rejected the convicted killer's appeal, stating "we are not convinced that the trial court abused its discretion when it refused to admit the artificial penis. There was no showing that an individual with such a device on his person was more likely to be an aggressor."[127]

Because physical "gay-bashing" by gangs or individuals is a significant and increasing threat to the safety of homosexuals, psychiatry and law must not permit an irrationally based hatred of homosexuals, sometimes termed homophobia, to masquerade as a psychiatric defense. Yet discarding those circumstances in which the "homosexual panic" defense is concocted to excuse a "hate crime," the question remains whether some males are so fragile in their self-concept of manliness, which is tethered tightly to their sense of heterosexuality, that their psychological defensive actions rise to the legal standards of mitigation or excuse. Those who would reject this defense outright should consider situations in which husbands happen upon wives and paramours *flagrante delicto* and kill in an explosion of jealousy. These men, too, may act in reaction to a threat to their masculine, heterosexual competence. To the limited extent that this latter "heat of passion" defense is admissible, perhaps there is also a limited justification for the former.

A number of lessons emerge from this stringing together of "sex-linked" defenses to criminal behavior as well as a number of questions. First, the misconception lingers that the "body" and the "mind" are separate. Yet even two classic authorities, one often cited as exalting the power of the mind over the body and the other as advancing the classic concept of mind-body dualism, were far more receptive to the integration of "the two."

Sigmund Freud, the father of psychoanalysis, persisted in his efforts to develop a theory grounding psychological events in physiology. For Freud, the "psychic apparatus is at bottom a system of neurons and . . . all events in the neurons can be considered ultimately as quantitative changes."[128] René Descartes, the seventeenth-century philosopher and mathematician who advocated the mind-body dichotomy, maintained that mental phenomena could occur "only after a rational soul had been joined to the body machine."[129]

Rejected by modern-day science as a false dichotomy, the mind-body separation persists in popular thinking as well as among some experts and courts. Their testimony and rulings give currency to the idea that physiological or anatomical phenomena are distinct from the causes of behavior.

Next there is the politics of diagnosis. In Chapter 1 we observed the science of psychiatry parading as a democracy when it polled its membership in a referendum on whether homosexuality is a mental illness. A subject of current debate is whether to include menstrual cycle disorders in the official diagnostic manual of mental illnesses. On the one hand is a body of data documenting, for some women, major behavioral changes associated with a phase of the menstrual cycle. On the other are concerns that relating female reproductive phenomena to antisocial behavior will perpetuate the stereotype of women as instruments of "raging hormones."

Third, the ethical issues in crime and punishment that surfaced in Chapter 12 reemerge here. What is appropriate long-term intervention for female offenders who successfully plead PMS and who respond favorably to hormone therapy? And should castration (or another form of sterilization, such as a birth control substance implanted under the skin) be mandated for those with a history of postpartum homicidal behavior? And, if the extra Y chromosome in a male is associated not only with crime but also with elevated male hormone levels, can antihormone intervention be mandated to treat "testosterone poisoning," the male equivalent of female "raging hormones"?

Finally, is there a meaningful dividing line between inexcusable actions labeled "prejudice," by definition irrationally (and perhaps unconsciously) based in part on fear, and excusable actions labeled "panic," also derived from irrational and unconscious fear? Can behavioral science distinguish early life experiences, which have taken their psychodynamic toll, that excuse or mitigate a crime of passion by a white latent homosexual against a black homosexual but not against a black heterosexual?

# · 14 ·

# Sexual Science and Sexual Privacy

Before his elevation to the United States Supreme Court, Louis Brandeis, as Counsel for the State of Oregon, pioneered the application of social and behavioral science to the law. In 1907, his 113-page brief supporting a limited workday of ten hours for females in factories and laundries argued: "When the health of women has been injured by long hours, not only is the working efficiency of the community impaired, but the deterioration is handed down to succeeding generations. Infant mortality rises, while the children of married working-women, who survive, are injured by inevitable neglect."[1] Brandeis quoted data from over ninety sources, including the Massachusetts State Board of Health, the Berlin International Conference in Relation to Labor Legislation, the Proceedings of the French Senate, the Report of the New York Bureau of Labor Statistics, a book by the sexual scientist Havelock Ellis, and articles published in the *Journal of Political Economy* and *Hygiene of Occupations*. In upholding the work limitation law, the Supreme Court observed that these works "may not be, technically speaking, authorities, and in them is little or no discussion of the constitutional questions presented to us for determination, yet they are significant of a widespread belief . . . [Although] Constitutional questions, it is true, are not settled by even a consensus of present public opinion . . . we take judicial cognizance of all matters of general knowledge."[2]

Four decades later racially segregated public schools provided the Supreme Court with another memorable opportunity for applying social and behavioral science. In a poll of eight hundred social scientists, 90 percent concluded that racial segregation had harmful effects on black students; 82 percent agreed that it also had a negative effect on white students.[3] These data were joined by behavioral studies of black children, some of whom were from racially segregated schools, some from integrated schools.[4] Children were shown white and brown dolls and told to select their favorite doll for play, the "nice doll," the "bad" doll, and the doll that was a "nice color." Kenneth Clark argued that the children's selections showed that black children in segregated schools were more "adjusted to the feeling that they were not as good as whites."[5] In another doll study demonstrating that segregated black children were "definitely harmed in the development of their personalities," eleven of sixteen black children thought the brown doll looked "bad," nine considered the white doll "nice," and seven picked the white doll as the one "like themselves."[6]

After Clark testified to the significance of these studies in an unsuccessful lower court challenge to segregation,[7] the findings were included in a social science brief in the landmark case *Brown v. Board of Education*.[8] The *Brown* decision cited this research in holding that segregation into allegedly "separate but equal facilities" was detrimental to black children and led to a sense of inferiority that affected their motivation to learn.[9]

The preceding chapters have illustrated areas in which the data of sexual science may have an impact on the law. In some, the data have been heeded—as in child custody decisions where a parent is homosexual or in sex-related criminal defenses; in others the data have been ignored—as in immigration or prostitution law. Still others are characterized by conclusions in search of data—such as the effects of sex education.

## Theories of Sexual Privacy

Several factors affect the extent to which sexual science data will find application in courts of law. One is the legal concept of "sexual privacy."

"Men often say that one cannot legislate morality. I should say that we legislate hardly anything else."[10] Eugene Rostow of Yale Law School wrote this in 1960, when I was a medical student at

Johns Hopkins, twenty-four years before I was a law student at Yale. The continuing vitality of his observation reverberates throughout this text.

When the nineteenth-century libertarian John Stuart Mill argued that the state has no legitimate moral concern for physically non-harmful acts and the twentieth-century conservative Lord Devlin warned that objectionable sexual acts tear society's "seamless web," legislation about morality was the essence of sexual privacy. Though we may attempt to sidestep the issue by demurring that our exceptions to sexual privacy engage issues of consent and the protection of children as in adult-minor sex, or regulating the commercialization of sex as in prostitution, or preventing vandalized portrayals of women as in pornography, legislatures and morals constitute the heart and soul of sexual privacy.

In writing *On Liberty* in 1859, Mill set the standard for the contemporary libertarian argument for privacy.[11] Society has jurisdiction over a person's conduct when it prejudicially affects the interests of others. "But there is no room for entertaining any such question when a person's conduct affects the interests of no persons beside himself."[12] No one has the right to say to another adult "that he shall not do with his life for his own benefit what he chooses to do with it. He is the person most interested in his own well-being."[13]

Mill confronted the "no man is an island" value system: "I fully admit that the mischief which a person does to himself may seriously affect, both through their sympathies and their interests, those nearly connected with him and, in a minor degree, society at large."[14] But for Mill, when a man neglects his family through intemperance and cannot pay his debts, he is to be punished not for his intemperance but for having neglected his family. "No person ought to be punished simply for being drunk; but a soldier or policeman should be punished for being drunk on duty."[15]

Mill's contemporary, the critic James Stephen, countered, "How can the State or the public be competent to determine any question whatever if it is not competent to decide that gross vice is a bad thing?"[16] For enforcement of moral behavior "[s]ociety has at its disposal two great instruments by which vice may be prevented and virtue promoted—namely, law and public opinion."[17]

Stephen's view was expanded a century later by the articulate English critic of sexual privacy, Lord Devlin. Society has the right to legislate against immorality, according to Devlin, there being no area of private immorality which is not the law's business.[18] The basis of morals is not that it derives from the law of God, even though that is "how it got there," or from its rational status as the law of reason. It is a feeling "that no right-minded man could behave in any other way without admitting that he was doing wrong."[19] For this feeling to become public morality, there must be agreement by the "man in the street"—a "reasonable man" standard. Disgust toward a particular behavior is not enough. For that behavior to be justifiably within the reach of the law, there must be "intolerance, indignation, and disgust."[20]

Whether individual liberty should be restricted is for Devlin a question of balance between the danger posed by an incursion on individual liberty and the danger to society if the behavior is permitted.[21] A collection of individuals does not make a society; rather, the cement that fashions a society from individuals is a shared morality. Vice is subversion, and because society can eradicate treason and sedition, it can also eradicate vice.[22]

Devlin's eloquent combatant, H. L. A. Hart,[23] agreed that "a consensus of moral opinion on certain matters is essential if society is to be worth living in,"[24] and observed that "[l]aws against murder, theft, and much else would be of little use if they were not supported by a widely diffused conviction that what these laws forbid is also immoral."[25] But Hart objects to the view of society as a "seamless web" that will disintegrate "unless all its emphatic vetoes are enforced by law."[26] He requires a considered answer to the question of whether a practice "which offends moral feeling" harms society, independent of its effect on the moral code and whether the fabric of society is jeopardized if the code is not enforced.[27]

Devlin considered homosexuality analogous to treason because he saw both as destroying society through the process of changing society. But Hart argued that if respect for homosexuals who are accomplished citizens changes society's views on sexuality, the analogy with government "is not the overthrow of ordered government, but a peaceful change in its form."[28] To Hart, the risk of democratic rule by the majority is to tell the man in the street that if "only he feels sick enough about what other people do in private to demand its suppression by law no theoretical criticism can be made of his demand."[29]

To frame his analysis of potential societal restraints on sexuality, Devlin set for himself three "interrogatories."[30] First, he asked whether society has "the right to pass judgement at all on matters of morals." Second, if that answer is affirmative, may society use the "weapon of the law" for enforcement? Third, if the second answer is affirmative, should the law be used "in all cases or only in some; and if only in some, on what principles should it distinguish?"[31]

The assumption that common values are essential for a society's survival provides the response to the first question. Society is a "community of ideas . . . [i]f men and women try to create a society in which there is no fundamental agreement about good and evil, they will fail; . . . society is not something that is kept together physically; it is held by the invisible bonds of common thought . . . [a] common morality."[32] Answering the second question, Devlin asserts that a "society may use the law to preserve morality in the same way as it uses it to safeguard anything else that is essential to its existence."[33] He attacked Mill's hypothetical example of the solitary drunkard who drinks in the privacy of his home, with no one except himself the worse for it: "Suppose a quarter or a half of the population got drunk every night, what sort of society would it be? You cannot set a theoretical limit to the number of people who can get drunk before society is entitled to legislate against drunkeness."[34]

With the first two questions answered in the affirmative, Devlin then asks how the lawmaker is to ascertain the moral judgments of society. The answer is not majority vote. It is the judgment of the "reasonable man," "the man in the street," the man on the Clapham omnibus (public transport in outer London). His judgment may be largely a matter of feeling. He is the "right-minded man, . . . the man in the jury box . . . Immorality then . . . is what every right-minded person is presumed to consider immoral[35] . . . It is not nearly enough to say that a majority dislike a practice; there must be a real feeling of reprobation."[36]

But not every offensive sexual behavior can be controlled. Devlin saw adultery that breaks up a marriage as harmful to the social fabric in the manner of homosexuality or bigamy. But adultery might be placed outside the law because of the difficulty of enforcement. As for fornication, "[a]ll that the law can do . . . is to act against its worst manifestations; there is a general abhorrence of the commercialization of vice."[37] Thus there is strength to the laws against brothels and pimping. Homosexuality, however, is vulnerable to societal control. "Those who are dissatisfied with the present law [against] homosexuality often say that the opponents of reform are swayed simply by disgust. If that were so it would be wrong, but I do not think one can ignore disgust . . . No society can do without intolerance, indignation, and disgust; they are the forces behind the moral law."[38] Noting a "general abhorrence of homosexuality," Devlin[39] asserted that people should ask themselves whether homosexuality is regarded "as a vice so abominable that its mere presence is an offence." If so, society cannot be denied "the right to eradicate it."[40]

In the United States, Kenneth Karst has advanced a principle for upholding sexual privacy: the principle of intimate association.[41] Karst's view is not one of unbridled sexual civil liberties, however. Sexual and emotional commitment, "intimate associations," are favored over "casual associations." The necessity of protecting the latter is recognized so that they may ripen into the former, rather than being inherently valued and so protected: "While commitment means an expectation of constancy over a period of time, any effective legal shelter for this value must offer some protection to casual associations as well as lasting ones. Suppose John and Mary become sexually intimate. Will their encounter amount to nothing more than one of those 'surface relationships' and 'quick exchanges' that are an American disease, or will it be the beginning of an intimate association that endures?"[42]

But Karst's principle stops short of protecting all enduring "intimate associations." Sibling marriage can be forbidden because the "force of conventional morality" acts as a "political constraint."[43] The state's power to protect the "social interest in . . . morality" is exemplified by the Supreme Court decision regulating the showing of pornographic films in a public theater.[44] The contested law was upheld as an effort to preserve the "tone of the society."[45] Karst is not bothered by that case's basic premise: "One need not agree with the decision . . . to agree with the general proposition that the state can legitimately seek to foster a particular morality."[46] The kernel to Karst is "whether the state has offered sufficient justification for a given type of impairment of intimate associational values."[47]

The grading of types of sexual privacy, where casual sex is to be protected because it may blossom into commitment, is reminiscent of the grading of types of speech by Justice Stevens in another pornography case, in which he wrote, "Pornography is not the type of speech for which we would march our sons and daughters off to war."[48] But, some would ask, why not? Why not fully protect pornography if for no other reason than to protect the next grade of speech? Why not fully protect promiscuity if for no other reason than to protect the next grade of intimacy? When does pornography become erotica and perhaps worthy of more protection? When does promiscuity become continuity and continuity interpersonal commitment?

Although a theoretical principle may be fashioned to provide (some) sexual privacy, finding a constitutional underpinning for it has challenged judges and professors alike. The framers of the Constitution embraced no specific philosophy of sexuality; sex is not mentioned. They could scarcely have anticipated the evolution of sexual attitudes and behaviors. Perhaps in formulating the Ninth Amendment they provided a shock absorber on the road to socio-sexual change. That amendment, which supports the principle that individual rights are not limited to those enumerated in the Constitution, provided the basis for Justice Goldberg's concurrence in *Griswold*, which struck down Connecticut's anti-contraception law.[49] Although the Ninth Amendment may open the door to additional liberties, it does not grant entrance to all. Similarly, Justice Stewart's concurrence in *Roe v. Wade*, which found a Fourteenth Amendment right to abortion, is also vulnerable to line drawing. He described liberty as "a rational continuum which, broadly speaking, includes a freedom from all substantial arbitrary impositions and purposeless restraints,"[50] The momentum of sexual privacy cases, from contraception through abortion rights, did not extend to consensual private homosexual behavior.[51] It also left behind common *heterosexual* behaviors.

## Laws

Justice Goldberg's concurring opinion in *Griswold* (joined by Justices Warren and Brennan) advised that Connecticut "does have statutes, the constitutionality of which is beyond dispute, which prohibit adultery and fornication."[52] This pronouncement followed that of Justice Harlan in his dissent in a 1961 case, *Poe v. Ullman, Griswold*'s predecessor: "Laws forbidding adultery [and] fornication . . . form a pattern so deeply pressed into the substance of our social life that any Constitutional doctrine in this area must build upon that basis[53] . . . I would not suggest that adultery [and] fornication . . . are immune from criminal enquiry, however privately practiced."[54]

Today, individual states have not lost interest in regulating consenting intercourse between unmarried persons (fornication) or where one person is married (adultery). Although law review articles frequently cite the statistic that nearly half the states and the District of Columbia continue to criminalize private consenting homosexual sodomy (another activity included in Justice Harlan's list of the unprotected), the perpetuation of anti-adultery and anti-fornication statutes receives rare attention. Yet the number of states that penalize adultery is comparable to the number that penalize homosexual behavior (twenty-five states and the District of Columbia), and the number of states that penalize fornication is not negligible (thirteen and the District of Columbia).[55]

It may not be reassuring to advocates of sexual privacy that adultery and fornication statutes are rarely enforced. Aside from the concern that generally unenforced and unenforceable laws denigrate the law, circumstances do arise in which the statutes are enforced and their consequences fall on violators. Historically, such statutes were used to punish interracial sexual conduct.[56] More recently, they have been used to deny employment[57] and child custody.[58] The conduct may also be included as a lesser offense in charges of a more serious sexual violation: an acquittal for rape, for example, may dictate a conviction for fornication. This was the charge to the jury in *Saunders*[59] that resulted in the challenge to New Jersey's two-hundred-year-old prohibition of fornication. Permitting a conviction for fornication when one for rape is not obtained could mean that every person tried for the rape of an unmarried woman would be convicted of a crime.

The Supreme Court has not squarely faced the extent to which private, consenting heterosexual behaviors may be penalized by the state. When the Court held in *Bowers v. Hardwick* that no fundamental (privacy) right existed to engage in homosexual sodomy, it finessed the section of the Georgia statute that also proscribed heterosexual sodomy.[60] Only Justice Stevens stated that such a prohibition would surely be unconstitutional: "Our prior cases . . . establish that a State may not prohibit sodomy within 'the sacred precincts of marital bedrooms,' or, indeed between unmarried heterosexual adults."[61]

Some, but not all, states agree. In a five to four decision involving heterosexual fellatio, the Iowa supreme court in 1976 struck down that state's sodomy law, which prohibited both heterosexual and homosexual sodomy, although it did not "reach the question of homosexuality since the applicability of the statute to such conduct was not made an issue in [the] case."[62] Sexual science data were not found relevant by the court, however, in reaching its decision: "Defense counsel has referred the court to numerous publications which might be adequately described as 'sex manuals' . . . we do not deem these publications to be of such compelling force or effect that we may take judicial notice of the supposed data, arguments and recommendation of the authors (even though they may have been bestsellers). The publications have no place in a quest involving determination of the constitutional validity of a criminal statute."[63] Nevertheless, the court held that the statute was "an invasion of fundamental rights, such as the personal right of privacy."[64]

Pennsylvania struck down its Voluntary Deviate Sexual Intercourse Statute, which criminalized oral or anal sex between unmarried consenting adults, in 1980 on the grounds that it impermissibly discriminated on the basis of marital status and exceeded the state's police power in regulating private conduct. (The heterosexual acts at issue had been performed on stage in an adult entertainment theater.) The court devoted a full page of its decision to quoting John Stuart Mill.[65]

Oklahoma, in 1986, found that an individual's constitutional right of privacy encompassed private, consensual acts of sodomy between heterosexual adults.[66]

Maryland, in 1990, found the state's heterosexual oral sex law, under which a man had been sentenced to five years probation for an act of fellatio, to be unconstitutional, but did not reach the issue of homosexual oral sex.[67]

By contrast, a New Mexico court overturned a conviction for heterosexual sodomy between unmarried parties in 1975 but was reversed on appeal because the case did not engage the protected rights of marital privacy or the nurturing of family life.[68] Similarly, an Arizona lower court held in 1975 that a conviction for heterosexual fellatio violated the right of privacy but was reversed because the state may "regulate sexual misconduct in its rightful concern for the moral welfare of the people" and sodomy has been considered wrong since antiquity.[69] North Carolina upheld a conviction for "the crime against nature" in 1979, in this case heterosexual fellatio, on the ground that, assuming for argument that married persons could not be prosecuted, unmarrieds could be treated differently. The court pointed to the state's law forbidding fornication, a statute since 1805.[70] Similarly, Rhode Island upheld a conviction for "committing an abominable and detestable crime against nature" in 1980, here, anal intercourse between an unmarried male and female. Because the offense did not involve child bearing and because the Supreme Court had summarily affirmed a homosexual sodomy case, the court held that the right of privacy was inapplicable to "private unnatural copulation between unmarried adults."[71]

## The Limits of the Applicability of Sexual Science

An exploration of the limits of sexual science's future impact on law may be informed by reflecting on the ghosts of sexuality past. Changes in both public opinion and scientific wisdom regarding sexuality in the twentieth century are illustrated in two patterns of behavior, one solitary, the other interpersonal. Both at one time preoccupied medical sexual science and society; both were seen as contributing to personal degradation, if not societal disintegration.

To learned physicians well into this century, masturbation was the cause of a panorama of medical problems, extending from acne (especially on the forehead)[72] to idiocy and insanity. As recently as 1946, a medical text referred to masturbation as "the most widespread of all sexual diseases."[73] The legacy of this concern for the calamity of sexual "self-abuse" is found in two of today's most commonly consumed foods. Sylvester Graham, who lived in the first half of the nineteenth century, is best remembered for the cracker that bears his name. Graham preached against eating meat, because carnivorous food "caused carnal desire"[74] and drove children to practice the "secret vice." John Kellogg, a medical student much influenced by Graham, later invented the cornflake as an antimasturbatory food intended to be even more effective than the crackers of Graham.[75] Twentieth-century American youth continued to learn of the dire consequences of masturbation in the Boy Scout manual, which warned against "caus[ing] this [seminal] fluid to be discharged from the body [because it] tends to weaken [one's] strength, [and] to make [one] less able to resist disease."[76]

Medicine's second untouchable was homosexuality. An 1825 text observed that "[this] [u]nnatural propensity is a variety of partial insanity, the principal feature of which is an irresistible propensity to the crime against nature . . . [but] [b]eing of so detestable a character it is a *consolation* to know that it is sometimes the consequence of insanity."[77] In the second half of the twentieth century, psychiatrists continued to characterize homosexuality as "an outcome of exposure to highly pathologic parent-child relationships and early life situations"[78] or of "massive childhood fears"[79] culminating in a "masquerade of life."[80] Not until 1973, when an overwhelming body of sexual science data demonstrated that a homosexual orientation did not meet the criteria for mental illness, was homosexuality per se removed from psychiatry's catalogue of illnesses.

To put the change in attitudes toward masturbation and homosexuality in perspective, I have chosen incest, which has been called "the last taboo,"[81] as a hypothetical example of the potential outer limit of sexual science's application to law because of its nearly universal condemnation. To set the emotional and political climate for considering this example, let us, while recoiling from the prospect that incest will ever be normalized, imagine living during the time when scientific and general wisdom concluded unequivocally that masturbation and homosexuality were evil, sick, and destructive.

Let us next imagine that the National Institute of Mental Health has concluded a twenty-year study in which parents engaging in incestuous relations with daughters and sons were granted immunity from prosecution, thus enabling a representative sample of families to come forward for periodic evaluations. The results demonstrate that in most families, the short-term effects are enhanced family stability, with less marital discord, and a more positive parent-child relationship, and that in the longer term, the children as young adults have fewer sexual problems than a control group of adults without a history of incest.

Would society and the courts find themselves willing to accommodate such hypothetical findings? Or would the study's fate be that of the $2 million government-funded research project reported in the 1970 Presidential Commission on Obscenity and Pornography, which concluded that pornography was beneficial and should be legalized.[82] That extensive report was rejected by Congress without a reading and condemned by President Nixon as "morally bankrupt." If the incest data were similarly rejected, where is the point at which "common sense" would mark the termination of scientific credibility?

Let us consider next society's revulsion toward another pattern of sexuality that tests the limits of sexual privacy. This second hypothetical example proceeds without the "benefit" of provocative (and unlikely) research data. The linchpin issue here is that of sanctioning a sexual relationship between siblings separated at birth who first meet as adults. Not relevant here are the usual arguments against incest, such as the victimization of the young due to unequal power of the parties (invoked by father-daughter sex) or incest's psychological disruption of the nuclear family of parents and young children. What may be present, however, is the debatable genetic concern over "inbreeding"; yet conception need not follow from the sexual union. What ultimately remains is society's abhorrence of brother-sister sex.

Now let us extend the example: the siblings are twins of the same sex who want to marry. Society's contempt attains Lord Devlin's test of the hypothetical average person's ultimate revulsion—the triumvirate of intolerance, indignation, and disgust. The Englishman on the Clapham omnibus has just thrown up.

## Future Tests

At a more realistic level than that of the hypothetical normalization of incest, test issues for sexual science and sexual privacy could emerge in both heterosexual and homosexual contexts. Undoubtedly they will stimulate political and religious responses. Yet such issues are amenable to study. Same-sex marriage and plural marriage (polygamy and polyandry), for example, may gauge the elasticity of the traditional concepts of marriage and family.

Whereas the gay community has long been criticized for its "promiscuity," medically dramatized in the United States by the AIDS pandemic, one explanation is that when relationships are given neither the recognition of law nor the sanction of society, their vitality cannot be expected. But although marriage has been recognized by the Supreme Court as a fundamental right, marital status for same-sex partners has not been permitted. Social and behavioral science can inform courts about the psychological and social effects of same-sex marriage. Denmark permits homosexual persons to achieve the civil equivalent of marriage. Are individual and societal needs met by this innovation?

If marriage is allowed only between men and women, then *how many* men or women? The nineteenth-century Supreme Court forbade the practice of polygamy by the Mormon church out of concern for the exploitation of women,[83] but would this concern prevail against a new court challenge? A lawyer in Utah who is one of nine wives has argued that "compelling social reasons make the lifestyle [of polygamy] attractive to the modern career woman . . . it enables women, who live in a society full of obstacles, to fully meet their career, mothering, and marriage obligations."[84] Particularly in older age groups, where females considerably outnumber males, would polygamy serve a societal good? Would a renewed argument, if again brought to the Supreme Court by the Mormon church, be disparaged by the Court and analogy made to the use of hallucinogenic drugs by religious groups during ceremonies? The Supreme Court has denied the Native American church the right to use peyote if prohibited by state law.[85] Governmental concern for the control of "illicit drugs" trumped the importance of religious tradition or any psychological benefits of the hallucinatory experience. Social and behavioral science may also inform courts about the effects of plural marriage. Polygamy is practiced openly by millions of persons in other nations and furtively by thousands in the United States. What are its effects on children and wives?

## Is Sexuality Different?

Whatever sexuality cases do come to court, philosophers and legal scholars will continue to argue over the relative weight to be given to the desires of the individual, the standards of society, and the powers of the state in limiting sexual autonomy. The relevance of sexual science to these considerations of law is underscored by the nature of human sexuality.

Sexuality in humans evolved in a manner distinct from its expression in other mammals because it dissociated the drive for sexual intercourse from the requirement of procreation. Unlike other mammals, which generally copulate periodically in concert with the periodic capacity for pregnancy, human males and females engage in sexual behavior that is largely independent of the brief time of fertility. The removal of the biological imperative of species propagation from uniquely pleasurable conduct permitted humans to enclothe sexuality in variegated symbols that capture a lifetime of experience and meaning.

To ignore sexual science in legal controversy is to ignore this essential aspect of human motivation and behavior. What is at stake is not casual, inadvertent, or peripheral. Sexual identity is experienced as the seamless web of personhood. No other quality—not race, not religion—so defines self-concept, overt behavior, and the reactions of others. No other quality is driven by the biological imperative. If jurisprudential analysis ignores the science of this uncommonly human dimension of meaning and expression, it ignores the foundation from which all sexuality cases and controversies spring. Sexuality is the bedrock human element, whether viewed with the negative awe of Saint Augustine as the feared "genital commotion," with the positive awe of Sigmund Freud as the celebrated libido, or with the dispassionate reflection of the evolutionist as the guarantor of humankind's continuity.

Sexuality is different.

Notes

Index

# Notes

## 1. Fornication

1. 381 U.S. 479 (1965).
2. 75 N.J. 200, 381 A.2d 333 (1977).
3. *Black's Law Dictionary,* 5th ed. (1979). St. Paul: West Publishing. The term is derived from the Latin word *fornix,* which originally meant the forceps of a beetle, then an arch, then an underground vault or cavern, and then a brothel. The last description derives from the Roman custom of keeping brothels in underground caverns and vaults. *Oxford English Dictionary,* s.v. "fornication"; *Corpus Juris* 26:986.
4. J. Money (1985). *The Destroying Angel.* Buffalo, N.Y.: Prometheus Books.
5. *Boy Scouts of America Official Handbook for Boys* (1911). Garden City, N.Y.: Doubleday, Page and Co.
6. A. Augustine. *Concerning the City of God against the Pagans,* trans. H. Bettenson (1972). Harmondsworth, England: Penguin Books.
7. A. Kinsey, W. Pomeroy, and C. Martin (1948). *Sexual Behavior in the Human Male.* Philadelphia: Saunders; and A. Kinsey, W. Pomeroy, C. Martin, and P. Gebhard (1953). *Sexual Behavior in the Human Female.* Philadelphia: Saunders.
8. Id.
9. 1 Thessalonians 4:3.
10. W. Blackstone. *Commentaries, Book IV,* chap. IV, 64–65.
11. Reg. v. Pierson, Salk, 382, 91 Reprint 333.
12. E. Haeberle (1978). *The Sex Atlas.* New York: Seabury Press, p. 350.
13. Note (1978). Fornication, Cohabitation, and the Constitution. *Michigan Law Review* 77:252–306.
14. An Act for the Punishment of Crimes L. 1796 S. XV.
15. L. 1899, C. 235, 48. An Act for the Punishment of Crimes, Revision of 1898.

16. New Jersey Statutes Annotated, S. 2A:110–111 (West 1973).
17. Smith v. Minor, 1 N.J.L. 19, 1 Coxe 19 (Sup. Ct. 1790).
18. Id., p. 19.
19. Id., p. 20.
20. Id., p. 21.
21. Id., p. 23.
22. Id., pp. 23–24.
23. Id., p. 24.
24. Id., p. 26.
25. Petition of Smith, 71 F. Supp. 968, 971, n.1 (N.J.1947).
26. State v. Barr, 265 A.2d 817 (1970).
27. 265 A.2d 817 (1970).
28. 272 A.2d 753 (1971).
29. 275 A.2d 137, 139 (1971).
30. Weiner v. Weiner, 293 A.2d 299 (1972).
31. M. Hunt (1974). *Sexual Behavior in the 1970's*. Chicago: Playboy Press.
32. Appellant's Brief, pp. 15–16.
33. Appellant's Brief, p. 7.
34. Appellant's Brief, pp. 7–8.
35. State v. Saunders, 326 A.2d 84 (1974).
36. State v. Saunders, 381 A.2d 333 (1977).
37. Id., p. 339.
38. Id., p. 342.
39. The distribution of many phenomena follows an expected, or normal dispersion. Graphing this disperson results in a bell-shaped curve. As a person or feature moves further from the center of the bell (the mean or average of all the values), it becomes less normal. Standard segments of the curve define the extent to which a person or feature deviates from the average of the distribution. These segments are standard deviations. The portion of the bell encompassing one standard deviation on each side of the center accounts for about 65 percent of the distribution, that encompassing two standard deviations about 95 percent, and that encompassing three standard deviations about 99 percent.
40. 413 U.S. 49, 60–61 (1973).
41. Id., p. 57.
42. *Report of the Commission on Obscenity and Pornography* (1970). New York: Bantam Books.
43. R. Bayer (1981). *Homosexuality and American Psychiatry*. New York: Basic Books.
44. S. Freud (1905). *Three Contributions to the Theory of Sex*, in *Standard Edition of the Complete Psychological Works of Sigmund Freud* (1953). London: Hogarth.
45. Kinsey et al., *Sexual Behavior in the Human Male;* and Kinsey et al., *Sexual Behavior in the Human Female.*
46. W. Masters and V. Johnson (1966). *Human Sexual Response;* (1970) *Human Sexual Inadequacy.* Boston: Little, Brown.

## 2. Child Custody and Homosexual Parents

1. J. Wallerstein and J. Kelly (1977). Divorce counseling. *American Journal of Orthopsychiatry* 47:4–22.
2. H. Biller (1969). Father absence, maternal encouragement, and sex role development in kindergarten-age boys. *Child Development* 40:539–546.
3. R. Green, J. Mandel, M. Hotvedt, J. Gray, and L. Smith (1986). Lesbian mothers and their children: A comparison with solo parent heterosexual mothers and their children. *Archives of Sexual Behavior* 15:167–184.
4. E. Koppitz (1968). *Psychological Evaluation of Children's Human Figure Drawings*. New York: Grune and Stratton.
5. D. Brown (1956). Sex role preference in young children. *Psychology Monographs* 70, no. 14 (whole no. 421).
6. R. Green, M. Fuller, and B. Rutley (1972). It-Scale for Children and Draw-a-Person Test: Thirty feminine vs. 25 masculine boys. *Journal of Personality Assessment* 36:349–352.
7. R. Green (1987). *The "Sissy Boy Syndrome" and the Development of Homosexuality*. New Haven: Yale University Press.
8. Id.
9. M. Kirkpatrick, K. Smith, and R. Roy (1983). Lesbian mothers and their children. *American Journal of Orthopsychiatry* 51:545–551.
10. S. Golombok, A. Spencer, and M. Rutter (1983). Children of lesbian and single-parent households. *Journal of Child Psychology and Psychiatry* 24:551–572.
11. Id., p. 571.
12. F. Bozett (1987). Children of Gay Fathers. In *Gay and Lesbian Parents*, ed. F. Bozett. New York: Praeger.
13. B. Miller (1979). Gay fathers and their children. *Family Coordinator* 28:544–552.
14. Holland v. Holland, 75 N.E. 2d 489 (Ohio, 1947).
15. Id., p. 490.
16. Id.
17. Id., p. 493.
18. Immerman v. Immerman, 176 Cal. App. 2d 122, 127 (1959).
19. Nadler v. Superior Court, 255 Cal. App. 2d 523 (1967).
20. Id., p. 525.
21. Nadler v. Nadler, No. 177331, Cal. Superior Court Sacramento, 1967, cited by Rivera (1979), *Hastings Law Journal* 30:890–891.
22. Chaffin v. Frye, 45 Cal. App. 3d 39 (1975).
23. Hall v. Hall, No. 55900, Ohio C.P. Court Domestic Relations Div., Licking County, October 31, 1974.
24. R. Rivera (1979). *Hastings Law Journal* 30:898.
25. Townend v. Townend, No. 74 CV 0670, Court of Common Pleas, Portage County, Ohio, April 4, 1975.
26. Transcript, p. 540.
27. Transcript, pp. 547–548, emphasis added.

28. Townend v. Townend, No. 639, County of Portage, Court of Appeals of Ohio, September 30, 1976, p. 3.
29. Id., p. 4.
30. Id., p. 9.
31. Id., p. 13.
32. Schuster v. Schuster and Isaacson v. Isaacson, No. D36868, 36867, Superior Court, State of Washington, King County, 1974.
33. Id., p. 4.
34. Id., p. 5.
35. Id., p. 8.
36. Id., p. 11.
37. Schuster v. Schuster, 585 P.2d 130 (Wash. 1978).
38. Matter of Marriage of Cabalquinto, 669 P.2d 886, 888 (Wash. 1983).
39. Madeiros v. Madeiros, No. 5196-80BC, Vermont Superior Court, Bennington County, 1982.
40. Irish v. Irish, 300 N.W. 2d 739 (Mich. App. 1980).
41. Ashling v. Ashling, 599 P.2d 475, 476 (Ore. App. 1979).
42. Peyton v. Peyton, 457 So. 2d 321 (La. App. 2 Cir. 1984).
43. Id., p. 324.
44. May 4, 1977, p. 3A.
45. Id.
46. Stamper v. Stamper, No. 75-054-550 DM, Circuit Court, County of Wayne, Michigan, 1976.
47. Bezio v. Patenaude, 410 N.E. 2d 1207 (Mass. 1980).
48. Id., pp. 1215–1216.
49. Id., p. 1216.
50. Kehoe v. Kehoe, No. 140795, Probate and Family Court, Middlesex City, Massachusetts, 1981.
51. Slip opinion, pp. 10–11.
52. Doe v. Doe, 452 N.E. 2d 293 (Mass. App. 1983).
53. Id., p. 295.
54. Id., p. 296.
55. Id., note 2.
56. Id., p. 296.
57. Smith v. Smith, Family Law Reporter 3: 2692–2693 (N.Y. Family Ct., Richmond Cty. Sept. 20, 1977).
58. 466 U.S. 429 (1984).
59. 466 U.S. 433.
60. S.N.E. v. R.L.B., No. S426 (Alaska Sup. Ct. 1985).
61. Belmont v. Belmont, N.J. Super. Ct. Hunterdon Cty. (1980), and Silverweig v. Wales (unreported).
62. Family Law Reporter 6:2785–2786.
63. R. Rivera, *University of Dayton Law Review* 11:359.
64. M.P. v. S.P., 404 A.2d 1256 (N.J. Super. 1979).
65. Id., p. 1261.
66. Id., p. 1262.

67. Id., p. 1263.
68. Jacobson v. Jacobson, 314 N.W. 2d 78, 81 (N.D. 1981).
69. Petersen v. Petersen, No. D-66634, District Court, Denver County, Colorado, 1978.
70. Mueller v. Mueller, No. 79-DR-1246, Colo. Dist. Ct., Jefferson County, March 27, 1980, *aff'd.* No. 80-0392, Colo. Ct. App. 1981, discussed by Rivera (1986), *University of Dayton Law Review* 11:363.
71. S.v.S., 608 S.W. 2d 64, 66 (Ky. App. 1980).
72. Commonwealth v. Bradley, 91 A.2d 379 (Pa. 1952).
73. In re: J.S. and C., 324 A.2d 90 (Super. Ct. N.J. 1974), *affd.* 362 A.2d 54 (1976).
74. Id., p. 92.
75. Id., p. 94.
76. Id., p. 95.
77. Id., p. 96.
78. Id.
79. Id.
80. 362 A.2d 54 (1976).
81. Gottlieb v. Gottlieb, 488 N.Y.S. 2d 180, 181 (1985).
82. Stone v. Stone, No. 71-2-D111, District Court, Knox County, Maine, 1979.
83. Id., p. 5.
84. Id.
85. Id., p. 6.
86. Id., p. 7.
87. Roe v. Roe, 324 S.E. 2d 691 (Va. 1985).
88. Id., p. 692.
89. Id., p. 694.
90. Id.
91. Id.
92. Birdsall v. Birdsall, 197 Cal. App. 3d 1024 (1988).
93. Walsh v. Walsh, 451 N.W. 2d 492 (Iowa Sup. 1990).
94. *Lesbian/Gay Law Notes,* (1990) April, p. 22.
95. J.L.P.(H.) v. D.J.P., 643 S.W. 2d 865 (Mo. App. 1982).
96. Id., p. 868.
97. Id., p. 869.

### 3. Homosexuality as a Fundamental Right

1. Skinner v. Oklahoma, 316 U.S. 535 (1942).
2. Griswold v. Connecticut, 381 U.S. 479 (1965).
3. Roe v. Wade, 410 U.S. 113 (1973).
4. Zablocki v. Redhail, 434 U.S. 374 (1978).
5. R. Green (1974). *Sexual Identity Conflict in Children and Adults.* New York: Basic Books; London: Gerald Duckworth.
6. M. Lewis and M. Weinraub (1974). Sex of parent X child: Socioemotional development. In *Sex Differences in Behavior,* ed. R. Friedman, R. Richart,

and R. Van de Wiele. New York: John Wiley; L. Michalson, J. Brooks, and M. Lewis (1974). Peers, parents, people: Social relationships in infancy. Study cited in M. Lewis (1975). Early sex differences in the human. *Archives of Sexual Behavior* 4:329–335.

7. J. Money, J. Hampson, and J. Hampson (1955). An examination of some basic sexual concepts: The evidence of human hermaphroditism. *Bulletin of The Johns Hopkins Hospital* 97:301–319.

8. J. Money and A. Ehrhardt (1972). *Man and Woman, Boy and Girl.* Baltimore: The Johns Hopkins University Press.

9. Money, Hampson, and Hampson (1955).

10. Money and Ehrhardt (1972).

11. Money, Hampson, and Hampson (1955).

12. W. Eaton and D. Von Bargen (1981). Asynchronous development of gender understanding in preschool children. *Child Development* 52:1020–1027.

13. R. Green (1987). *The "Sissy Boy Syndrome" and the Development of Homosexuality.* New Haven: Yale University Press.

14. R. Green (1987); F. Whitam and R. Mathy (1991). Childhood cross-gender behavior of homosexual females in Brazil, Peru, the Philippines, and the United States. *Archives of Sexual Behavior* 20:151–170; F. Whitam and R. Mathy (1986). *Male Homosexuality in Four Societies.* New York: Praeger.

15. J. Gagnon and W. Simon (1973). *Sexual Conduct: The Social Sources of Human Sexuality.* Chicago: Aldine, p. 137.

16. R. Green (1987).

17. C. Socarides (1968). *The Overt Homosexual.* New York: Grune and Stratton; I. Bieber et al. (1961). *Homosexuality.* New York: Basic Books; L. Hatterer (1984). *Changing Homosexuality in the Male.* New York: McGraw-Hill.

18. J. Schippers (1989). *Voorkeur Voor Mannen* (A Preference for Men). The Hague: S.D.U./Schorer, cited by J. Gonsiorek and J. Rudolph (1991), in chap. 11, Homosexual Identity, in *Homosexuality,* ed. J. Gonsiorek and J. Weinrich. Newbury Park, Calif.: Sage.

19. L. Humphreys and B. Miller (1980). Identities in the Emerging Gay Culture. In *Homosexual Behavior,* J. Marmor. New York: Basic Books, p. 153.

20. B. Ponse (1980). Lesbians and their Worlds. In Marmor, p. 173.

21. D. Sanders (1980). A Psychotherapeutic Approach to Homosexual Men. In Marmor, p. 352.

22. M. McIntosh (1981). The Homosexual Role. In *The Making of the Modern Homosexual,* ed. K. Plummer. Totowa, N.J.: Barnes and Noble, pp. 30–44.

23. M. Weinberg and C. Williams (1974). *Male Homosexuals: Their Problems and Adaptations.* New York: Oxford University Press, p. 200.

24. Id., p. 160.

25. Id.

26. R. Green (1989). *Griswold's* Legacy. *Ohio Northern University Law Review* 16:545–549.

27. Weinberg and Williams (1974), p. 268.
28. J. Gonsiorek and J. Rudolph (1991). Homosexual Identity. In *Homosexuality*. Newbury Park, Calif.: Sage, p. 173.
29. K. Karst (1980). The Freedom of Intimate Association. *Yale Law Journal* 89:624–692, p. 658.
30. Id., p. 654.
31. Id., p. 683.
32. Id., p. 651.
33. Id., p. 658, n.155.
34. D. Richards (1979). Sexual Autonomy and the Constitutional Right to Privacy: A Case Study in Human Rights and the Unwritten Constitution. *Hastings Law Journal* 30:957–1018, p. 960; D. Richards (1982). *Sex, Drugs, Death, and the Law*. Totowa, N.J.: Rowman and Littlefield.
35. Richards (1982), p. 31; (1979), p. 961.
36. Id.
37. Richards (1982), p. 41.
38. Id.
39. Id., p. 42.
40. S. Freud (1910). A special type of object choice made by men. Reprinted in *Sexuality and the Psychology of Love* (1963). New York: Collier Books, p. 49.
41. S. Freud (1920). Preface to *Three Contributions to the Theory of Sex* (1962). New York: Dutton, p. xx.
42. Richards (1982), p. 52; (1979) p. 1003.
43. Richards (1982), p. 51; (1979) pp. 1001–1002.
44. Bowers v. Hardwick, 478 U.S. 186, 106 S.Ct. 2841 (1986).
45. Id., pp. 190, 191, 192, 196.
46. 468 U.S. 609, 615 (1984).
47. Carey v. Population Services International, 431 U.S. 678, 705 (1977), (Powell, J., concurring).
48. 277 U.S. 438 (1928).
49. 277 U.S. 478.
50. 478 U.S. 186.
51. Id., p. 203.
52. Id., p. 204.
53. Id., p. 205.
54. Id., emphasis in original.
55. Id., p. 206.
56. Id., p. 211.
57. People v. Onofre, 51 N.Y. S.2d 476, 415 N.E. 2d 936 (1980), *cert. denied*, 451 U.S. 987 (1981).
58. 381 A.2d 333 (1977).
59. State v. Ciuffini, 164 N.J. Super. 145, 395 A.2d 904 (App. Div. 1978).
60. 415 N.E. 2d 941.
61. Act of December 6, 1972. P.L. 1482. No. 334, Sec. 1, Pa. Cons. Stat. Ann. Sec. 3101 (Purdon 1973).

62. Commonwealth v. Bonadio, 490 Pa. 91, 415 A.2d 47, 49 (Pa. 1980).
63. 106 S.Ct. 2856.
64. A. Kinsey, W. Pomeroy, and C. Martin (1948). *Sexual Behavior in the Human Male.* Philadelphia: Saunders; A. Kinsey, W. Pomeroy, C. Martin, and P. Gebhard (1953). *Sexual Behavior in the Human Female.* Philadelphia: Saunders; P. Gebhard (1972). Incidence of overt homosexuality in the United States and Western Europe. In J. Livingood, ed. National Institute of Mental Health Task Force on Homosexuality Publication 72-9116. Washington, D.C.: Dept. of Health, Education, and Welfare, pp. 22–29.

## 4. Homosexuals as a Suspect Class

1. Plyler v. Doe, 457 U.S. 202, 216, n.14 (1982), Frontiero v. Richardson, 411 U.S. 677 (1973).
2. Parham v. Hughes, 441 U.S. 347, 351 (1979).
3. Bowers v. Hardwick, 478 U.S. 186 (1986).
4. D. Bailey (1955). *Homosexuality and the Western Christian Tradition.* London: Longmans, Green; D. Cory (1956). *Homosexuality: A Cross Cultural Approach.* New York: Julian Press.
5. R. Rivera (1979). Our straight-laced judges: the legal position of homosexual persons in the United States. *Hastings Law Journal* 30:799–955; (1986). Special project: survey on the constitutional right to privacy in the context of homosexual activity. *University of Miami Law Review* 40:521–638. The six antidiscrimination states are Wisconsin, Massachusetts, Hawaii, and Connecticut, New Jersey, and Vermont.
6. S. Freud (1920). The Psychogenesis of a Case of Homosexuality in a Woman. In *Standard Edition of the Complete Psychological Works of Sigmund Freud* (1955). London: Hogarth Press.
7. See generally, R. Fieve, D. Rosenthal, and H. Brill, eds. (1975). *Genetic Research in Psychiatry.* Baltimore: The Johns Hopkins University Press.
8. J. Sanders (1934). Homosexueele tweelingen, *Nederlands Tijdschrift Geneeskunde* 78:3346–3352.
9. F. Kallman (1952). Comparative twin study on genetic aspects of male homosexuality. *Journal of Nervous and Mental Disease* 115:283–298.
10. Id., p. 290.
11. A. Kinsey, W. Pomeroy, and C. Martin (1948). *Sexual Behavior in the Human Male.* Philadelphia: Saunders.
12. See, for example, N. McConaghy and O. Blaszczwski (1980). A pair of monozygotic twins discordant for homosexuality: Sex-dimorphic behavior and penile volume responses. *Archives of Sexual Behavior* 9:123–131; B. Zuger (1976). Monozygotic twins discordant for homosexuality—Report of a pair and significance of phenomenon. *Comprehensive Psychiatry* 17:661–669; J. Rainer, A. Mesinkoff, L. C. Kolb, and A. Carr (1960). Homosexuality and heterosexuality in identical twins. *Psychosomatic Medicine* 22:251–259; R. C. Friedman, F. Wollesen, and R. Tendler (1976). Psycho-

logical development and blood levels of sex steroids in male identical twins of divergent sexual orientation. *Journal of Nervous and Mental Disease* 163:282–288; and N. Parker (1964). Homosexuality in twins: A report on three discordant pairs. *British Journal of Psychiatry* 110:489–495.

13. F. Kallman (1953). In *Heredity in Health and Mental Disorder.* New York: W. W. Norton.

14. L. Heston and J. Shields (1968). Homosexuality in twins. *Archives of General Psychiatry* 18:149–160.

15. Id., p. 154.

16. J. Bailey and R. Pillard (1991). A genetic study of male sexual orientation. *Archives of General Psychiatry* 48:1089–1096.

17. J. Bailey, R. Pillard, and Y. Agyei. A genetic study of female sexual orientation. Unpublished.

18. E. Eckert, T. Bouchard, J. Bohlen, and L. Heston (1986). Homosexuality in monozygotic twins reared apart. *British Journal of Psychiatry* 148:421–425.

19. R. Pillard, J. Poumadere, and R. Carretta (1982). A family study of sexual orientation. *Archives of Sexual Behavior* 11:511–520.

20. J. Bailey, L. Willerman, and C. Parks (1991). A test of the maternal stress theory of human male homosexuality. *Archives of Sexual Behavior* 20:277–294.

21. Bailey, Pillard, and Agyei, unpublished.

22. G. Henry (1941). *Sex Variants: A Study of Homosexual Patterns.* New York: Paul B. Hoeber.

23. R. Pillard, J. Poumadere, and R. Carretta (1982).

24. R. Krafft-Ebing (1898). *Psychopathia Sexualis,* 10th ed., Stuttgart: Enke.

25. R. Kolodny, W. Masters, J. Hendryx et al. (1971). Plasma testosterone and semen analysis in male homosexuals. *New England Journal of Medicine* 285:1170–1174; R. Pillard, R. Rose, and M. Sherwood (1974). Plasma testosterone levels in homosexual men. *Archives of Sexual Behavior* 3:453–458; L. Starka, I. Sipova, and J. Hynie (1975). Plasma testosterone in male transsexuals and homosexuals. *Journal of Sex Research* 11:134–138.

26. H. Meyer-Bahlburg (1984). Psychoendocrine research on sexual orientation: Current status and future options. *Progress in Brain Research* 61:375–398.

27. W. Rohde, F. Stahl, G. Dorner (1977). Plasma basal levels of FSH, LH and testosterone in homosexual men. *Endokrinologie* 70:241–248; F. Stahl, G. Dorner, L. Ahrens et al. (1976). Significantly decreased apparently free testosterone levels in plasma of male homosexuals. *Endokrinologie* 68:115–117.

28. P. Doerr (1976). Further studies on sex hormones in male homosexuals. *Archives of General Psychiatry* 33:611–614.

29. P. Doerr, G. Kockott, H. J. Vogt et al. (1973). Plasma testosterone, estradiol, and semen analysis in male homosexuals. *Archives of General Psychiatry* 29:829–833.

30. S. R. Newmark, L. I. Rose, R. Todd et al. (1979). Gonadotropin, estradiol, and testosterone profiles in homosexual men. *American Journal of Psychiatry* 136:767–771.
31. See generally, H. Meyer-Bahlburg (1984).
32. J. Loraine, D. Adamopoulos, K. Kirkham et al. (1971). Patterns of hormone excretion in male and female homosexuals. *Nature* 234:552–555; N. K. Gartrell, D. L. Loriaux, and T. N. Chase (1977). Plasma testosterone in homosexual and heterosexual women. *American Journal of Psychiatry* 134:1117–1119; I. Sipova and L. Starka (1977). Plasma testosterone values in transsexual women. *Archives of Sexual Behavior* 6:477–481.
33. A. Jost (1947). Recherches sur la différenciation sexuelle de l'embryon de lapin. *Archives d'Anatomie Microscopique et de Morphologie Experimentale* 36:151–200, 242–319.
34. W. Young, R. Goy, and C. Phoenix (1964). Hormones and sexual behavior. *Science* 143:212–218.
35. C. H. Phoenix, J. N. Jensen, and K. C. Chambers (1983). Female sexual behavior displayed by androgenized female rhesus macaques. *Hormones and Behavior* 17:146–151.
36. J. Money and A. Ehrhardt (1972). *Man and Woman, Boy and Girl.* Baltimore: The Johns Hopkins University Press.
37. A. Ehrhardt and S. Baker (1974). Fetal Androgens, Human Central Nervous System Differentiation, and Behavior Sex Differences. In *Sex Differences in Behavior,* ed. R. Friedman, R. Richart and R. Van de Wiele. New York: John Wiley.
38. A. Ehrhardt, K. Evers, and J. Money (1968). Influence of androgen on some aspects of sexually dimorphic behavior in women with late-treated adrenogenital syndrome. *Johns Hopkins Medical Journal* 123:115–122.
39. J. Money, M. Schwartz, and V. Lewis (1984). Adult erotosexual status and fetal hormonal masculinization and demasculinization: 46 XX congenital virilizing adrenal hyperplasia and 46 XY androgen-insensitivity syndrome compared. *Psychoneuroendocrinology* 9:405–414.
40. J. Money and D. Alexander (1969). Psychosexual development and absence of homosexuality in males with precocious puberty: Review of 18 cases. *Journal of Nervous and Mental Disease* 148:111–213; J. Money and V. Lewis (1982). Homosexual/heterosexual status in boys at puberty: Idiopathic adolescent gynecomastia and congenital virilizing adrenocorticism compared. *Psychoneuroendocrinology* 7:339–346.
41. Money and Ehrhardt (1972).
42. J. Imperato-McGinley, R. E. Peterson, T. Gautier, and E. Sturia (1979). Androgens and the evolution of male gender identity among male pseudohermaphrodites with 5α reductase deficiency. *New England Journal of Medicine* 300:1233–1237.
43. See generally, B. McEwen (1983). Gonadal Steroid Influences on Brain Development and Sexual Differentiation. In R. Greep, ed. *Reproductive Physiology IV, International Review of Physiology,* vol. 27. Baltimore: University Park Press, pp. 99–145.

44. A. Ehrhardt, H. Meyer-Bahlburg, L. Rosen et al. (1985). Sexual orientation after prenatal exposure to exogenous estrogen. *Archives of Sexual Behavior* 14:57–75.
45. G. Dorner, W. Rohde, F. Stahl et al. (1975). A neuroendocrine predisposition for homosexuality in men. *Archives of Sexual Behavior* 4:1–8.
46. B. Gladue, R. Green, and R. Hellman (1984). Neuroendocrine response to estrogen and sexual orientation. *Science* 225:1496–1499.
47. L. Gooren (1986). The neuroendocrine response of luteinizing hormone to estrogen administration in heterosexual, homosexual and transsexual subjects. *Journal of Clinical Endocrinology and Metabolism* 63:583–588.
48. S. Hendricks, B. Graber, and J. Rodriguez-Sierra (1989). Neuroendocrine responses to exogenous estrogen: No differences between heterosexual and homosexual men. *Psychoneuroendocrinology* 14:177–185.
49. See generally, I. Ward (1984). The prenatal stress syndrome: Current status. *Psychoneuroendocrinology* 9:3–11.
50. G. Dorner, T. Geiser, L. Ahrens et al. (1980). Prenatal stress and possible aetiogenic factor for homosexuality in human males. *Endokrinologie* 75:365–368.
51. G. Dorner, B. Schenk, B. Schmiedel, and L. Ahrens (1983). Stressful events in prenatal life of bi- and homosexual men. *Experimental and Clinical Endocrinology* 81:83–87.
52. L. Ellis, M. Ames, W. Peckham, and D. Burke (1988). Sexual orientation of human offspring may be altered by severe maternal stress during pregnancy. *Journal of Sex Research* 25:152–157.
53. G. Schmidt and V. Clement (1990). Does peace prevent homosexuality? *Archives of Sexual Behavior* 19:183–187; R. Wille, D. Borchers, and W. Schultz (1987). Prenatal distress: A disposition for homosexuality. International Academy of Sex Research meeting, Tutzing, Federal Republic of Germany.
54. J. Bailey, L. Willerman, and C. Parks (1991). A test of the maternal stress theory of human male homosexuality. *Archives of Sexual Behavior* 20:277–294.
55. D. Swaab and M. Hofman (1990). An enlarged suprachiasmatic nucleus in homosexual men. *Brain Research* 537:141–148.
56. S. Le Vay (1991). A difference in hypothalamic structure between heterosexual and homosexual men. *Science* 253:1034–1037.
57. G. Sanders and L. Ross-Field (1986a). Sexual orientation and visuo-spatial ability. *Brain and Cognition* 5:280–290.
58. G. Sanders and L. Ross-Field (1986b). Sexual orientation, cognitive abilities and cerebral symmetry: A review and a hypothesis tested. *Monitore Zoologico Italiano* 20:459–470.
59. G. Sanders and L. Ross-Field (1986a), p. 287.
60. H. Breuer and E. Neischlag (1975). Antibodies to Hormones in Endocrinology. In E. Neischlag, ed. *Immunization with Hormones in Reproduction Research,* Amsterdam: Elsevier.
61. T. Fainstat and N. Bhat (1983). Recurrent Abortion and Progesterone Ther-

apy. In C. Bardin, E. Milgrom, and P. Mauvais-Jarvis, eds. *Progesterone and Progestins*. New York: Raven Press.

62. M. Wintrobe (1956). *Clinical Hematology*. Philadelphia: Lea and Feibiger.
63. E. Slater (1962). Birth order and maternal age of homosexuals. *Lancet* 1:69–71; E. Hare and P. Moran (1979). Parental age and birth order in homosexual patients: A replication of Slater's study. *British Journal of Psychiatry* 134:178–182; R. Blanchard and P. Sheridan (in press). Sibship size, sibling sex ratio, birth order, and parental age in homosexual and nonhomosexual gender dysphorics. *Journal of Nervous and Mental Disease*.
64. S. Freud (1920). The Psychogenesis of a Case of Homosexuality in a Woman. *Collected Papers*, vol. 2. New York: Basic Books (1957).
65. I. Bieber, H. Dain, P. Dince et al. (1962). *Homosexuality*. New York: Basic Books.
66. Id., p. 276, emphasis added.
67. P. Mayerson and H. Lief (1965). Psychotherapy of Homosexuals. In J. Marmor, ed. *Sexual Inversion*. New York: Basic Books.
68. E. Coleman (1978). Toward a new model of treatment of homosexuality. *Journal of Homosexuality* 3:345–359.
69. M. Woodward (1956). The diagnosis and treatment of homosexual offenders. *British Journal of Delinquency* 9:44–59.
70. D. Curran and D. Parr (1957). Homosexuality: An analysis of 100 male cases seen in private practice. *British Medical Journal* 1:797–801.
71. B. Fookes (1960). Some experiences in the use of aversion therapy in male homosexuality, exhibitionism, and fetishism-transvestism. *British Journal of Psychiatry* 115:339–341.
72. M. MacCullough and M. Feldman (1967). Aversion therapy in management of 43 homosexuals. *British Medical Journal* 2:594–597.
73. J. Bancroft (1969). Aversion therapy of homosexuality. *British Journal of Psychiatry* 115:1417–1431.
74. W. Freeman and R. Meyer (1975). A behavioral alteration of sexual preferences in the human male. *Behavior Therapy* 6:206–212.
75. L. Birk, W. Huddleston, E. Muller et al. (1971). Avoidance conditioning for homosexuality. *Archives of General Psychiatry* 25:314–323.
76. M. Adams and E. Sturgis (1977). Status of behavioral reorientation techniques in the modification of homosexuality: A review. *Psychological Bulletin* 84:1171–1188.
77. K. Freund (1960). Some Problems in the Treatment of Homosexuality. In H. Eysenck, ed. *Behavioural Therapy and the Neuroses*. Oxford: Pergamon.
78. N. McConaghy (1976). Is a homosexual orientation irreversible? *British Journal of Psychiatry* 129:556–563, pp. 561–562.
79. Id., p. 563, emphasis added.
80. E. Pattison and M. Pattison (1980). "Ex-gays": Religiously mediated change in homosexuals. *American Journal of Psychiatry* 137:1553–1562.
81. D. Haldeman (1991). Sexual orientation conversion therapy for gay men

and lesbians. In *Homosexuality: Research Implications for Public Policy,* ed. J. Gonsiorek and J. Weinrich. Newbury Park, Calif.: Sage, p. 158.
82. R. Green (1987). *The "Sissy Boy Syndrome" and the Development of Homosexuality.* New Haven: Yale University Press.
83. Watkins v. U.S. Army, 847 F.2d 1329 (9th Cir. 1988).
84. Watkins v. U.S. Army, 875 F.2d 699 (9th Cir. 1989) (Norris, J. dissenting).
85. 875 F.2d 724, citations omitted.
86. Id., p. 727.
87. Id., p. 726.

## 5. Immigration and Homosexuality

1. The Immigration Act of 1917 (Ch. 29, S. 3, 39 Stat. 847 [1917]).
2. P. Draper (1939). Mental abnormality in relation to crime. *American Journal of Medical Jurisprudence* 2:161–165.
3. Quoted in In re La Rochelle, 11 I. and N. Dec. 436, 440 (1965).
4. Id.
5. Senate Committee on the Judiciary, The Immigration and Naturalization · Systems of the United States, S. Rep. No. 1515, 81st Congress, 2d Session 343 (1950).
6. H.R. Rep. No. 1365, 82d Congress, 2d Session 46–48 (1952) in *United States Code Congressional and Administrative News,* pp. 1699–1702.
7. S. Rep. No. 1515, 81st Congress, 2d Session, 345 (1950).
8. S. 3455, 81st Congress 2d Session, S. 212 (a) (1950), S. 716, 82nd Congress, 1st Session, S. 212 (a) (1951).
9. S. Rep. No. 1137, 82nd Congress, 2d Session 9 (1952), emphasis added.
10. H.R. Rep. No. 1365, 82nd Congress, 2d Session 46–48 (1952).
11. American Psychiatric Association (1957). *A Psychiatric Glossary.* Washington, D.C.: American Psychiatric Association, p. 551.
12. Public Health Service, Report on the Medical Aspects of H.R. 2379, in H.R. Rep. No. 1365, 82d Congress, 2d Session 46 (1952), in *United States Code Congressional and Administrative News,* pp. 1653, 1700 (1952).
13. Id., p. 1701, emphasis added. Presumably the psychological test referred to was the Rorschach ink blot test, which was experiencing its heyday.
14. 302 F.2d 652 (9th Cir. 1962).
15. Section 15(G) of the Act of October 3, 1965, 79 Stat. 919 in *United States Code Congressional and Administrative News,* p. 3328 (1965).
16. *New York Times* (1974) April 9, p. 12.
17. Interpreter Releases 56:387, 398 (1979), Memorandum of Julius Richmond to William Foege and George Lythcort (August 2, 1979), INS, No. 79–85, OP Office of Legal Counsel 3:457, 458 (1979).
18. *New York Times* (1979) August 15, p. A14.
19. Memorandum of David L. Crossland, General Counsel, INS, to Carl T. Wach, Jr., Associate Commissioner, INS, October 21, 1978.
20. Memorandum of John M. Harmon, Assistant Attorney General, to David L. Crossland, Acting Commissioner, INS, December 10, 1979, p. 8.

21. Interpreter Releases 557:440 (1980).
22. 8 U.S.C. S. 1182(a) (4) (1990).
23. *New York Times* (1986) April 23, p. 1.
24. Bar Association for Human Rights of Greater New York (February, 1990). *Lesbian/Gay Law Notes,* p. 11.
25. 302 F.2d 652 (9th Cir. 1962).
26. Rosenberg v. Fleuti, 374 U.S. 449 (1963).
27. 363 F.2d 488 (2nd Cir. 1966).
28. Id., p. 491.
29. Id.
30. Boutilier v. Immigration Service, 387 U.S. 118 (1967).
31. Id., p. 120.
32. Citing Sen. Rep. No. 1137, 82 Cong., 2d Sess. p. 9.
33. 387 U.S. 125.
34. 291 F.2d 906, 907 (5th Cir. 1961).
35. Lesbian/Gay Freedom Day Co. Inc., v. U.S. I.N.S., 541 F. Supp. 569 (1982).
36. Id., pp. 557–578.
37. Id., p. 579.
38. Hill v. United States I.N.S., 714 F.2d 1470 (9th Cir. 1983).
39. No. A-12402065 - Boston (March 13, 1968).
40. 12 I & N Dec. 528 (1967).
41. No. A-10379108 - New York (July 12, 1967).
42. No. A-12944125 - (September 8, 1965).
43. In re La Rochelle, 11 I. and N. December 436 (1965).
44. 714 F.2d 1480.
45. 716 F.2d 1439 (5th Cir. 1983), *cert. denied,* 467 U.S. 1219 (1984).
46. Id., p. 1447.
47. Id.
48. Id., p. 1448.
49. 326 F. Supp. 924 (S.D.N.Y. 1971).
50. Id., p. 926.
51. Id., p. 930.
52. State courts are vested with concurrent jurisdiction in naturalization matters. 8 U.S.C. S. 1421.
53. 289 N.Y.S. 2d 89, 92 (1968).
54. 394 F. Supp. 1208, 1209 (D. Oregon 1975).
55. 647 F.2d 432 (4th Cir. 1981).
56. Id., pp. 436–437.
57. Bowers v. Hardwick, 478 U.S. 186 (1986).
58. *Record of the Association of the Bar of New York City* (1985).
59. *Congressional Record* 111:21, 772 (1965) (emphasis added).
60. Testimony of John Spiegel, November 19, 1979, in *Staff Report* of the Select Commission, p. 754.
61. *Los Angeles Times* (1990) October 29, p. A1.

## 6. Transsexualism

1. Previously published in R. Green (1974). *Sexual Identity Conflict in Children and Adults*. New York: Basic Books; London: Gerald Duckworth; (1975) Baltimore: Penguin.
2. R. Stoller (1969). Parental Influences in Male Transsexualism. In *Transsexualism and Sex Reassignment*, ed. R. Green and J. Money. Baltimore: The Johns Hopkins Press.
3. R. Hellman, R. Green, J. Gray, and K. Williams (1981). Childhood sexual identity, childhood religiosity, and homophobia as influences in the development of transsexualism, homosexuality and heterosexuality. *Archives of General Psychiatry* 38:910–915.
4. G. Dorner (1988). Neuroendocrine response to estrogen and brain differentiation in heterosexuals and transsexuals. *Archives of Sexual Behavior* 17:57–96.
5. D. Swaab, E. Fliers, and T. Partiman (1985). The suprachiasmatic nucleus of the human brain in relation to sex, age, and senile dementia. *Brain Research* 342:37–44.
6. J. Hoenig and J. Kenna (1979). EEG abnormalities and transsexualism. *British Journal of Psychology* 134:293–300.
7. D. Watson (1991). Laterality and handedness in adult transsexuals. *SIEC-CAN Journal* 6:22–26.
8. W. Futterweit, R. Weiss, and R. Fagerstrom (1986). Endocrine evaluation of forty female-to-male transsexuals. *Archives of Sexual Behavior* 15:69–78.
9. R. Richards and J. Ames (1983). *Second Serve: The Renee Richards Story*. Briarcliff Manor, N.Y.: Stein and Day.
10. Standards of Care (1985). The hormonal and surgical sex reassignment of gender dysphoric persons. *Archives of Sexual Behavior* 14:79–90.
11. Title VII, S.703 of the Civil Rights Act of 1964 (42 U.S.C. 2000e-2) (1982).
12. Ulane v. Eastern Airlines, 581 F. Supp. 821 (N.D. Ill. 1983) *rev'd*, 742 F.2d 1081 (7th Cir., 1984), *cert. denied*, 471 U.S. 1017 (1985).
13. Transcript of Trial Court Proceedings, p. 35 (Sept. 26, 1983) (Dean Dickie, attorney for plaintiff).
14. Id., p. 252 (Sept. 27, 1983).
15. 581 F. Supp. 821.
16. 742 F.2d 1081.
17. Kirkpatrick v. Seligman and Latz, Inc., 636 F.2d 1047 (5th Cir. 1981).
18. Terry v. EEOC, 25 Empl. Prac. Dec. (CCH) para. 31, 638, p. 19, 733 (E.D. Wis. Dec. 10, 1980).
19. Smith v. Liberty Mutual Insurance Co., 569 F.2d 325 (5th Cir. 1978).
20. Sommers v. Budget Marketing, Inc., 667 F.2d 748, 749 (8th Cir. 1982).
21. Voyles v. Ralph K. Davies Medical Center, 403 F. Supp. 456, 457 (N.D. Cal. 1975), *aff'd. mem.* 570 F.2d 354 (9th Cir. 1978).
22. Sommers v. Budget Marketing, 667 F.2d 750.

23. American Psychiatric Association (1988). *Diagnostic and Statistical Manual of Mental Disorders IIIR* (DSM IIIR). Washington, D.C.: American Psychiatric Association.
24. 29 U.S.C. S.701 *et seq.* (1982).
25. 29 U.S.C. S.794, S.706 (6) (1982).
26. *DSM IIIR,* p. 75.
27. Guerriero v. Schultz, 557 F. Supp. 511 (D.D.C. 1983).
28. Doe v. New York University, 666 F.2d 761 (2d Cir. 1981).
29. Doe v. Region 13 Mental Health–Mental Retardation Commission, 704 F.2d 1402 (5th Cir. 1983).
30. 45 C.F.R. S.84.3 (1985).
31. 42 U.S.C. 12101 *et seq.* (1991).
32. In re Grossman, 127 N.J. Super. 13, 316 A.2d 39 (1974), *cert. denied* 65 N.J. 292, 321 A.2d 253 (1974).
33. H. Benjamin (1966). *The Transsexual Phenomenon.* New York: Julian Press.
34. In re Grossman, 127 N.J. Super. 25.
35. Ashlie, a/k/a Komarnicki v. Chester-Upland School District, Civil Action No. 78-4037, D.C., E.D. Penn., May 9, 1979, p. 9, n.6.
36. R. Stoller (1968). *Sex and Gender.* New York: Science House; R. Green, and J. Money (eds.) (1969). *Transsexualism and Sex Reassignment.* Baltimore: The Johns Hopkins Press.
37. In re Leber (Neuchatel Cantonal Court, July 2, 1945).
38. Corbett v. Corbett 2 A11 E.R. 33 (1970).
39. 2 A11 E.R. 33, 46–49.
40. *London Times* (1990). Sex change woman loses legal case. September 28.
41. J. Money (1968). *Sex Errors of the Body.* Baltimore: The Johns Hopkins University Press.
42. M.T. v. J.T., 140 N.J. Super. 77, 355 A. 2d 204 (1976), *cert. denied* 71 N.J. 345, 364 A.2d 1076 (1976).
43. I. Kennedy (1973). Transsexualism and single sex marriage. *Anglo-American Law Review* 2:112–129.
44. R. Green (1978). Sexual identity of 37 children raised by homosexual or transsexual parents. *American Journal of Psychiatry* 135:692–697.
45. P. Crane (undated). *Gays and the Law.* London: Pluto Press, p. 193.
46. W. Eaton and D. Von Bargen (1981). Asynchronous development of gender understanding in preschool children. *Child Development* 52:1020–1027.
47. In re Application of John William Eck, *New Jersey Law Journal* 127:562 (1991), February 28, reported in *Lesbian/Gay Law Notes* (1990) April, p. 25.
48. Richards v. United States Tennis Association, 400 N.Y.S. 2d 267 (1977).
49. Id.
50. Id., p. 273.
51. Id.
52. Id.
53. Id.

54. Merriwether v. Faulkner, 821 F.2d 408 (7th Cir. 1987), *cert. denied* 484 U.S. 935 (1987).
55. Lamb v. Maschner, 633 F. Supp. 351 (DC Kansas, 1986).
56. White v. Farrier, 849 F.2d 322 (8th Cir. 1988).
57. Supre v. Ricketts, 792 F.2d 958 (10th Cir. 1986).
58. Phillips v. Michigan Dept. Corrections, 731 F. Supp. 792 (W.D. Mich. 1990), *aff'd.* 932 F.2d 969 (6th Cir. 1991).
59. R. Green and J. Money (1969). *Transsexualism and Sex Reassignment.*
60. D. Hunt and J. Hampson (1980). Follow-up of 17 biological male transsexuals after sex-reassignment surgery. *American Journal of Psychiatry* 137: 432–438.
61. T. Sorenson (1981). A follow-up study of operated transsexual males. *Acta Psychiatrica Scandinavica* 63:486–503.
62. T. Sorenson (1981). A follow-up study of operated transsexual females. *Acta Psychiatrica Scandinavica* 64:50–64.
63. G. Lindemalm, D. Korlin, and N. Uddenberg (1987). Prognostic factors vs. outcome in male-to-female transsexualism. *Acta Psychiatrica Scandinavica* 75:268–274.
64. S. Abramowitz (1986). Psychosocial outcomes of sex reassignment surgery. *Journal of Consulting and Clinical Psychology* 54:183–189.
65. B. Lundstrom, I. Pauly, and J. Walinder (1984). Outcome of sex reassignment surgery. *Acta Psychiatrica Scandinavica* 70:289–294.
66. R. Green and D. Fleming (1990). Transsexual surgery follow-up: Status in the 1990's. In *Annual Review of Sex Research,* ed. J. Bancroft, C. Davis, and H. Ruppel. Mt. Vernon, Iowa: Society for the Scientific Study of Sex.
67. Benjamin (1966); Green and Money (1969).
68. J.D. v. Lackner, 80 Cal. App. 3d 90 (1978); G.B. v. Lackner, 80 Cal. App. 3d 64 (1978); Rush v. Parham, 440 F. Supp. 383 (N.D. Ga. 1977), *rev'd;* Rush v. Parham, 625 F.2d 1150 (5th Cir. 1980); Pinneke v. Preisser, 623 F.2d 546 (8th Cir. 1980); Doe v. State Department of Public Welfare, 257 N.W. 2d 816 (Minn. 1977).
69. Pinneke v. Preisser, 623 F.2d 549.
70. Rush v. Johnson, 565 F. Supp. 856 (N.D. Ga. 1983).

## 7. Pornography

1. B. Kutchinsky (1973). The effect of easy availability of pornography on the incidence of sex crimes: The Danish experience. *Journal of Social Issues* 29:163–181; (1983). Obscenity and Pornography. In *Encyclopedia of Criminal Justice,* vol. 3, ed. S. Kadish. New York: Free Press, pp. 1077–1086; (1985). Pornography and its effects in Denmark and the United States. In *Comparative Social Research,* vol. 8, ed. R. Thomasson. Greenwich, Ct.: JAI Press, pp. 301–330.
2. Id.
3. Polizeiliche Kriminalstatistik (1983). Bundesrepublik Deutschland. Bundeskriminalamt Wiesbaden, cited by Kutchinsky (1985).

4. Kutchinsky (1973, 1983, 1985).
5. Committee on Obscenity and Film Censorship (1979). *Report of the Committee on Obscenity and Film Censorship.* London: Her Majesty's Printing Office, p. 80.
6. J. Money (1984). Committee on the Judiciary, Congressional Hearings, 98th Congress, 2nd Session, p. 342.
7. FBI Uniform Crime Reports, U.S. Department of Justice, cited by Kutchinsky (1983, 1985).
8. J. Scott (1985). Violence and erotic material: The relationship between adult entertainment and rape. Paper read at the annual meeting of the American Association for the Advancement of Science, Los Angeles.
9. L. Baron and M. Straus (1984). Sexual stratification, pornography and rape in the United States. In *Pornography and Sexual Aggression,* ed. N. Malamuth and E. Donnerstein. Orlando, Fla.: Academic Press; L. Baron and M. Straus (1985). Legitimate violence, pornography, and sexual inadequacy as explanations for state and regional differences in rape. Paper read at the annual meeting of the American Association for the Advancement of Science, Los Angeles.
10. *Report of the Commission on Obscenity and Pornography* (1970). New York: Bantam Books, p. 32.
11. *New York Times* (1990). Keating Indicted in Savings Fraud and Goes to Jail. September 19, p. 1; *New York Times* (1991). Keating is Convicted of Securities Fraud. December 5, p. 1.
12. *Report of the Commission on Obscenity and Pornography* (1970) pp. 580–581.
13. Id., p. 584.
14. V. Cline (1976). The scientists vs. pornography, an untold story. *Intellect Magazine,* May-June, 574–576, p. 576.
15. U.S. Department of Justice (1986). *Attorney General's Commission on Pornography,* vol. 1. Washington, D.C.: U.S. Government Printing Office, p. 326.
16. Reuters (1990). Father Bruce Ritter, Covenant House Head Resigns. February 28.
17. U.S. Department of Justice (1986), p. 206.
18. R. Baron and P. Bell (1977). Sexual arousal and aggression by males: Effects of type of erotic stimuli and prior provocation. *Journal of Personality and Social Psychology* 35:78–87.
19. E. Donnerstein, N. Donnerstein, and R. Evans (1975). Erotic stimuli and aggression: Facilitation or inhibition. *Journal of Personality and Social Psychology* 32:237–244.
20. E. Donnerstein (1980). Aggressive erotica and violence against women. *Journal of Personality and Social Psychology* 39:269–277.
21. N. Malamuth and J. Check (1981). The effects of mass media exposure on acceptance of violence against women. *Journal of Research in Personality* 15:436–446.
22. E. Donnerstein (1984). Pornography: Its effects on violence against

women. In *Pornography and Sexual Aggression,* ed. N. Malamuth and E. Donnerstein. Orlando, Fla.: Academic Press, pp. 53–81.

23. D. Zillmann and J. Bryant (1982). Pornography, sexual callousness, and the trivialization of rape. *Journal of Communication* 32:1–21.

24. D. Linz, E. Donnerstein, and S. Penrod (1984). The effects of multiple exposure to filmed violence against women. *Journal of Communication* 34:130–147.

25. J. Ceniti and N. Malamuth (1984). Effects of repeated exposure to sexually violent or nonviolent stimuli on sexual arousal to rape and non-rape depictions. *Behavior Research and Therapy* 22:535–548.

26. M. Goldstein, H. Kant, L. Judd, E. Rice, and R. Green (1971). Experience with pornography: Rapists, pedophiles, homosexuals, transsexuals and controls. *Archives of Sexual Behavior* 1:1–15.

27. P. Gebhard, J. Gagnon, W. Pomeroy, and H. Christenson (1965). *Sex Offenders.* New York: Harper and Row.

28. R. Cook, R. Fosen, and A. Pacht (1971). Pornography and the sex offender. *Journal of Applied Psychology* 55:503–511.

29. R. Lang and R. Langevin (1990). Pornography and Sexual Offences. International Academy of Sex Research, Sigtuna, Sweden.

30. R. Green (1987). *The "Sissy Boy Syndrome" and the Development of Homosexuality.* New Haven: Yale University Press.

31. M. Vandervoert and T. McIlvenna (1979). The Use Of Sexually Explicit Teaching Materials. In *Human Sexuality: A Health Practitioner's Text,* 2nd ed., ed. R. Green. Baltimore: Williams and Wilkins.

32. Interstate Circuit, Inc. v. Dallas, 390 U.S. 676, 704–705; (1968) (Harlan, J., dissenting).

33. 354 U.S. 476 (1957).

34. 383 U.S. 413 (1966).

35. Id., p. 418.

36. Paris Adult Theatre I v. Slaton, 413 U.S. 49 (1973) (Brennan, J., dissenting).

37. 413 U.S. 15.

38. Smith v. California, 361 U.S. 147, 164–166 (1959) (Frankfurter, J., concurring).

39. Paris Adult Theatre I. v. Slaton, 413 U.S. 49, 56 (1973).

40. Kahm v. United States, 300 F.2d 78, 84, n.3 (5th Cir. 1962), *cert. denied,* 369 U.S. 859 (1962).

41. United States v. Groner, 479 F.2d 577, 587 (5th Cir. 1973) (Ainsworth, J., concurring), vacated Groner v. U.S., 414 U.S. 969 (1973), 494 F.2d. 499 (5th Cir. 1974), *cert. denied,* 419 U.S. 1010 (1974).

42. 413 U.S. 56, n.6.

43. Roth v. United States, 354 U.S. 476, 487, n.20.

44. Queen v. Hicklin, L.R. 3 Q.B. (1868).

45. United States v. Gugliemi, 819 F.2d 451 (4th Cir. 1987), *cert. denied,* 484 U.S. 1019 (1988).

46. Illinois Revised Statutes, ch. 38, par. 11–20(c) (4) (1977).

47. People v. Nelson, 410 N.E. 2d 476 (App. Ct. Ill. 1980).
48. Commonwealth v. Trainor, 374 N.E. 2d 1216 (Sup. Jud. Ct. Mass., Suffolk, 1978).
49. Saliba v. State, 475 N.E. 2d 1181 (Ind. App. 1985).
50. United States v. Pryba, 678 F. Supp. 1225, 1233 (E.D. Va. 1988), 680 F. Supp. 790 (E.D. Va. 1988), 900 F.2d 748 (1990), *cert. denied,* 111 S. Ct. 305 (1990).
51. People v. Parker, 33 Cal. App. 3d 842 (1973).
52. 395 U.S. 444 (1969).
53. Olivia N. v. National Broadcasting Co., 126 Cal. App. 3d 488 (1981), *cert. denied,* 458 U.S. 1108 (1982).
54. 126 Cal. App. 3d 494–495, citations omitted.
55. Zamora v. Columbia Broadcasting System, 480 F. Supp. 199 (S.D. Fla. 1979).
56. 480 F. Supp. 202.
57. Id., p. 203.
58. Id., p. 206–207.
59. Barnes v. Glen Theatre, 111 S. Ct. 2456 (1991).
60. 111 S.Ct. 2463.
61. Id., p. 2461.
62. Id., p. 2474, White, J., joined by Marshall, Blackmun and Stevens, J.J.
63. State v. Kam, 748 P.2d 372 (Haw. 1988).
64. State v. Henry, 732 P.2d 9 (Ore. 1987).
65. 394 U.S. 557 (1969).
66. New York v. Ferber, 458 U.S. 747, 756–757 (1982).
67. Id., p. 759.
68. 495 U.S. 103, 110 S. Ct. 1691 (1990).
69. 110 S. Ct. 1691, 1714 n.18. (Brennan, J., dissenting, joined by Marshall and Stevens, J.J.)
70. U.S. Department of Justice (1986), pp. 600–601.
71. R. Pierce (1984). Child pornography: A hidden dimension of child abuse. *Child Abuse and Neglect* 8:483–493, p. 486.

## 8. Intergenerational Sexuality

1. R. Kourany, R. Hill, and M. Hollender (1986). The age of sexual consent. *Bulletin of the American Academy of Psychiatry and Law* 14:171–176.
2. Id.
3. C. Greenland (1983). Sex law reform in an international perspective. *Bulletin of the American Academy of Psychiatry and Law* 11:309–330.
3. Greenland (1983), p. 315.
4. Cmnd 8216, Her Majesty's Stationery Office (1981), cited in *New Law Journal* 131, no. 5998, April 23, 1981, p. 433.
5. Greenland (1983).
6. Wilson v. State, 109 A.2d 381 (Del. 1954), Kourany et al. (1986).

7. T. O'Carroll (1982). *Paedophilia: The Radical Case*. Boston: Alyson Publications, p. 153.
8. O'Carroll (1982), p. 153.
9. Id., p. 154.
10. Id.
11. P. Wilson (1981). *The Man They Called a Monster*. New South Wales: Cassell, p. 133.
12. Greenland (1983), p. 319.
13. D. West (1975). Thoughts on sex law reform. In *Crime, Criminology and Public Policy,* ed. R. Hood. New York: Free Press, pp. 469–487.
14. Kourany et al. (1986), p. 174.
15. P. Skegg (1977). English law relating to experimentation on children. *Lancet* 2:754–755, p. 754; (1973) Consent to medical procedures on minors. *Modern Law Review* 36:370–381.
16. B. Tomkins (1974–1975). Minors: Right to consent. *Saskatchewan Law Review* 40:41–62.
17. W. Gaylin (1982). The competence of children: No longer all or none. *The Hastings Center Report,* April, pp. 33–38, p. 34.
18. R. Green (1972). Homosexuality as a mental illness. *International Journal of Psychiatry* 10:77–98; R. Bayer (1981). *Homosexuality and American Psychiatry*. New York: Basic Books.
19. N. Lukianowicz (1972). Incest. *British Journal of Psychiatry* 120:301–313.
20. L. Bender and A. Grugett (1952). A follow-up report on children who had atypical sexual development. *American Journal of Orthopsychiatry* 29: 825–836.
21. Id., p. 827.
22. Quoted in R. Farson (1974). *Birthrights*. New York: MacMillan, p. 150.
23. D. Finkelhor (1979). *Sexually Victimized Children*. New York: Free Press.
24. J. Stein, J. Golding, J. Siegel, M. Burnam, and S. Sorenson (1988). Long-term Psychological Sequences of Child Sexual Abuse. In *Lasting Effects of Child Sexual Abuse,* ed. G. Wyatt and G. Powell. Newbury Park, Calif.: Sage.
25. D. Russell (1983). Incidence and prevalence of intrafamilial and extrafamilial sexual abuse of female children. *Child Abuse and Neglect* 7:133–146.
26. A. Baker (1985). Child sexual abuse: A study of prevalence in Great Britain. *Child Abuse and Neglect* 9:457–467.
27. Report of the Committee on Sexual Offenses Against Children and Youth (1984). Ottawa: Ministry of Justice and Ministry of National Health and Welfare.
28. W. Friedrich, A. Urquiza, and R. Beilke (1985). Behavioral problems in sexually abused young children. *Journal of Pediatric Psychology* 11: 47–57.
29. Id., p. 55.
30. Id., p. 49.

31. J. Conte and J. Schuerman (1987). Factors associated with an increased impact of child sexual abuse. *Child Abuse and Neglect* 11:201–211.
32. Tufts New England Medical Center, Division of Child Psychiatry (1984). Sexually Exploited Children: Service and Research Project. Washington, D.C., Office of Juvenile Justice and Delinquency Prevention, U.S. Department of Justice.
33. A. Browne and D. Finkelhor (1986). Impact of child sexual abuse: A review of the research. *Psychological Bulletin* 99:66–72, p. 72.
34. J. Beitchman, K. Zucker, J. Hood, G. Da Coste, and D. Akman (1991a). A review of the short-term effects of child sexual abuse. *Child Abuse and Neglect* 15:537–556, p. 552.
35. Id., p. 543.
36. Id., p. 544.
37. J. Stein et al. (1988), pp. 135–154.
38. Id., p. 150.
39. P. Mullen, S. Romano-Clarkson, V. Walton, and G. Herbison (1988). Impact of sexual and physical abuse on women's mental health. *Lancet* 1:841–845.
40. M. Fromuth (1986). The relationship of childhood sexual abuse with later psychological and sexual adjustment in a sample of college women. *Child Abuse and Neglect* 10:5–15, p. 9.
41. Id., p. 13.
42. A. Kilpatrick (1986). Some correlates of women's childhood sexual experiences: A retrospective study. *Journal of Sex Research* 22:221–242.
43. M. Tsai, S. Feldman-Summers, and M. Edgar (1979). Childhood molestation: Variables related to differential impacts on psychosexual functioning in adult women. *Journal of Abnormal Psychology* 88:407–417.
44. Browne and Finkelhor (1986), p. 72.
45. Id., p. 74.
46. Id., p. 74.
47. Id., p. 72.
48. Beitchman et al. (1991), p. 549.
49. Browne and Finkelhor (1986), p. 73.
50. Id.
51. Id.
52. Id., pp. 74–75.
53. Id., p. 75.
54. J. Briere (1988). Longterm clinical correlates of childhood sexual victimization. *Annals of the New York Academy of Science* 528:327–334.
55. A. Green (1988). Overview of the Literature on Child Sexual Abuse. In *Child Sexual Abuse*, ed. D. Shetkey and A. Green. New York: Brunner/Mazel, pp. 40–41.
56. Browne and Finkelhor (1986), p. 69.
57. Id., p. 72.
58. Id., p. 75.
59. J. Beitchman, K. Zucker, J. Hood, G. Da Costa, D. Akman, and E. Cas-

savia (1992). A review of the short-term and long-term effects of childhood sexual abuse. Part II. Long-term effects. *Child Abuse and Neglect* 16:101–118.

60. J. Briere and M. Runtz (1986). Suicidal thoughts and behaviours in former sexual abuse victims. *Canadian Journal of Behavioural Science* 18:413–423.

61. Beitchman et al. (1992).

62. J. Briere and M. Runtz (1988). Symptomatology associated with childhood sexual victimization in a non-clinical adult sample. *Child Abuse and Neglect* 12:51–59, p. 52.

63. J. Briere (1988). Controlling for family variables in abuse effects research. *Journal of Interpersonal Violence* 3:80–89, p. 82.

64. J. Briere and M. Runtz (1988). Post Sexual Abuse Trauma. In Wyatt and Powell, pp. 85–99; in nearly identical form, (1987) *Journal of Interpersonal Violence* 2:367–379.

65. Id., (1987), p. 376; (1988), p. 96.

66. G. Herdt (1984). Semen Transaction in Sambia Culture. In *Ritualized Homosexuality in Melanesia,* ed. G. Herdt. Berkeley: University of California Press, pp. 173–174; G. Herdt and R. Stoller (1990). *Intimate Communications.* New York: Columbia University Press, pp. 70–71.

67. R. Freeman-Longo (1986). The impact of sexual victimization on males. *Child Abuse and Neglect* 10:411–414; B. Vander Mey (1988). The sexual victimization of male children. *Child Abuse and Neglect* 12:61–72.

68. A. Urquiza and M. Capra (1990). The Impact of Sexual Abuse: Initial and Long-term Effects. In *The Sexually Abused Male: Prevalance, Impact and Treatment,* ed. M. Hunter. Lexington, Mass.: D. C. Heath, p. 108.

69. J. Briere, D. Evans, M. Runtz, and T. Wall (1988). Symptomatology in men who were molested as children. *American Journal of Orthopsychiatry* 58:457–461.

70. A. Groth (1979). Sexual trauma in the life histories of rapists and child molesters. *Victimology* 4:10–16.

71. P. Rossman (1976). *Sexual Experience between Men and Boys.* New York: Association Press.

72. Id., p. 164.

73. Id., p. 144.

74. T. Sandfort (1987). *Boys on Their Contacts with Men.* Elmhurst, N.Y.: Global Academic.

75. Id., p. 134.

76. P. Okami (1991). Self-reports of "positive" childhood and adolescent sexual contacts with older persons: An exploratory study. *Archives of Sexual Behavior* 20:437–458.

77. Vander Mey (1988), p. 69.

78. Urquiza and Capra (1990), p. 127.

79. E. Seemanova (1971). A study of children of incestuous matings. *Human Heredity* 21:108–128; M. Adams and J. Neel (1967). Children of incest. *Pediatrics* 40:55–62.

80. S. Parker (1987). The waning of the incest taboo. *Legal Studies Forum,* 205–215; M. Noble and J. Mason (1978). Incest. *Journal of Medical Ethics* 4:64–68.

81. T. Parsons (1954). The incest taboo in relation to social structure and the socialization of the child. *British Journal of Sociology* 5:101–117.

82. R. Middleton (1962). Brother-sister and father-daughter marriage in ancient Egypt. *American Sociological Review* 27:603–611.

83. R. Masters (1963). *Patterns of Incest.* New York: Julian Press, p. 18.

84. Id., pp. 44–45.

85. T. Schroeder (1915). Incest in Mormonism. *American Journal of Urology and Sexology* 11:409–416.

86. C. Bagley (1969). Incest behavior and incest taboo. *Social Problems* 16:505–519, p. 511.

87. S. Riemer (1940). A research note on incest. *American Journal of Sociology* 45:566.

88. S. Kubo (1959). Researchers and studies on incest in Japan. *Hiroshima Journal of Medical Sciences* 8:99–159; See generally, review by C. Bagley (1969). Incest behavior and incest taboo. *Social Problems* 16:505–519.

89. J. Herman, D. Russell, and K. Trochi (1986). Long-term effects of incestuous abuse in childhood. *American Journal of Psychiatry* 143:1293–1296.

90. J. Jackson, K. Calhoun, A. Amick, H. Maddever, and V. Habit (1990). Young adult women who report childhood intrafamilial sexual abuse: Subsequent adjustment. *Archives of Sexual Behavior* 19:211–221.

91. Id., p. 218.

92. E. Pribor and S. Dinwiddie (1992). Psychiatric correlates of incest in childhood. *American Journal of Psychiatry* 149:52–56.

93. R. Krug (1989). Adult male report of childhood sexual abuse by mothers. *Child Abuse and Neglect* 13:111–119.

94. P. Olson (1990). The Sexual Abuse of Boys: A Study of the Long-Term Psychological Effect. In *The Sexually Abused Male,* ed. M. Hunter. Lexington, Mass.: Lexington Books.

95. A. Yorukoglu, and J. Kemph (1966). Children not severely damaged by incest with a parent. *Journal of the American Academy of Child Psychiatry* 5:111–124.

96. J. Weiner (1978). A clinical perspective on incest. *American Journal of Diseases of Children* 132:123.

97. J. Henderson (1983). Is incest harmful? *Canadian Journal of Psychiatry* 28:34–40.

98. Id., p. 38.

99. A. Yates (1982). Children eroticized by incest. *American Journal of Psychiatry* 139:482–485, p. 483.

100. M. Ploscowe (1951). *Sex and the Law.* New York: Prentice-Hall, p. 184.

101. H. Giarreto (1989). Community-based treatment of the incest family. *Psychiatric Clinics of North America* 12:352–360.

102. M. Meinig and B. Bonner (1991). *Violence Update,* October. Newbury Park, California.

103. T. Gibbens and J. Prince (1963). *Child Victims of Sex Offences*. London: Institute for the Study and Treatment of Delinquency.
104. D. Walters (1975). *Physical and Sexual Abuse of Children*. Bloomington: Indiana University Press, p. 113.
105. Howard League Working Party (1985). *Unlawful Sex*. London: Waterlow Publishers, p. 161.
106. W. Wolters, E. Zwaan, P. Wagener-Schwenche, and T. Deenen (1985). A review of cases of sexually exploited children reported to the Netherlands State Police. *Child Abuse and Neglect* 9:591–674.
107. Annotated California Codes, Penal Code Sections 11165 et. seq., 11172(e) West (1991).
108. People v. Younghanz, 156 Cal. App. 3d 811 (1984).
109. People v. Farrow, 183 Mich. App. 436 (1990).
110. J. James, W. Womack, and F. Strauss (1978). Physician reporting of sexual abuse of children. *Journal of the American Medical Association* 240:1145–1146.
111. K. Pope, B. Tabachnick, P. Keith-Spiegel (1987). Ethics of practice: The beliefs and behaviors of psychologists as therapists. *American Psychologist* 42:993–1006.
112. F. Berlin, H. Malin, and S. Dean (1991). Effects of statutes requiring psychiatrists to report suspected sexual abuse of children. *American Journal of Psychiatry* 148:449–453.
113. Id., p. 452.
114. Coy v. Iowa, 487 U.S. 1012 (1988).
115. Maryland v. Craig, 110 S.Ct. 3157 (1990).
116. 110 S.Ct. 3171.
117. Wheeler v. United States, 159 U.S. 523, 524 (1895).
118. Annotated California Codes, Evidence Section 700, West (1991).
119. Glendening v. State, 536 So. 2d 212 (Fla. 1988).
120. Michigan Compiled Laws Annotated. Section 600.2163a, West (1990).
121. S. White, G. Strom, G. Santilli, and B. Halpin (1986). Interviewing young sexual abuse victims with anatomically correct dolls. *Child Abuse and Neglect* 10:519–529.
122. L. Lampole and M. Weber (1987). An assessment of the behavior of sexually abused and nonsexually abused children with anatomically correct dolls. *Child Abuse and Neglect* 11:187–192.
123. In re Amber B., 191 Cal. App. 3d 682 (1987).
124. State v. Fletcher, 368 S.E. 2d 633 (N.C. 1988).
125. State v. Rimmasch, 775 P.2d 388, 401 (Utah, 1989).
126. State v. Black, 537 A.2d 1154, 1157 (Me. 1988).
127. State v. Lawrence, 541 A.2d. 1291, 1292 (Me. 1988).
128. Id., emphasis in original.
129. State v. York, 564 A.2d 389, 390 (Me. 1989).
130. State v. Lamb, 427 N.W.2d 142 (Wis. 1988).
131. 427 N.W.2d 145.
132. People v. Roscoe, 168 Cal. App. 3d 1093 (1985).

133. State v. Kim, 645 P.2d 1330, 1338 (Haw. 1982).
134. State v. Batangan, 799 P.2d 48 (Haw. 1990).
135. Kruse v. State 483 So. 2d 1383 (Fla. App. 4 Dist. 1986).
136. R. Summit (1983). The child sexual abuse accommodation syndrome. *Child Abuse and Neglect* 7:177–193.
137. State v. Myers, 359 N.W.2d 604, 610 (Minn. 1984).
138. Allison v. State, 346 S.E.2d 380, 384–385 (Ga. 1986).
139. Allison v. State, 353 S.E.2d 805 (Ga. App. 1987).
140. Seering v. Department of Social Services, 194 Cal. App. 3d 298 (1987).
141. People v. Bowker, 203 Cal. App. 3d 385 (1988).
142. *New York Times* (1990) January 19, pp. A1, 14; (1990) July 28, pp. A1, 9; (1990) March 5, p. B7; *Los Angeles Times* (1990) January 19, pp. A21–22; (1990) July 6, p. A7; (1990) July 28, p. A18; *Time* (1990) August 6, p. 28.
143. L. Coleman (1986). Learning from the McMartin Hoax. Vocal Convention, October 24–26. Torrance, California, p. 3, cited in P. O'Kami (1990). Sociopolitical Biases in the Literature on Sexual Behavior. In *Pedophilia: Biosocial Dimensions,* ed. J. Feierman. New York: Springer-Verlag.
144. *Los Angeles Times* (1990), January 19, p. B6.
145. 110 S.Ct. 3157.
146. Id., p. 3176.
147. Id.
148. Id.
149. Lord Justice Butler-Sloss (1988). *Report of the Inquiry into Child Abuse in Cleveland, 1987.* London: Her Majesty's Stationery Office, p. 243.
150. M. Everson and B. Boat (1989). False allegations of sexual abuse. *Journal of the American Academy of Child and Adolescent Psychiatry* 28:230–235.
151. A. Green (1986). True and false allegations of sexual abuse in child custody disputes. *Journal of the American Academy of Child Psychiatry* 5: 449–456.
152. J. Groner (1991). *Hilary's Trial: The Elizabeth Morgan Case: A Child's Ordeal in America's Legal System.* New York: Simon and Schuster.
153. M. Zackin (1988). The discovery rule and father-daughter incest: A legislative response. *Boston College Law Review* 29:941–968, p. 949.
154. 727 P.2d 226 (Wash. 1986).
155. Citing M. Wesson (1985). Historical truth, narrative truth, and expert testimony. *Washington Law Review* 6:331.
156. Wash. Rev. Code ch. 144, S.S.B. No. 6305.
157. De Rose v. Carswell, 196 Cal. App. 3d 1011 (1987).
158. Mary D. v. John D., 216 Cal. App. 3d 285 (1989).
159. Evans v. Eckelman. 216 Cal. App. 3d 1609 (1990).
160. E. W. v. D. C. H., 754 P.2d 817 (Mont. 1988).
161. Hammer v. Hammer, 418 N.W. 2d 23 (Wis. 1987).
162. Johnson v. Johnson, 701 F. Supp. 1363 (N.D. Ill. 1988); 766 F. Supp. 662 (N.D. Ill. 1991).

163. Meiers-Post v. Schafer, 427 N.W. 2d 606 (Mich. 1988).
164. Annotated California Codes, Civil Procedure, Section 340.1, West (1991).
165. J. Herman and E. Schatzow (1987). Recovery and verification of memories of childhood sexual trauma. *Psychoanalytic Psychology* 4:1–14.
166. Id., pp. 7–8.
167. VOCAL Brochure, undated, Santa Ana, California.
168. J. Goodwin (1988). Obstacles to Policymaking about Incest. In Wyatt and Powell, p. 30, emphasis added.
169. M. Guyer (1991). Psychiatry, Law, and Child Sexual Abuse. In *Annual Review of Psychiatry 10,* ed. A. Tasman and S. Goldfinger. Washington, D.C.: American Psychiatric Association, p. 386.
170. P. Okami (1990). Sociopolitical biases in the literature on sexual behavior. In *Pedophilia: Biosocial Dimensions,* ed. J. Feierman. New York: Springer-Verlag, p. 92.
171. L. Brunngraber (1986). Father-daughter incest. *Advances in Nursing Science* 8:15–35, p. 21, emphasis added.
172. D. Russell, p. 138, emphasized in Okami (1990).
173. D. Finkelhor, p. 141, emphasized in Okami (1990).
174. J. James and J. Meyerding (1977). Early sexual experiences as a factor in prostitution. *American Journal of Psychiatry* 134:1381–1385.
175. P. Fields (1981). Parent-child relationships, childhood sexual abuse, and adult interpersonal behavior in female prostitutes. *Dissertation Abstracts International* 42:2053B.

## 9. Sex Education

1. No author (1968). *Is the Schoolhouse the Proper Place to Teach Raw Sex?* Tulsa, Okla.: Christian Crusade Publications, p. 31.
2. Id., p. 20.
3. G. Ramsey (1950). *Factors in the Sex Life of 291 Boys.* No publisher, p. 93.
4. Id.
5. State ex. rel. Andrew v. Webber, 108 Ind. 31, 8 N.E. 708 (1886).
6. Sewell v. Board of Education, 29 Ohio St. 89 (1876).
7. Samuel Benedict Memorial School v. Bradford, 111 Ga. 801, 36 S.E. 920 (1900).
8. Wisconsin v. Yoder, 406 U.S. 205 (1972).
9. Meyer v. Nebraska 262 U.S. 390 (1923).
10. 262 U.S. 399, 401.
11. Pierce v. Society of Sisters, 268 U.S. 510 (1925).
12. Prince v. Massachusetts 321 U.S. 158 (1943).
13. In re Gault 387 U.S. 1 (1967).
14. Tinker vs. Des Moines School District, 393 U.S. 503, 511 (1969).

15. Keyishian v. Board of Regents, 385 U.S. 589, 603 (1967).
16. Keyishian (university level), Webb v. Lake Mills Community School District, 344 F.Supp. 791 (Iowa, 1972) (high school and elementary).
17. Valent v. New Jersey State Board of Education, 274 A.2d 832 (N.J. 1971), 288 A.2d.52 (N.J. 1972).
18. Id., p. 835.
19. Id.
20. Id., p. 839.
21. Id., pp. 840–841.
22. Smith v. Ricci, 446 A.2d 501 (N.J. 1982).
23. Id., p. 503.
24. Abington School District v. Schempp, 374 U.S. 203 (1963).
25. 446 A.2d 507.
26. Madeiros v. Kiyosaki, 478 P.2d 314 (Haw. 1970).
27. Epperson v. Arkansas 393 U.S. 97 (1968).
28. 393 U.S. 106.
29. Citizens for Parental Rights v. San Mateo County Board of Education, 51 Cal. App. 3d 1; (1975), *appeal dismissed,* 425 U.S. 908 (1976).
30. Id., p. 9.
31. Id., p. 32.
32. Trachtman v. Ankar, 426 F.Supp. 198 (S.D. N.Y. 1976).
33. Id., p. 202.
34. Trachtman v. Ankar, 563 F.2d 512 (2nd Cir. 1977), *cert. denied* 435 U.S. 925 (1978).
35. Id., p. 517.
36. Id., p. 518.
37. Id.
38. Id.
39. Id., p. 523, emphasis in original.
40. Id., p. 524.
41. Id., p. 525.
42. Id.
43. Id.
44. Gambine v. Fairfax County School Board, 429 F.Supp. 731 (1977), *aff'd.* 564 F.2d 157 (4th Cir. 1977).
45. Chesebrough v. State, 255 So. 2d 675 (Fla. 1971), *cert. denied* 406 U.S. 976 (1972).
46. Id., p. 676.
47. Id., p. 679.
48. Id.
49. E. Robert and S. Holt (1980). Parent-child communications about sexuality. *SIECUS Report* 8:1–10.
50. D. Dawson (1986). The effects of sex education on adolescent behavior. *Family Planning Perspectives* 18:162–70, p. 162.
51. National Center for Health Statistics (1972), (1973) United States, 1950–67. Vital and Health Statistics, Series 3, No. 15, Series 20, No. 14.

52. R. Record, T. McKeown, and J. Edwards (1969). The relation of measured intelligence to birth order and maternal age. *Annals of Human Genetics* 33:61–69.
53. P. Sarrel and C. Davis (1966). The young unwed primipara. *American Journal of Obstetrics and Gynecology* 95:722–725.
54. M. Exner (1915). *Problems and Principles of Sex Education.* New York: International Committee of Young Men's Christian Associates.
55. W. Hughes (1926). Sex experiences of boyhood. *Journal of Social Hygiene* 12:262–273.
56. H. Thornburg (1981). Adolescent sources of information on sex. *Journal of School Health* 51:274–277.
57. Id.
58. W. Marsiglio and F. Mott (1986). The impact of sex education on sexual activity, contraceptive use and premarital pregnancy among American teenagers. *Family Planning Perspectives* 18:151–162.
59. M. Zelnik and Y. Kim (1982). Sex education and its association with teenage sexual activity, pregnancy and contraceptive use. *Family Planning Perspectives* 14:117–126.
60. Id., p. 119.
61. Id., p. 123.
62. Id.
63. D. Dawson (1986). The effects of sex education on adolescent behavior. *Family Planning Perspectives* 18:162–170.
64. E. Brann, L. Edwards, T. Calicott et al. (1979). Strategies for the prevention of pregnancy in adolescents. *Advances in Planned Parenthood* 14: 68–76.
65. D. Kirby (1985). The effects of selected sexuality education programs: Towards a more realistic view. *Journal of Sex Education and Therapy* 11:28–37.
66. Id., p. 37.
67. Id., p. 36.

## 10. Prostitution

1. V. Bullough and B. Bullough (1987). *Women and Prostitution.* Buffalo: Prometheus, p. 27.
2. H. Benjamin and R. Masters (1964). *Prostitution and Morality.* New York: Julian Press, p. 36.
3. Id.
4. Id., pp. 40–41.
5. Bullough and Bullough (1987), p. 35.
6. Id., p. 48.
7. Benjamin and Masters (1964), p. 286.
8. Id., p. 289.
9. A. Kinsey, W. Pomeroy, and C. Martin (1948). *Sexual Behavior in the Human Male.* Philadelphia: Saunders, p. 597.

10. M. Stein (1974). *Lovers, Friends, Slaves* . . . New York: Berkeley Publishing and G. P. Putnam's Sons.
11. Id., pp. 1–2.
12. Id., p. 25.
13. Id., p. 317.
14. Id., p. 320.
15. Id., p. 21.
16. Id., p. 22.
17. M. Choisy (1961). *Psychoanalysis of the Prostitute*. New York: Philosophical Library.
18. Id., pp. 62–63.
19. Benjamin and Masters (1964), p. 91.
20. Id., pp. 117–118.
21. J. Exner, J. Wylie, A. Leura, and T. Parrill (1977). Some psychological characteristics of prostitutes. *Journal of Personality Assessment* 41:474–485.
22. Id., p. 483.
23. U.S. Department of Health, Education, and Welfare (1978). *Juvenile Prostitution*. Washington, D.C.: U.S. Government Printing Office.
24. I. Gibson-Ainyette, D. Templer, R. Brown, and L. Veaco (1988). Adolescent female prostitutes. *Archives of Sexual Behavior* 17:431–438.
25. J. James and J. Meyerding (1977). Early sexual experience and prostitution. *American Journal of Psychiatry* 134:1381–1385; (1978) Early sexual experience as a factor in prostitution. *Archives of Sexual Behavior* 7: 31–42.
26. James and Meyerding (1978), p. 40.
27. S. Caukins and N. Coombs (1976). The psychodynamics of male prostitution. *American Journal of Psychotherapy* 30:441–451, p. 441.
28. Id., p. 446.
29. Id., p. 450.
30. Id., p. 446.
31. N. Coombs (1974). Male prostitution: A psychosocial view of behavior. *American Journal of Orthopsychiatry* 44:782–789.
32. C. Earls and H. David (1989). A psychosocial study of male prostitution. *Archives of Sexual Behavior* 18:401–419.
33. D. MacNamara (1965). Male prostitution in American cities: A socioeconomic or pathological phenomenon? *American Journal of Orthopsychiatry* 35:204.
34. P. Simon, E. Morse, H. Osofsky et al. (1992). Psychological characteristics of a sample of male street prostitutes. *Archives of Sexual Behavior* 21.
35. D. Allen (1980). Young male prostitutes: A psychosocial study. *Archives of Sexual Behavior* 9:399–426.
36. Id., p. 415.
37. Id., p. 404.
38. Id., p. 418.

39. Id., pp. 419–20.
40. Id., p. 422.
41. W. Butts (1947). Boy prostitutes of the metropolis. *Journal of Clinical Psychopathology* 8:673–681.
42. A. Reiss (1961). The social integration of queers and peers, reprinted in *Sexual Deviance,* ed. J. Gagnon and W. Simon (1967). New York: Harper and Row.
43. American Law Institute (1959). *Model Penal Code 207.12* Tent. Draft No. 9, Comment, pp. 169–174. Philadelphia: American Law Institute.
44. Id.
45. 413 U.S. 49 (1973).
46. Caeser's Health Club v. St. Louis County., 565 S.W. 2d 783 (Mo. App. 1978), *cert. denied* 439 U.S. 955 (1978).
47. Id., p. 788.
48. Id., p. 789.
49. J.B.K. Inc. v. Caron, 600 F.2d 710 (8th Cir. 1979), *cert. denied* 444 U.S. 1016 (1980).
50. Morgan v. City of Detroit, 389 F.Supp. 922 (E.D. Mich. 1975).
51. Id., p. 926.
52. Id., p. 927.
53. Commonwealth v. King, 372 N.E. 2d 196 (Mass. 1977).
54. Id., p. 204.
55. Id., p. 207.
56. IDK, Inc. v. Clark County, 836 F.2d 1185 (9th Cir. 1988).
57. Id., p. 1191.
58. Citing Roberts v. United States Jaycees, 468 U.S. 619 (1984).
59. 836 F.2d 1193.
60. Id., p. 1195.
61. Id., p. 1201.
62. Commonwealth v. Finnegan, 421 A.2d 1086 (Pa. Super. 1980).
63. Commonwealth v. Dodge, 429 A.2d 1143 (Pa. Super. 1981).
64. Id., pp. 1148–1149, emphasis in original.
65. Coyote v. Roberts, 502 F.Supp. 1342 (R.I. 1980); 523 F.Supp. 352 (R.I. 1981).
66. Brown v. Brannon, 399 F.Supp. 133, 135 (N.C. 1975), *aff'd.* 535 F.2d 1249 (4th Cir. 1976).
67. Id., p. 139.
68. 413 U.S. 49, 65 (1973).
69. In re P., 400 N.Y.S. 2d 455 (Fam. Ct. 1977).
70. 400 N.Y.S. 2d 462–463.
71. M. Hunt (1974). *Sexual Behavior in the 1970's.* Chicago: Playboy Press, pp. 166–167.
72. 400 N.Y.S. 2d 463.
73. Id., p. 468.
74. In the Matter of Dora P., 68 A.D. 2d 719, 418 N.Y.S. 2d 597 (1979).

75. Oregon v. Cordray, 755 P.2d 735 (Ore. 1988).
76. L. Ullerstam (1966). *The Erotic Minorities*. New York: Grove Press, pp. 150–152.
77. R. Barber (1969). Prostitution and the increasing number of convictions for rape in Queensland. *Australian and New Zealand Journal of Criminology* 2:169–174.
78. C. Winick and P. Kinsie (1971). *The Lively Commerce*. Chicago: Quadrangle, p. 64.
79. O. Idsoe and T. Guthe (1967). The rise and fall of treponematoses. *British Journal of Venereal Disease* 43:227–243; R. Wilcox (1962). Prostitution and venereal disease. *British Journal of Venereal Disease* 38:37–42.

## *11. Abortion*

1. 410 U.S. 113 (1973).
2. 410 U.S. 153.
3. R. Pasnau (1972). Psychiatric complications of therapeutic abortion. *Obstetrics and Gynecology* 40:252–256.
4. World Health Organization (1978). Technical Report Series. Induced Abortion. #623. Geneva: World Health Organization.
5. P. Gebhard, W. Pomeroy, C. Martin, and C. Christenson (1958). *Pregnancy, Birth and Abortion*. New York: Harper and Row, p. 208.
6. J. Kummer (1963). Post-abortion psychiatric illness: A myth. *American Journal of Psychiatry* 119:980–983.
7. A. Peck and H. Marcus (1966). Psychiatric sequelae of therapeutic interruption of pregnancy. *Journal of Nervous and Mental Disease* 143:417–425.
8. K. Niswander and R. Patterson (1967). Psychological reaction to therapeutic abortion. *Obstetrics and Gynecology* 29:702–706.
9. L. Marder (1970). Psychiatric experience with a liberalized therapeutic abortion law. *American Journal of Psychiatry* 126:1230–1236.
10. C. Ford, P. Castelauevo-Tedesco, and K. Long (1971). Abortion—Is it a therapeutic procedure in psychiatry? *Journal of the American Medical Association* 218:1173–1178.
11. Institute of Medicine/National Academy of Sciences (1975). *Legalized Abortion and the Public Health*. Washington, D.C.: National Academy of Sciences.
12. N. Adler (1975). Emotional response of women following therapeutic abortion. *American Journal of Orthopsychiatry* 45:446–454.
13. E. Freeman, K. Rickels, G. Huggins, C. Garcia, and J. Polin (1980). Emotional distress patterns among women having first or repeat abortions. *Obstetrics and Gynecology* 55:630–636.
14. Alan Guttmacher Institute (1981). *Teenage Pregnancy: The Problem That Hasn't Gone Away*. New York: Alan Guttmacher Institute.
15. L. Zabin, M. Hirsch, and M. Emerson (1989). When urban adolescents

choose abortion: Effects on education, psychological status and subsequent pregnancy. *Family Planning Perspectives* 21:248–255.

16. H. Greer, S. Lal, S. Lewis, E. Belsey, and R. Beard (1976). Psychosocial consequences of therapeutic abortion. *British Journal of Psychiatry* 128: 74–79.

17. B. Lask (1975). Short-term psychiatric sequelae to therapeutic termination of pregnancy. *British Journal of Psychiatry* 126:173–177.

18. J. Ashton (1980). The psychosocial outcome of induced abortion. *British Journal of Obstetrics and Gynaecology* 87:1115–1122.

19. C. Brewer (1977). Incidence of post-abortion psychosis. *British Medical Journal* 1:476–478.

20. C. Pare and H. Raven (1970). Follow-up of patients referred for termination of pregnancy. *Lancet* 1:635–638.

21. C. McCance, P. Olley, and E. Vivien (1973). Longterm Psychiatric Followup. In *Experience with Abortion: A Case Study of North-East Scotland,* ed. G. Horobin. Cambridge: Cambridge University Press.

22. M. Ekblad (1955). Induced abortion on psychiatric grounds: A follow-up study of 479 women. *Acta Psychiatrica Scandinavica Supplement* 99.

23. K. Hook (1963). Refused abortion. *Acta Psychiatrica Scandinavica* 39: Supplement 168.

24. H. David, N. Rasmussen, and E. Holst (1981). Postpartum and post abortions psychotic reactions. *Family Planning Perspectives* 13:88–92.

25. N. Adler, H. David, B. Major, S. Roth, N. Russo, and G. Wyatt (1990). Psychological responses to abortion. *Science* 248:41–44.

26. Id., p. 42.

27. Gebhard et al. (1958).

28. W. Barnett, N. Freudenberg, and R. Wille (1992). Partnership after induced abortion. *Archives of Sexual Behavior* 21.

29. P. Resnick (1970). Murder of the newborn: A psychiatric review of neonaticide. *American Journal of Psychiatry* 126:1414–1420.

30. H. Forssman and I. Thuwe (1966). One hundred and twenty children born after application for therapeutic abortion refused. *Acta Psychiatrica Scandinavica* 42:71–88.

31. H. Forssman and I. Thuwe (1988). The Goteborg Cohort, 1939–1977. In *Born Unwanted,* ed. H. David, Z. Dytrych, Z. Matejcek et al. New York: Springer.

32. Z. Dytrych, Z. Matejcek, V. Schuller, H. David, and H. Friedman (1975). Children born to women denied abortion. *Family Planning Perspectives* 7:165–171.

33. Z. Matejcek (1985). Follow-up study of children born to women denied abortion. *Ciba Foundation Symposium* 115:136–149.

34. Z. Dytrych, Z. Matejcek, and V. Schuller (1988). The Prague cohort: Adolescence and early adulthood. In David et al.

35. K. Hook (1963). Refused abortion. *Acta Psychiatrica Scandinavica* 39: Supplement 168.

36. Planned Parenthood of Central Missouri v. Danforth, 428 U.S. 52 (1976), (Brief for Missouri, pp. 34, 38).
37. 428 U.S. 69–70.
38. Id., p. 71.
39. Id., p. 93 (White, J., dissenting, joined by Burger and Rehnquist, J.J.).
40. Pursley v. State, 730 S.W. 2d 250, 252 (Ark. 1987).
41. Akron v. Akron Center for Reproductive Health, 462 U.S. 416, (1983).
42. 462 U.S. 445.
43. Id., p. 458.
44. Committee on Government Operations, House of Representatives. The Federal Role in Determining the Medical and Psychological Impact of Abortions on Women, 101st. Cong. 2d sess., December 11, 1989, House Report 101-392, p. 14.
45. P. Dagg (1991). The psychological sequelae of therapeutic abortion— denied and completed. *American Journal of Psychiatry* 148:578–585.
46. Id., p. 583.
47. Id., p. 584.

## 12. Surgical or Chemical Castration of Sex Offenders

1. J. Bancroft (1978). The relationship between hormones and sexual behaviour in humans. *Biological Determinants of Human Behavior,* ed. J. Hutchison. Chichester: Wiley.
2. A. Groth (1979). *Men Who Rape.* New York: Plenum.
3. P. Gebhard, J. Gagnon, W. Pomeroy, and C. Christenson (1965). *Sex Offenders.* New York: Harper and Row, p. 197.
4. H. Persky, K. Smith, and G. Basu (1971). Relations of psychological measures of aggression and hostility to testosterone production in man. *Psychosomatic Medicine* 33:265–277.
5. N. Heim and C. Hursch (1979). Castration for sex offenders. *Archives of Sexual Behavior* 8:281–304.
6. A. Langeluddeke (1963). *Castration of Sexual Criminals.* Berlin: de Gruyter (in German); reviewed by Heim and Hursch.
7. F. Cornu (1973). *Catamnestic Studies on Castrated Sex Delinquents from a Forensic Psychiatric Viewpoint.* Basel: Karger (in German); reviewed by Heim and Hursch.
8. J. Bremer (1959). *Asexualization.* New York: Macmillan.
9. K. Christiansen, M. Elers-Nielson, L. Le Maire, and G. Sturup (1965). Recidivism among sexual offenders. In *Scandinavian Studies in Criminology.* London: Tavistock; Oslo: Universitetsforlaget, pp. 55–85.
10. G. Sturup (1972). Castration: The Total Treatment. In *Sexual Behaviors,* ed. H. Resnik and M. Wolfgang. Boston: Little, Brown, pp. 361–382.
11. N. Heim (1981). Sexual behavior of castrated sex offenders. *Archives of Sexual Behavior* 10:11–19.
12. L. Rousseau, M. Coutre, A. Dupont, F. Labrie, and N. Coutre (1990). Effect of combined androgen blockade with an LHRH agonist of flutamide

in one severe case of male exhibitionism. *Canadian Journal of Psychiatry* 35:338–341.

13. J. Money (1968). Discussion of hormonal inhibition of libido in male sex offenders. In *Endocrinology and Human Behavior,* ed. R. Michael. London: Oxford University Press; J. Money (1970). Use of an androgen depleting hormone in the treatment of male sex offenders. *Journal of Sex Research* 6:165–172; J. Money, C. Wiedeking, and P. Walker (1976). Combined anti-androgenic and counseling programs for treatment of 46 XY and XYY sex offenders. In *Hormones Behavior and Psychopathology,* ed. E. Sachar. New York: Raven Press.

14. F. Berlin and C. Meinecke (1981). Treatment of sex offenders with antiandrogenic medication. *American Journal of Psychiatry* 138:601–607.

15. P. Gagne (1981). Treatment of sex offenders with medroxyprogesterone acetate. *American Journal of Psychiatry* 138:644–646.

16. A. Cooper (1986). Progestogens in the treatment of male sex offenders: A review. *Canadian Journal of Psychiatry* 31:73–79.

17. U. Laschet and L. Laschet (1975). Antiandrogens in the treatment of sexual deviations in men. *Journal of Steroid Biochemistry* 6:821–826; A. Cooper, A. Ismail, A. Phanjoo, D. Love (1972). Antiandrogen (cyproterone acetate) therapy in deviant hypersexuality. *British Journal of Psychiatry* 120:59–63.

18. F. Neumann, K. Graf, S. Hasam, B. Schweck, and M. Steinbeck (1977). In *Androgens and Antiandrogens,* ed. L. Martini and M. Motta. New York: Raven Press, pp. 163–177.

19. J. Ortman (1980). Treatment of sexual offenders, castration and antihormone therapy. *International Journal of Law and Psychiatry* 3:443–451.

20. Cooper (1986), p. 74.

21. J. Bancroft, T. Tennent, K. Loucas, and J. Cass (1974). Control of deviant sexual behaviour by drugs. *British Journal of Psychiatry* 125:310–315.

22. J. Wincze, S. Bansal, and M. Malamud (1986). Effects of medroxyprogesterone acetate on subjective arousal, erotic stimulation, and nocturnal arousal to penile tumescence in male sex offenders. *Archives of Sexual Behavior* 15:293–305.

23. J. Bradford and A. Pawlak (1987). Sadistic homosexual pedophilic treatment with cyproterone acetate. *Canadian Journal of Psychiatry* 32:22–31; J. Bradford and A. Pawlak (unpublished).

24. S. Halleck (1981). Ethics of antiandrogen therapy. *American Journal of Psychiatry* 138:642–643.

25. People v. Gauntlett, 352 N.W.2d 310 (Mich. App. 1984).

26. Id., p. 313.

27. Id., p. 315.

28. Id., p. 316.

29. Arizona v. Christopher, 652 P.2d 1031 (Ariz. 1982).

30. Id., p. 1032.

31. Paoli v. Lally, 636 F. Supp. 1252 (MD 1986), *aff'd.* 812 F.2d 1489 (4th Cir. 1987), *cert. denied* 484 U.S. 864 (1987).

32. McDonald v. Warden, State Prison. Judicial District of Hartford, New Britain at Hartford #32654 (1983), case withdrawn, cited by Berlin (1989).
33. Estelle v. Gamble, 429 U.S. 97, 103 (1976).
34. Bowring v. Godwin, 551 F.2d 44 (4th Cir. 1977).
35. 551 F.2d 47.
36. Runnels v. Rosendale, 499 F.2d 733 (9th Cir. 1974).
37. Furman v. Georgia, 408 U.S. 238, 279 (1972) (Brennan, J., concurring).
38. State v. Feilen, 70 Wash. 65, 126 P. 75 (1912).
39. Davis v. Berry, 216 F.413 (D.C. Iowa 1914), *rev'd other grounds,* 242 U.S. 468 (1917).
40. Buck v. Bell, 274 U.S. 200 (1927).
41. Skinner v. Oklahoma, 316 U.S. 535 (1942).
42. Revised Code of Washington Annotated, Sections 71.09.010–.120 (West, 1975 and Supp. 1991).
43. T. Monahan (1981). *The Clinical Prediction of Violent Behavior.* Washington, D.C.: U.S. Government Printing Office.
44. L. Furby, M. Weinrott, and L. Blackshaw (1989). Sex offender recidivism: A review. *Psychological Bulletin* 105:3–30.
45. F. Berlin (1989). The paraphilias and Depo-Provera. *Bulletin of the American Academy of Psychiatry and Law* 17:233–239, p. 238.
46. F. Berlin, H. Malin, and S. Dean (1991). Effects of statutes requiring psychiatrists to report suspected sexual abuse of children. *American Journal of Psychiatry* 148:449–453.

## *13. Sex-Linked Defenses to Criminal Behavior*

1. W. LaFave and A. Scott (1986). *Criminal Law,* 2nd ed. St. Paul, Minn.: West Publishing, pp. 22–25.
2. W. Holdsworth (1942). *History of English Law,* 5th ed. London: Methuen, p. 311.
3. S. Glueck (1925). *Mental Disorder and the Criminal Law.* Boston: Little, Brown, p. 125.
4. R. Perkins (1977). *Criminal Law.* Minneola, N.Y.: Foundation Press, p. 739.
5. J. Hall (1947). *General Principles of Criminal Law.* Indianapolis: Bobbs-Merrill, p. 480; and Glueck (1925), pp. 138–139.
6. Queen v. M'Naghten, 8 Eng. Rep. 718 (1843).
7. LaFave and Scott (1986), p. 320.
8. Id., p. 323.
9. Id., p. 329; Model Penal Code, Section 4.01.
10. LaFave and Scott (1986), p. 368.
11. Id., p. 359.
12. *New York Times* (1968). April 21, p. 1.
13. *Washington Post* (1968). October 23, p. B6.
14. A. Bartholomew and G. Sutherland (1969). A defence of insanity and the

extra Y chromosome: R v Hannell. *Australian and New Zealand Journal of Criminology* 2:29–37, p. 36.

15. A. Sandberg, G. Koepf, T. Ishihara, and T. Hauschka (1961). An XYY human male. *Lancet* 2:488–489.
16. P. Jacobs, M. Brunton, M. Melville et al. (1965). Aggressive behaviour, mental sub-normality and the XYY male. *Nature* 208:1351–1352.
17. K. Burke (1969). The "XYY Syndrome": Genetics, behavior and the law. *Denver Law Journal* 46:261–284.
18. E. Hook (1973). Behavioral implications of the human XYY genotype. *Science* 179:139–150; E. Hook (1975). Rates of XYY genotype in penal and mental settings. *Lancet* 1:98.
19. S. Shah (1970). *Report on the XYY Chromosomal Abnormality.* National Institute of Mental Health, Public Health Service Publication 2103.
20. R. Goodman, F. Miller, and C. North (1968). Chromosomes of tall men. *Lancet* 1:1318.
21. H. Witkin, S. Mednick, F. Schulsinger et al. (1976). Criminality in XYY and XXY men. *Science* 193:547–555.
22. Id.
23. R. Schiavi, A. Theilgaard, D. Owen, and D. White (1988). Sex chromosome anomalies, hormones, and sexuality. *Archives of General Psychiatry* 45:19–24.
24. R. Schiavi, A. Theilgaard, D. Owen, and D. White (1984). Sex chromosome anomalies, hormones, and aggressivity. *Archives of General Psychiatry* 41:93–98.
25. Id.
26. Schiavi et al. (1988).
27. B. Noel, J. Dupont, D. Revil et al. (1974). The XYY syndrome: Reality or myth? *Clinical Genetics* 5:387–394.
28. Frye v. United States, 293 F. 1013 (D.C. Cir. 1923).
29. Id., p. 1014, emphasis added.
30. McCormick (1984). *On Evidence,* 3rd ed. Sec. 203, p. 606.
31. 261 A.2d 227 (Md. 1970).
32. 13 Cal. App. 3d 596 (1970).
33. Id., p. 600.
34. Id., pp. 600–601.
35. People v. Yukl, 372 N.Y.S. 2d 313 (1975).
36. 372 N.Y.S. p. 318.
37. Supreme Court, Queens County, Indictment No. 1827, April 30, 1969.
38. 372 N.Y.S. 2d 320.
39. Id.
40. C. Wiedeking, J. Money, and P. Walker (1979). Follow-up of 11 XYY males with impulse and/or sex offending behaviors. *Psychological Medicine* 9:287–292.
41. Semonides (6th c. B.C.), quoted in H. Lloyd-Jones (1975). *Females of the Species: Semonides on Women.* Park Ridge, N.J.: Noyes Press, p. 43.

42. R. Frank (1929). *The Female Sex Hormone.* Springfield: Charles C. Thomas, p. 236.
43. R. Greene and K. Dalton (1953). The premenstrual syndrome. *British Medical Journal* 1:1007–1014.
44. C. Boorse (1987). Premenstrual Syndrome and Criminal Responsibility. In *Premenstrual Syndrome,* ed. B. Ginsburg and B. Carter. New York: Plenum, p. 88.
45. J. Morton, H. Additon, R. Addison, L. Hunt, and J. Sullivan (1953). A clinical study of premenstrual tension. *American Journal of Obstetrics and Gynecology* 65:1182–1191.
46. K. Dalton (1960). Menstruation and accidents. *British Medical Journal* 2:1425–1426.
47. K. Dalton (1959). Menstruation and acute psychiatric illnesses. *British Medical Journal* 1:148–149.
48. K. Dalton (1980). Cyclical criminal acts in premenstrual syndrome. *Lancet* 2:1070–1071.
49. Regina v. Craddock, 1 C.L. 49 (1981).
50. K. Dalton (1987). Should premenstrual syndrome be a legal defense? In *Premenstrual Syndrome,* ed. B. Ginsburg and B. Carter. New York: Plenum, pp. 287–300, p. 295.
51. Dalton (1987), p. 289.
52. C. Boorse (1987), p. 83, citing R. Carney and B. Williams (1983). Premenstrual syndrome: A criminal defense. *Notre Dame Law Review* 59: 253–69.
53. Carney and Williams (1983), p. 261.
54. Dalton (1987), p. 288.
55. Dalton (1980), p. 1071.
56. Id.
57. Homicide Act, 1957, 5 and 6 Eliz. II, ch. 11 § 2 (1), cited by Carney and Williams.
58. Reported in R. Norris (1987). Historical Development of Progesterone Therapy. In Ginsburg and Carter, pp. 277–278; S. Israel (1938). Premenstrual tension. *Journal of the American Medical Association* 110:1721–1723.
59. Greene and Dalton (1953).
60. G. Sampson (1979). Premenstrual Syndrome—a double-blind controlled trial of progesterone and placebo. *British Journal of Psychiatry* 135:209–215; U. Halbreich and J. Endicott (1985). Methodological issues in studies of premenstrual changes. *Psychoneuroendocrinology* 10:15–32.
61. K. Dalton (1984). *Premenstrual Syndrome and Progesterone,* 2nd ed. Chicago: Year Book Publishers.
62. *The Times* (London) (1981). Letters to the Editor. Premenstrual Tension and Equality. November 19, p. 13.
63. Dalton (1987), p. 298.
64. R. Norris (1987). In Ginsburg and Carter, pp. 277–278, emphasis in original.
65. Dalton (1987), p. 288.

66. Id.
67. Cited by Carney and Williams (1983), p. 255.
68. Id., p. 287.
69. In re Irvin, 31 B.R. 251 (Bkrtcy. Colo. 1983).
70. Reid v. Florida Real Estate Comm'n., 188 So. 2d 846 (Fla. 1966).
71. State v. Lashwood, 384 N.W. 2d 319 (S.D. 1986).
72. Swanson v. State, 759 P.2d 898 (Idaho 1988).
73. People v. Santos, No. 1K046229 (Criminal Court, New York, 1982).
74. K. Paige (1987). Menstrual Symptoms and Menstrual Beliefs. In Ginsburg and Carter, p. 186.
75. American Psychiatric Association (1987). *Diagnostic and Statistical Manual of Mental Disorders, IIIR.* Washington, D.C.: American Psychiatric Association, p. 367.
76. American Psychiatric Association, *DSM-IV Options Book,* 9-1-91. Washington, D.C.: American Psychiatric Association.
77. G. Zilboorg (1929). The dynamics of schizophrenic reactions related to pregnancy and childbirth. *American Journal of Psychiatry* 85:733–767, p. 733.
78. Id.
79. Id.
80. J. Hamilton (1962). *Postpartum Psychiatric Problems.* St. Louis: C. V. Mosby.
81. G. Robinson and D. Stewart (1986). Postpartum psychiatric disorders. *Canadian Medical Association Journal* 31–37; F. Kane (1980). Postpartum Disorders. In *Comprehensive Textbook of Psychiatry,* vol. 3, ed. H. Kaplan, A. Freedman and B. Sadock. Baltimore: Williams and Wilkins, p. 1346.
82. *Washington Post* (1988). Mother Charged in Slaying in Md. Diagnosed as Psychotic. December 3, P. B5.
83. People v. Thompson, No. 7995 California Superior Court, Yolo County, July 30, 1984.
84. L. Button (1989). Postpartum psychosis: The birth of a new defense? *Cooley Law Review* 6:323–344, p. 333.
85. People v. Molina, 202 Cal. App. 3d 1168 (1988).
86. People v. Saille, 54 Cal. 3d 1103 (1991).
87. 229 Cal. App. 3d 1400 (1990).
88. Id., p. 1405.
89. Id., p. 1406.
90. Id., p. 1407, 1415.
91. People v. Massip, 824 P.2d 568 (1992), 54 Cal.3d 1103 (1991).
92. People v. Wing, No. 84-53731 Ingham County, Circuit Court, Mich. September 9, 1985, cited by Button, p. 335.
93. People v. Penguelly, No. 85667, California Superior Court, San Diego County, June 6, 1989, cited by Button, p. 335.
94. People v. Green, No. 1273/86, New York Supreme Court, New York County, September 30, 1988, cited by Button, p. 334.
95. Commonwealth v. Comitz, 530 A.2d 473 (Pa. Super. 1987).

96. 530 A.2d 478–479.
97. American Psychiatric Association (1987). *Diagnostic and Statistical Manual of Mental Disorders, IIIR.* Washington, D.C.: American Psychiatric Association.
98. American Psychiatric Association, *Diagnostic and Statistical Manual of Mental Disorders, IV, Options Book* 9-1-91. Washington, D.C.: American Psychiatric Association.
99. England Infanticide Act of 1938, 1 and 2 Geo. 6, Ch. 36, *Halsbury's Statutes of England and Wales, Fourth Edition* (1988), 12:221.
100. E. Kempf (1920). *Psychopathology.* St. Louis: C. V. Mosby.
101. B. Glueck (1959). Homosexual panic: Clinical and theoretical considerations. *Journal of Nervous and Mental Disease* 129:20–28.
102. Id., p. 26.
103. Id., p. 25.
104. L. Ovesey and S. Woods (1980). Pseudohomosexuality and Homosexuality in Men. In *Homosexual Behavior,* ed. J. Marmor. New York: Basic Books, p. 329.
105. Id., p. 329–330.
106. American Psychiatric Association (1952). *Diagnostic and Statistical Manual of Mental Disorders.* Washington, D.C.: American Psychiatric Association.
107. San Francisco Superior Court. No. 125603, Court of Appeal, First Appellate, Division Five, No. A042962, 1989.
108. Record of Transcript (RT) 174.
109. RT 176-177.
110. Appellant's Opening Brief, 15.
111. RT 177.
112. 462 N.E. 2d 1084 (Mass. 1984).
113. Id., p. 1097.
114. People v. Parisie, 287 N.E. 2d 310 (Ill. 1972).
115. 671 F.2d 1011 (7th Cir. 1988).
116. Id., p. 1014.
117. Id.
118. Id.
119. Id., p. 1015.
120. Id., p. 1016.
121. Id.
122. Parisie v. Greer, 705 F.2d 882 (7th Cir. 1982), *cert. denied,* 464 U.S. 918 (1983).
123. 705 F.2d 893.
124. Id., p. 899.
125. People v. Limas, 359 N.E. 2d 1194 (Ill. App. 1977).
126. 359 N.E.2d 1199.
127. Id., p. 1200.
128. R. Stewart (1980). Psychotherapies. In *Comprehensive Textbook of Psychiatry,* vol. 2, ed. H. Kaplan, A. Freedman, and B. Sadock. Baltimore: Williams and Wilkins, p. 2115.

129. G. Mora (1980). Historical and Theoretical Trends in Psychiatry. In Kaplan, Freedman, and Sadock, vol. 1, p. 48.

## 14. Sexual Science and Sexual Privacy

1. Muller v. Oregon, 208 U.S. 412 (1907). Brief for the State of Oregon, in P. Kurland and G. Casper, eds. (1975). *Landmark Briefs and Arguments of the Supreme Court of the United States: Constitutional Law,* vol. 16. Arlington, Va.: University Publications of America.
2. 208 U.S. 420–421.
3. M. Deutscher and I. Chein (1948). The psychological effects of enforced segregation: A survey of social science opinion. *Journal of Psychology* 26:259–287.
4. K. Clark and M. Clark (1947). Racial identification and preference in Negro children. In *Readings in Social Psychology,* 2nd ed., ed. T. Newcomb and E. Hartley. New York: Holt, Rinehart and Winston.
5. R. Kluger (1976). *Simple Justice.* New York: Alfred A. Knopf, p. 354.
6. Kluger (1976), pp. 330, 354.
7. Briggs v. Elliot, 98 F.Supp. 529 (E.D.S.C. 1951).
8. The Effects of Segregation and the Consequences of Desegregation: A Social Science Statement. In *Landmark Briefs and Arguments of the Supreme Court: Constitutional Law,* vol. 49.
9. 347 U.S. 483, 494 n. 11 (1954).
10. E. Rostow (1960). The Enforcement of Morals. *Cambridge Law Journal* 174, 197.
11. J. Mill (1859). *On Liberty,* ed. E. Rapaport. Indianapolis: Hackett Publishing (1978).
12. Id., p. 73.
13. Id., p. 74.
14. Id., p. 79.
15. Id., p. 80.
16. J. Stephen (1873). *Liberty, Equality, Fraternity.* London: Smith Elder and Co., p. 125.
17. Id., p. 146.
18. P. Devlin (1965). Morals and the Criminal Law. In *The Enforcement of Morals.* Oxford: Oxford University Press.
19. Id., p. 17.
20. Id.
21. Id., p. 22.
22. Id., p. 14.
23. H. Hart (1961). Immorality and Treason. In *The Law as Literature,* ed. L. Blom-Cooper. London: The Bodley Head.
24. Id., p. 224.
25. Id.
26. Id.
27. Id.
28. Id., p. 225.

29. Id., p. 227.
30. Devlin (1965) p. 7.
31. Id., pp. 7–8.
32. Id., p. 10.
33. Id., p. 11.
34. Id., p. 14.
35. Id., p. 15.
36. Id., p. 17.
37. Id., p. 22.
38. Id., p. 17.
39. Id.
40. Id.
41. K. Karst (1980). The Freedom of Intimate Association. *Yale Law Journal* 89:624–692.
42. Id., p. 633.
43. Id., p. 673.
44. Paris Adult Theatre I v. Slaton, 413 U.S. 49, 61 (1973), Karst, p. 690.
45. 413 U.S. 59.
46. Karst, p. 690.
47. Id., p. 691.
48. Young v. American Mini Theatres, 427 U.S. 50, 56 (1976).
49. 381 U.S. 479, 488–489 (Goldberg, J., concurring).
50. 410 U.S. 113, 169–170 (Stewart, J., concurring).
51. Bowers v. Hardwick, 478 U.S. 186 (1986).
52. 381 U.S. 479, 498.
53. 367 U.S. 497, 546 (1961) (Harlan, J., dissenting).
54. Id., p. 552.
55. R. Green (1989). *Griswold's* Legacy: Fornication and Adultery as Crimes. *Ohio Northern Law Review* 16:545–549.
56. Pace v. Alabama, 106 U.S. 583 (1882).
57. Hollenbaugh v. Carnegie Free Library, 578 F.2d 1374 (3d Cir. 1978), *cert. denied,* 439 U.S. 1052 (1978) (Marshall, J., dissenting).
58. Jarrett v. Jarrett, 400 N.E. 2d 421, 424 (Ill. 1979), *cert. denied,* 449 U.S. 927 (1980).
59. 75 N.J. 200, 381 A.2d 333 (1977).
60. 478 U.S. 186.
61. 478 U.S. 218 (Stevens, J., dissenting), citations omitted.
62. Iowa v. Pilcher, 242 N.W. 2d 348, 359 (Iowa, 1976).
63. Id.
64. Id.
65. Commonwealth v. Bonadio, 415 A.2d 47 (Pa. 1980).
66. Post v. State, 715 P.2d 1105 (Okla. Crim. 1986), *cert. denied,* 479 U.S. 890 (1986).
67. Schochet v. Maryland, 580 A.2d 176 (1990).
68. State v. Elliot, 539 P.2d 207 (N.M. 1975), *reversed,* State v. Elliot, 551 P.2d 1352 (N.M. 1976).

69. State v. Callaway, 542 P.2d 1147 (Ariz. 1975), State v. Bateman, 540 P.2d 732 (Ariz. 1975), *vacated,* State v. Bateman 547 P.2d 6 (Ariz. 1976), *cert. denied,* 429 U.S. 864 (1977).
70. State v. Poe, 252 S.E. 2d 843 (N.C. App. 1979), *cert. denied,* 259 S.E. 2d 304 (1979), *appeal dismissed,* Poe v. North Carolina, 445 U.S. 947 (1980).
71. State v. Santos, 413 A.2d 58 (R.I. 1980).
72. J. Money (1985). *The Destroying Angel.* Buffalo, N.Y.: Prometheus Books, p. 96.
73. M. Huhner (1946). *The Diagnosis and Treatment of Sexual Disorders in the Male and Female.* Philadelphia: F. A. Davis, p. 187.
74. Money (1985), p. 17.
75. Id., p. 24.
76. *Boy Scouts of America Official Handbook for Boys* (1911). Garden City, N.Y.: Doubleday, Page and Co.
77. A. Morison. *Outlines on Lectures on Mental Disease,* cited in R. Bayer (1981). *Homosexuality and American Psychiatry.* New York: Basic Books, pp. 18–19, emphasis added.
78. I. Bieber et al. (1962). *Homosexuality: A Psychoanalytic Study of Male Homosexuals.* New York: Basic Books, p. 173.
79. C. Socardides (1975). *Beyond Sexual Freedom.* New York: Quadrangle, p. 11.
80. C. Socardides (1968). *The Overt Homosexual.* New York: Grune and Stratton, p. 90.
81. *Time* (1980). Attacking the last taboo. April 14; J. Ramey (1979). Dealing with the last taboo. *Siecus Report* 7:1–2, 6–7.
82. *Report of the Commission on Obscenity and Pornography* (1970). New York: Bantam Books.
83. Reynolds v. United States, 98 U.S. 145 (1878).
84. E. Joseph (1991). My husband's nine wives. *New York Times,* May 23, p. A 31.
85. Employment Division, Department of Human Resources of Oregon v. Smith, 110 S.Ct. 1595 (1990).

# Index